Sweden in the Sixties

**Desire and
Transformation.**
*Tapestry by Max Walter
Svanberg (1964).
Rendered in textile by
Edna Martin for the
Friends of Textile Art
Association. Svanberg
(born 1912) has belonged
to the international
surrealist group since the
mid-1950's. His art pays
tribute to woman as a
mysterious erotic creature.
Photo : Sten Didrik
Bellander.*

Sweden

in the Sixties

A Symposium of Facts and Views
in 17 Chapters
Edited by Ingemar Wizelius

Almqvist & Wiksell

© Svenska Institutet
Almqvist & Wiksell / Gebers Förlag AB Stockholm 1967

Translated from the Swedish by Rudy Feichtner

Illustrated by Per Åhlin

Design by sig, studio för industriell grafik ab

Printed in Sweden by
Almqvist & Wiksells Boktryckeri AB, Uppsala 1967

Contents

Foreword

Dear
Reader:
Perhaps you are i
n the habit of skippin
g over forewords. If so, m
ake an exception this time.
As you read these lines your gaze
will travel over a map of Swede
n. Right now you're looking at the ar
ea of Lapland's ore fields north of the
A R C T I C   C I R C L E
This book was not written to dissuade peop
le of other nationalities from thinking of Swe
den as a country of "sin, sex and su
icide". These misconceptions have
already been waylaid so thoroughly
by foreign writers that we run the
risk of losing the mystique which has
glamourized our country for the past
20 years or so. The time has now come t
o strip a second veil from the Swedes: t
hey are, as it turns out, quite ordin
ary people. We regret to say that th
e disclosure lacks dramatic excit
ement, but it will surely serve
to present a much more accurate
picture. Contrary to the sit
uation 20 years ago a wealth
of literature on Sweden is n
ow available. In presenti
ng some important fact
s on and views of Sweden w
ithin the compass of one v
olume it has therefore been
possibe to apply a more impress
ionistic method. The articles are writ
ten by specialists, who were asked to brin
g their own lights to bear on the selecti
on of facts and their interpretation. By t
heir very nature, however, certain subjec
ts are better suited to pure descript
ion than to the expression of op
inion for or against. The resul
t, we think, is a judicious
mixture of the neutral and
the highly personal. Thank
you for reading the fore
word. You are now in S
weden's southernmost
province, which lies o
n the same parallel as
northernm
ost New
foundland

Hans L. Zetterberg

Born in 1927. Professor of sociology at Ohio State University, formerly associate professor at Columbia University. Specializes in social theory and the structure of advanced societies. Publications include *On Theory and Verification in Sociology* (3rd ed. 1964) and *Social Theory and Social Practice* (1962). Board chairman of Bedminster Press Inc. and the Swedish Institute of Public Opinion Research (SIFO).

Sweden—A Land of Tomorrow?

A Sociologist Looks at Sweden

In the history of the West events in one country have sometimes
signaled what is to come in other countries many years hence.
For example, the establishment of independence and democracy
in the United States foreshadowed by a hundred years or more
what was to come both to the continent of Europe and to
European colonies. As S. M. Lipset has shown in his book,
The First New Nation, the first 30 or 40 years of American
independence, if seen from this particular perspective, can be
read as a rough guide to the history of today's new nations in
Africa and Asia. A nationalist charismatic hero—a George
Washington—emerges to whom people give personal loyalty
to the point of breaking law and rejecting colonial order.
A democratic constitution is established, but the franchise is not
complete and civil liberties are somewhat curtailed. A neutralist
foreign policy is evolved that plays the big powers against one
another. Every effort is made to secure foreign aid. Governmental
units take charge of economic development through subsidies
and investments. An old order where status is based on family
and land is replaced by one based on achievement and industrial
goods. The risks of political cleavage, instability and civil war
loom large. On maturity (at least in North America) a stable
democracy emerges, and large organizations—corporations, unions,
military and scientific establishments—gain indisputable dominance.
 Such was the story of the United States in its first decades
and such is the story of the new nations today, however
annoying such an observation may seem to the intellectuals of
the new states. In those old days the United States was a remote

*There are no pointers to
the future other than a
mobile which the wind
blows as it pleases.
The mobile shown here,
combined with a wind
machine, is made of iron,
weighs 80 tons and is 85
feet high. It serves as a
seal for the iron mine at
Svappavaara in
northernmost Lapland,
where the first deposits
were worked in 1964. The
slightest breeze sets the
upper part in motion.
Architect: Örjan Lüning.
Photo: Rolf Dahlström.*

and rather insignificant country on the world stage; nevertheless, it set a pattern which was repeated in many other places. The young America was rather isolated from European wars and it was prosperous and well-educated. Ideas and tendencies that were repeatedly counteracted by other forces in Europe and in European colonies got a free play there. Thus, America, long before it became a world power, pioneered in developing a social structure which seemed radical and strange to the rest of the world, but which in due course was to be followed in its main outlines by a large number of other nations. Hegel once called young America "the land of tomorrow" and on this score at least the old man was proven right (although, as we now know, for the wrong reasons). Young America, indeed, was a model for the world; she knew it and she took pride in it. The sociologist who understood a little of this and wrote about it, Alexis de Tocqueville, is rightly counted among the great.

In looking around the world today for a land of tomorrow attention is immediately drawn to the Nordic countries, particularly to Sweden. There by a combination of circumstances which also includes a measure of isolation from world wars, relative prosperity, and high literacy in social and physical science, features of social structure have emerged that are in the cards for other developed countries. The trends may be present in other countries; but in Scandinavia they have grown longer and met with more favorable circumstances. The trends I have in mind are not measured in simple statistics of wealth and production. They rather represent new ways to enact basic cultural values, new arrangements between man and fellowman and between public roles and private pursuits; in short, a new social order. To be sure, this new order is not likely to emerge except in wealthy countries, but wealth as such is no guarantee for its success. If wealth alone could produce this new social order, the United States of America would still be in the forefront of development. But this is not the case today when Uncle Sam stands for an old order rather than one of the future.

Rationalism

The civilization of the West has two outstanding themes, both of which are thoroughly entrenched in Scandinavia: rationalism and humanitarianism. The defeat of Nazi Germany clinched their ascendancy, for Hitler was the incarnation of unreason and disregard for human dignity. The rationalists (who in Sweden sometimes are called "culture-radicals") have achieved a certain dominance in the climate of opinion. A pious Swede is often ashamed of admitting his allegiance to God, while a rationalist Swede is not a bit ashamed of admitting his allegiance to Reason. Irrational expressions, ranging from official Church doctrine about hell to the private mystic of Hammarskjöld's diaries, are often looked upon with question and even suspicion. The rationalists have the main say about the content of the programs of radio and television and they control the editorial and serious pages of the large newspapers. They have turned political discourse into seminars on economics, political science and sociology. The political debate in Sweden in the post-war years has been characterized by Herbert Tingsten as a "reduction of ideology":

Differences of opinion arise primarily over assumptions which have to be made regarding the development of the economy and the likely consequences of decisions taken. For example, will there be a depression in the United States? What causes international commodity prices to change? Do increased prices for agricultural products mean that the standard of living of the farmers will be unreasonably raised or does it simply mean that they now receive reasonable compensation? How much should wages be raised to replace what is lost through inflation, and how much inflation can be permitted in the interest of full employment? In what way can everyone be assured a suitable basic pension?

A democratic debate over issues like these is a debate among rational experts and the solutions proposed are applied social science. Gone are the rabble-rousing, folksy, electioneering politicians; enter the rationalist with his briefcase of statistics and research reports and his academic degree. In the same fashion the daring intuitive business entrepreneur is replaced by the expert in planned and programmed expansion, and the clergyman who surrenders to holy mysticism is replaced by the clergyman who treats Christianity as a rational, or at least sensible, blueprint for a good life in a good society.

Humanitarianism

The other great theme of the civilization of the West of which Scandinavia is the front-line bearer is humanitarianism. Humanitarianism is an independent theme in our civilization; it is not a consequence of our rationalism. There is little or nothing in rationalism that necessarily leads us to take care of the mentally ill, the deformed and the invalids, nothing that argues for medical aid for the aged and prolongation of the life of the seniles, nothing that forces us to guarantee that a child born to unfit imbecile parents shall be given as much care as other children.

There are, of course, varieties of mercy in all known societies but only the civilization of the West has developed a consistent concern for the dignity of every man and a consistent care for each and all individuals. As a streak in the history of the West, humanitarianism is said to owe much to Christianity. But its most elaborate manifestation—the one we find in Sweden—is a product of leftists in a rather secular state, often working in opposition to church officials. The welfare state may be unlikely to flourish except in a civilization in which values of neighborly love and charity have been preached for generations: yet its establishment in Scandinavia is mostly the work of a generation of atheists or lukewarm believers.

The humanitarian features of the Scandinavian societies are well known. We have, in Sweden in particular, a situation in which the war on poverty is won, in which urban rehabilitation is a fact, civil liberties are guaranteed in law and in practice, medical care for the aged (indeed for all) is available with only nominal fees, education is free up to and including the doctorate, and any able youngster in need will have support during his higher education. Unestablished newlyweds are given loans by the state for their dowries, every expectant mother is given care, and all families automatically receive child support, housewives are given free vacations away from the routines of housework and children, no one suffers financial destitution with loss of earning power, et cetera, et cetera. This care and help to the individual is not dependent on the whims of charitable rich men and ladies, not dependent on a humble and pious attitude of the recipient, not dependent on the persuasiveness of his pleas for help. The care and help are given as his *right*, as solid as his right to vote or his right to own property. They are given across the board to the good and the bad, the friendly and the obnoxious, in predetermined manners and amounts. Scandinavia has organized humanitarianism from top to bottom like no other part of the world.

Legal Aspects of the Development of a Society

One of the earliest and best sociological treatises on modernization of a society is Sir Henry Sumner Maine's *Ancient Law,* published in 1861. It traces the main line of modernization as a trend "from status to contract". In underdeveloped societies man's experience and destiny are predetermined by ascribed statuses: his birth and other events beyond his control. Tribal Africa, caste-dominated India, as well as feudal Europe are thus described as status-dominated, i.e. underdeveloped, societies. These ascribed statuses determine nearly all activities and affiliations, whether religious or secular, including occupational pursuit, business associates, marriage mate, home, style of life, and power and influence in the larger community. The modernization of a society, according to Sir Henry, consists of letting an ever increasing number of actions and life histories be dependent upon freely negotiated contracts rather than on predetermined statuses. In a developed society the individual himself can decide and negotiate his entry into a church, an occupation, a trade relation, a marriage, a neighborhood, a political body, et cetera. Modernization thus consists of a lifting of restrictions of status and an opening of opportunities for contract.

The history of Scandinavia from the time of the Napoleonic wars to the present is very much a history of a movement from status to contract, not unlike any other advanced country. The movement started fairly late and actually lagged behind many advanced nations, particularly the United States—as measured by such indicators as free trade laws, extension of franchise, right to education, right for women to own and inherit property, et

cetera. However, once started, the transformation has been swift.
In many instance the abolition of dependency on status in
Scandinavia has gone further than in the United States: the
right to dissolve marriages by mutual agreement of husband and
wife has been recognized for several decades, and recent
legislation grants women the right to retain the maiden name in
marriage. The marriage contract, in other words, is stripped of the
remnants of paternalistic status considerations and, like other
contracts, it can be declared null and void by mutual consent of
the contracting parties. Even the much discussed sexual freedom
can be interpreted as an illustration of the status restraints yielding
to more freely negotiated unions. Scandinavia has run the full
scale from status to contract and now reveals some very
intriguing trends of a post-contractual, or overdeveloped, society.
Rational humanitarianism is enacted through a variety of
modifications in conventional contract law, the right for voluntary
associations to sign contracts that are binding on their members,
and the widespread emergence of what one might call reinsured
contracts.

Humanitarian Checks on Contracts

In their book, *Legal Values in Modern Sweden,* Folke Schmidt
and Stig Strömholm have shown how Swedish contractual law
has broken both with the Anglo-Saxon and the Continental
tradition. Generally speaking, the offer to contract has binding
force in these countries only under special circumstances: if it is
made under seal, if it involves an exchange of a token payment
at the signing, et cetera. In Swedish law you cannot withdraw
an offer to contract. This, of course, gives the buyer of goods or
services an extra protection. Furthermore, Swedish courts consider
themselves fully entitled to adjust harsh and seemingly unfair
contracts even if they have been properly signed and executed.
If breach of contract causes injury to one party, tort law allows
the courts to distribute liability among all parties and to allocate
the damages among them; it does not have to rule one party
guilty and another party innocent. In numerous small ways, thus,
one makes sure that freedom of contract is restrained by
humanitarian considerations.

Even in areas where no legislation exists, informal norms have emerged which limit contracts causing excessive human pain.
In Sweden, as elsewhere, any taking of the wife or girl-friend of a neighbor, colleague or friend is not readily condoned. Sexual license in primary groups, i.e. groups on which one is dependent, cause too much agony to be tolerated.

Voluntary Associations Contracting on behalf of Their Members

The most important modifications of contract have given voluntary associations the right to enter into contracts that are binding upon their members. Before and during World War I the Swedish courts recognized and enforced collective bargaining contracts, and in 1929 a special Labor Court started to interpret and enforce collective agreements. The Swedish labor market is (at least in theory) self-governing; nationwide collective contracts are negotiated between the national association of the workers and the national association of the employers, and these contracts are enforceable in the Labor Court. Apart from providing the services of the court and the mediation services, the State is supposed to stay out of the picture. The individual laborer and the individual employer have to abide by the contract made. Thus, some effective right to contract and control one's own destiny has been taken from the individual and become vested in his organizations. Parallel trends, although less formal and codified, can be ascertained for farm groups, consumer cooperatives, and other voluntary organizations, even such esoteric ones as a club of authors, an association of academicians, a religious denomination. These groups also make enforceable contracts on behalf of their members. Sometimes the other party to the contract is an employer, sometimes it is the State itself acting as cosponsor of a welfare program.

An old-fashioned contract was achieved by shopping around for the best deal and by competitive bidding. Contracts made by large, powerful organizations acting on behalf of their members cannot be of this nature. A situation in which the winner takes all and the loser gets nothing is impossible. Rewards reaped from organization contracts tend to contain modest gains, and to be fairly equally distributed, regardless of the merit and effort of the individual.

The impact of organizations equipped with these rights is considerable. To a very great extent the political influence and economic life chances of a citizen depend on what associations he belongs to. This new pattern, however, is not quite the same as the feudal one of the past when a man's status as nobleman, farmer, or burgher determined his life cycle; the movement from status to contract has not been reversed. Although strong forces make for collective and compulsory joining of the large organizations, the citizen is still free to leave them, something not true of the feudal estates.

On balance, the various Swedish organizations of blue collar and white collar workers in industry and government have used their powers to consolidate the positions of the occupations they represent and to elaborate and develop the economic and honorific rewards available to each occupation. They have *not* used the powers to equalize the distribution of rewards and cut down the distance between well-paid and poorly paid jobs.

Security through Insured Contracts

A major consequence of the welfare state has been to preserve the individual's ambitions and motivations at the times when adversity strikes. Since the state steps in with a helping hand at the crises in one's employment history, one's family cycle, one's medical history, one is not easily pushed into a state of hopelessness, despair or fatalism. Contrary to conservative ideology, there is in fact much individual competition in the Swedish welfare state. And there is much ambition to achieve and get ahead.

The change is this: competitors do not have to face the roughest consequences of their losses. A system has evolved in which one can still gain both small and big winnings but one can only make small losses. The Swedish pension reform enacted a few years ago indicates the prevailing spirit: each citizen is guaranteed an annual old age pension amounting to some sixty percent of his average earnings during the ten best years of his employment. By retiring from the labor market he may lose some income, to be sure, but never more than forty percent of what he had in his best years. A floor is thus provided through which he will not sink. A floor of another kind is represented by the large number of positions, both in government and industry, that have tenure contracts. In these positions one's job is secure but promotion is dependent upon performance. Both these examples indicate a curious mixture of status and contract: a man's status is insured as in a feudal society but he can compete for better contracts as in the developed society. This kind of "insured contract" or secure advance will, I believe, be very characteristic of the society of tomorrow. When it was a society of the future, young America proclaimed man's inalienable right to the pursuit of happiness. This was a truly revolutionary principle when the prevailing world belief was that a man must remain at his given station. The Nordic nations endorse a pursuit of happiness and add to it a second revolutionary concept, a guaranteed minimum of happiness regardless of the success of the pursuit.

Per Olof Sundman

Born in 1922. Author of various novels, of which *The Expedition* (1962) has been translated into many languages. Shuns the psychological approach, preferring to rely solely on verifiable observations for his human portrayals. Likes to use documentary sources. Active as a politician in local government.

A 15-minute Baedeker

Since time immemorial, the Lapps used to live the life of nomad reindeer breeders in the mountainous and wooded tracts of the far north. In recent years, however, the majority have taken to settled ways and entered other occupations. Those who still tend reindeer have enlisted modern means of communication, such as planes and snow scooters, in their work. Even so, the lasso continues to come in handy. Photo : Pål-Nils Nilsson.

There's a little place in Sweden called *Märsta*. You have probably never heard of it, but bear the name in mind, anyway.

Until a few years ago Märsta was just a whistle stop on the railway between Stockholm and Uppsala. Today it is a thriving modern town of 14,000 inhabitants and all the forecasters predict its continued rapid expansion.

As befits a growing community, Märsta has a "center" with a post office, banks, shops and a department store grouped around a stone-paved square. Its completion was celebrated with an inaugural ceremony in May 1966. Several eloquent speeches were given; however, they did not pay tribute to Märsta Center, but to Märsta as the *Center of the World*.

Märsta, incidentally, lies in Uppland, the province of Sweden which is richest in memories of the past. It is located just south of Mora Stenar, the place where peasants of yore used to elect their kings, to the accompaniment of ear-splitting shouts and the clashing of swords and shields.

Sweden and her people were not unknown to the ancient Greeks. They knew that we lived somewhere way up north, and accordingly called us Hyperboreans. We were supposed to be beloved of Apollo and to live a free and happy life in our cool, deep forests—remote from disease, drought, swarms of locusts and other plagues.

It was another Greek, Pytheas of Massilia, who actually took the trouble of finding out where Sweden was in relation to the Mediterranean. He undertook a voyage to this part of the world some 2,300 years ago. In those days Sweden was called Thule, and his account placed Thule six days' voyage north of Britain.

The people of Thule, he found, were pretty normal types. Pytheas further noted that the sun shone for 22 hours per day. Either he never got as far as the Arctic Circle or he must have arrived there after Midsummer. North of the Arctic Circle, of course, the sun shines in late spring and early summer for 24 hours.

If we are to be sticklers for accuracy, it must be admitted that the region of Thule also includes Norway. This makes it a bit difficult to talk about Sweden and leave Norway out in the cold. Both countries, of course, occupy the Scandinavian peninsula (indeed, so does the northwest tip of Finland).

Actually, the differences between Norwegians and Swedes are not readily distinguishable, except that they each have their own king and speak their own language. However, the languages are so much alike that a Stockholmer finds it easier to understand a Norwegian from Oslo than a Swede from the island of Gotland. And a Norwegian from Trondheim communicates better with a Swede from Östersund than with a fellow countryman from, say, Hallingdalen.

For brevity and accuracy, nothing beats the description of Sweden to be found in my youngest son's geography textbook. It reads:

"Sweden is long and narrow. It has different climates in the north and south. The summer lasts only two months in the far north. It is twice as long in the far south."

Yes, Sweden is truly long and narrow. Its southernmost point is called Smygehuk, a name that few foreigners learn to pronounce correctly. The northernmost point is "Treriksröset", an imposing name for the cairn where the borders of Sweden, Norway and Finland meet. The cairn is actually a solid block of concrete deposited in a small shallow lake, Koltajaure. That name was bestowed by the Lapps.

The southern and northern tips of Sweden are separated by 980 crow-flying miles. A motorist, however, has to reckon with a distance of about 1,250 miles, with the only passable roads in the north going through Finland. And if he is really determined, he will have to cover the very last stretch on foot.

This is not to disparage the Swedish roads: they cover a lot

Sweden stretches very far to the north. The mining town of Kiruna, for example, lies on the same latitude as Verkhoyansk in Siberia, the coldest spot on the globe.

of ground, too, given the peculiar shape of our country. Indeed, if all our roads were laid end to end, they would circle the globe four times. Allowing for some bumpy surfaces, the last two laps might prove a bit jarring.

Sweden lies farther to the north than most foreigners think (and many Swedes, too, for that matter).

Take Moscow, for instance. In winter the snow piles high on the streets, the river is covered with ice, and the people wear fur caps with pull-down earmuffs. Yet Moscow straddles the same degree of latitude as Smygehuk in Sweden's far south.

Or take Archangel, the Soviet port near the Arctic Circle and on the White Sea. Although so far north, Archangel is still some 435 miles farther south than Treriksröset.

When we draw our comparisons westward, it turns out that Sweden's southern tip runs parallel with central Labrador. The

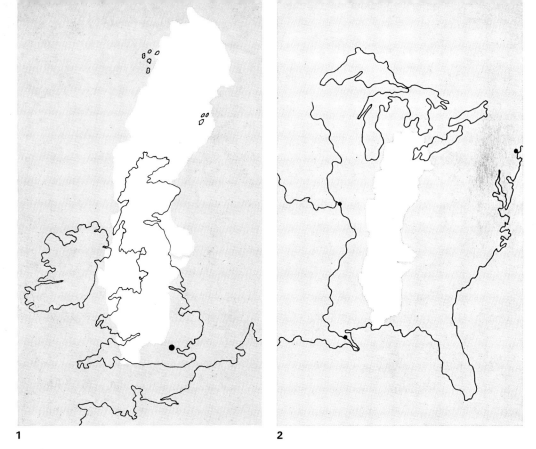

1 **2**

1. *Area of the British Isles compared with Sweden's. The Swedish forests cover an area roughly equal to England, Scotland and Wales put together.*
2. *The length of Sweden from north to south equals the distance separating the Gulf of Mexico from Lake Superior. The exact figure is 976 miles.*

Trotting races and the pari-mutuel betting on them are popular pastimes in Sweden.
Photo : Svante Hedin.

location of Stockholm works out at the northern end of Hudson Bay. As for Treriksröset, it lies well above the site where the Mackenzie River flows into the Arctic Ocean near Alaska.

It might be inferred from the foregoing that Sweden is a frigid, inhospitable place for human life. Actually, it wasn't more than about 14 to 15 thousand years ago that glacial ice began to retreat far enough to expose the southern plains.

Contrary to what one might expect, however, Sweden is a pretty warm country. Härnösand, the Bothnian port 310 miles north of Stockholm, has a mean temperature of 21.5 degrees Fahrenheit in January and an annual mean of 39 degrees. At the same latitude is Yakutsk in Siberia, but there the mean for January is 44.5 degrees below zero and the annual mean is 14 degrees.

Tornedalen, the valley of the river Torne, which here separates Sweden from Finland, is known for its vegetable crops. Yet it lies almost as far north as Verkhoyansk, where a temperature of minus 93.6 degrees has been recorded and the ground never thaws.

In case readers might think that these comparisons with Siberia have been deliberately picked to make Sweden look good, we can balance the picture with a Canadian example. In Winnipeg, the mean temperature for January hovers between five and six degrees lower than at Sweden's northern tip. And Winnipeg happens to be about 250 miles farther south than Smygehuk.

Not only is it fairly warm in Sweden, but sometimes it can get pretty hot, as an Italian, Giuseppe Acerbi, found out back in 1799 when he journeyed to the extreme north. Here is a passage in his diary: "It was terribly hot, with a midday temperature of 27 degrees Celsius, and the mosquitoes tormented us incessantly. We elected to travel by night and decided to do likewise in future."

Oh well, Sweden can hardly be called tropical. Nobody has to tell us how rugged our winters can sometimes be. On the other hand, our climate is favorable and pleasant on the whole, and for a good reason. We borrow our heat from America in the form of the world's largest central heating plant: the Gulf Stream. Originating in the Sargasso Sea, the Gulf Stream heats up to about 77 degrees and is ultimately deflected northward as it follows the western coast of Scandinavia. By the time it reaches our neighborhood, it moves at the inconceivable velocity of 25,000,000 cubic meters of warm water per second.

But for the Gulf Stream, Sweden would probably consist for the most part of one vast tundra—and the world would be one civilization poorer.

The ancient Greeks looked on Sweden as a very remote land in northern Europe. Hence their name for it, Thule. And Sweden can be very far away if the means chosen to get there are wind-powered seacraft or a pair of feet. But we live in different times now.

And that brings me back to Märsta, the fast-growing town I mentioned at the beginning.

Included in the borders of Märsta is Arlanda, the international airport serving the Stockholm area. From Märsta distances aren't counted in marches or miles, but in time. Which puts Märsta within 135 minutes of Moscow, 165 minutes of London, 220 minutes of Paris and 290 minutes of Rome.

When those inaugural speakers referred to Märsta (and, by extension, Arlanda) as "Center of the World", they weren't necessarily giving vent to the exaggerated rhetoric of local patriots. Their outlook was unprejudiced—call it global or mathematical, if you like.

A ship sailing from the United States to Europe doesn't head due east. The shortest route starts off at an angle to the north and then dips slightly southward. In other words, the captain simply follows the great circle of the earth's curvature.

As of ships, so of planes. Thus the shortest distance between New York and Moscow describes an arc which intersects Sweden just north of Stockholm. To reach the Far East from London or Paris, the traveller doesn't head east as Marco Polo did in his day. He goes by air over Denmark, Sweden and the North Pole. From the North Pole, of course, all roads lead south—strange as that may sound.

It is easy to be fooled by the old Mercator projections, the conventional travel routes, and the notion that nobody in his right mind goes to the North Pole if he can possibly avoid it.

So there it is: remote Thule with its Märsta and Arlanda stands midway between the inhabited continents. Or nearly so.

Whenever Sweden comes to mind (especially the minds of people far away from us), the associations it is most likely to evoke are Stockholm, Göteborg, Beautiful Women and the Midnight Sun. And the royal warship, Vasa.

As a man who has run a tourist resort for 14 years, I have had many occasions in the past to enlarge on this picture of Sweden, and I shall now have another go at it. The touches I propose to add will be chiefly of a geographic nature.

In a bygone day, as the chosen favorites of Apollo, we lived a gay and carefree life deep in our huge forests.

We still can today. Many of us make a living at it, and here I am speaking of the lumberjacks. Then there are the youngsters, large groups of them, who can be seen running hither and thither in the woods with a map and compass. Their activity is called "orienteering", a popular form of sport in our country. Still others get lost in the woods while out picking berries or mushrooms, causing no little headache for the search parties which have to be rounded up to find them.

Sweden is amply endowed with trees. All told, they cover an area roughly equivalent to England, Wales and Scotland put together.

The forests are valuable and form a cornerstone of the Swedish economy. In the past decade about 40,000,000 cubic meters of timber have been felled each year, most of it converted to wood pulp.

Although most of the logs are nowadays hauled by truck to the sawmills and processing plants, about one-fourth of them are still being transported by water, with 12 river systems functioning as floatways. In 1960, for instance, 160,000,000 logs were floated from inland forests down to the coast. The combined length of the floatways comes to more than 20,000 miles, which is five times the length of the Mississippi-Missouri.

Finland is called the "Land of a Thousand Lakes". This is not mere poetry but also truth: that figure of 1000 is certainly a minimum.

But how many lakes does Sweden have? According to available tables, we have 54 lakes larger than 20 square kilometers in area (about 7.7 square miles). But that doesn't tell us much.

It is further noted in the official statistics that Sweden's total water-covered area amounts to around 15,000 square miles. (The original figure, of course, is in square kilometers: 38,535.08; how the statisticians arrived at that .08 decimal is beyond me.) I have looked high and low, but found nobody who can tell me how many lakes there are.

The semblance of a clue is provided by the annual list of fishing waters compiled by the Association for the Promotion of Sport Fishing. This body enumerated more than 1300 licensed fishing areas in its 1965 list; each area comprises between 50 and 100 waterways and lakes.

That still doesn't account for all the lakes with fish in them.

A perennial favorite of the Swedish sports scene is the Vasa Ski Race, which has been run every winter since 1922. The course cuts across some 53 miles of Dalarna Province, with the finish line at Mora. Tradition has it that Gustavus Vasa covered this stretch in 1521 when fleeing to Norway. What looks like a swarm of bees in the picture is actually a packed crowd of starters. In recent years more than 6,000 skiers have taken part in the event. Photo: Olle Seijbold.

Once, when I lived in northern Jämtland near the Norwegian border, I figured out with the help of a map that there were about 600 lakes within a radius of 20 miles.

If I were to hazard a guesstimate, the number of fishable lakes in Sweden must be at least 150,000. Whether or not the authorities would permit fishing in all of them is another matter.

Many of the lakes are dotted with islands. I was once told that one such lake, Bolmen I believe, contains exactly 365. While I may be wrong about the lake, I remember the figure very well because it matches the number of days in the year.

Since then upright countryfolk have told me on two occasions that *their* lakes—the one in Värmland and the other in Hälsingland—contain 365 islands. It was easy to remember the figure because....

Similar reports have come to me about clusters of islands in our coastal areas. Before long I'll be doubting whether the year does have 365 days.

In 1681 the French comic dramatist, Jean-François Regnard,

made a visit to Sweden, and of course he wrote a book about it. Sweden was then still regarded as an exotic country on the fringe of the world. He came to Stockholm by sea, where he found the buildings magnificent and the people friendly. But the city's location, he thought, was "abominable". "It is incredible", he wrote, "that this place was deliberately chosen to found the capital of such a great kingdom". Regnard doesn't build up his case for Stockholm's "abominable location", but he probably thought it a chore for a ship to have to navigate snakewise into port past the myriad of islands that make up what is known as the Stockholm Archipelago.

How many islands are there in the archipelago? I haven't found a satisfying answer to that one, either.

We have excellent maps, based on meticulous surveys, and the name of every single island is given on them. But nobody at the National Hydrographic Office has ever bothered to count the number. An official there said he had heard of estimates ranging from 25,000 to 250,000—the latter figure no doubt including islets and skerries.

Other towns with archipelagoes are Luleå and Haparanda at the northern end of the Gulf of Bothnia; Piteå, Umeå, Örnsköldsvik and Härnösand farther south; Norrköping and Västervik on the Baltic. Then there are chains of islands along the southern coast and along the entire western coast from Mölndal past Göteborg up to the Norwegian border.

Even an estimate of the number of islands along our coasts and in our lakes seems to defy human powers. Let's just call Sweden the land with the uncounted hundreds of thousands of islands.

Getting back to my own unofficial estimate of fishing waters in Jämtland, it also resulted in a curious discovery. In Norway, about $4\frac{1}{2}$ miles from the Swedish border, there is a mountain called Nobrientjåkko, located at 65°15'N and 13°20'E. One of its effluents is a stream running south. After a half-mile or so, the stream bifurcates into two channels. The one channel flows east into Sweden, eventually draining into the Ångermanälven, which in turn empties into the Gulf of Bothnia. The other channel flows west, empties into Namnsvandet, and ends up in the Atlantic.

All of which means that a nameless stream emerging from Nobrientjåkko cuts across Scandinavia. So only the northern bank and beyond can properly be called a peninsula; the remaining and larger part of Scandinavia is an island.

Sweden is rather densely populated in the southern parts and along the Bothnian coast. The far northern inland, with its poor wind-lashed forests, peat bogs, vast unwooded expanses and high fjelds have always been either desolate or sparsely populated.
Backsettlers were clearing land in the north as late as the 1930's. Not so today, however. The population keeps thinning out as factories in the south and along the coasts cry for more manpower. Once again Sweden's "outback" is growing in extent.
For all the wealth of minerals and hydroelectric power in these open spaces, Swedes cannot help but regard them as one big impediment, the more so since they comprise between 20 and 25 percent of the country's total area.
Other Europeans may think differently: from the vantage point of their crowded continent, all that unused land must look mighty attractive. Not only does it constitute the largest tract of wilderness in Europe, but much of it is of rare scenic beauty.
Indeed, our great botanist, Carolus Linnaeus, seems to have anticipated man's need for unspoilt nature. Here is what he wrote back in 1748:

"To behold nature is to have a foretaste of heavenly bliss, of constant joy to the soul, and the first beginnings of its complete refreshment. When the soul partakes thereof, it is like being aroused from a heavy coma. One wanders about in the light, forgetful of self, and life is spent, so to speak, in a heavenly land or an earthly paradise".

Or, to put these thoughts in simpler terms: If you're ailing from the rat race, let nature cure you.

Kurt Ågren

Born in 1926. Docent of history at Uppsala University. Painstaking researcher in the social history of 17th century Sweden, but also known as a bizarre humorist in press and radio. Disposed to take the irreverent view of past Swedish feats in the military sphere.

A History of Sweden

The Viking period is regarded in the popular imagination as a heroic age of Swedish history. Posterity has attached considerably less glamour to the element of merchant trading which informed much of the Viking lust for travel.

The Ancient Glory

Even though neutrality and the will for peace have given rise to other ideals, the martial exploits of former days bulk large in the generally known facts of Swedish history. To be sure, chauvinism —sometimes euphemistically called "love of the fatherland"— must subsist on a meager diet after so many years in which Sweden has played a minor military and political role. However, the Swedish people still like to think that their forefathers, at any rate, were paragons of manly vigor and wartime bravery.

Indeed, the popular folklore would appear to be corroborated by the first written references to Sweden. Around 100 A.D. the Roman historian, Tacitus, held up the pristine and virile Svear as examples for his supposedly degenerate countrymen. Unfortunately for the Swedes, Tacitus was less concerned with sound scholarship than with the dissemination of propaganda at home, so he drew for his comparisons on a source so remote that it could not possibly be verified.

We have much more reliable sources to draw on 700 years later, when the Swedes again turn up on the international stage, this time in joint performances with their Scandinavian neighbors under the name of Vikings. Recent historians have tended to stress the non-military causes of the Viking raids, in terms of overpopulation, a deteriorating climate, and so on; in the popular Swedish mind, however, the Viking Age stands for epic adventure, and as such well meets the need for a glorious past. The ideals attributed to these aggressive Northmen are still cherished: when Swedish athletes compete abroad they are often called Vikings— as long as they win, that is.

Most of the Viking forays from Sweden headed east, following a course of expansion that had been set in an earlier, lesser-known period. One of these penetrations resulted in the founding of a Russian state, a historical fact generally accepted in Sweden but vehemently denied by Soviet scholars.

Better known, and perhaps more glamorous, were the westward forays, with landfalls in France, the conquest of England and the early discovery of Vinland, America. Although these feats were largely performed by the neighboring Danes and Norwegians the average Swede usually includes them as part of his own history.

At the same time, however, the outside world was also showing some solicitude for Scandinavia. One of its manifestations was the despatch of a Christian mission to Sweden, which was then pagan. Foreign interest in Swedish sin is thus of long standing, even though the missionaries were motivated by other considerations than 20th century tourists.

The first missionary to Sweden was St. Ansgar, who in the course of his travels built the first church in 830 at Birka, located on Lake Mälaren and then the land's chief commercial center. Actually, paganism in Sweden was not fully stamped out until the 12th century. But since history so often eulogizes the initiator at the expense of his successors, St. Ansgar has come to be known as the "Apostle of the North", and as such he is the best known of all the missionaries.

As the Swedes became increasingly less disposed to embark on foreign ventures, other external influences began to assert themselves with greater force. Those emanating from Germany were particularly great during the Middle Ages. The language of commerce, handcraft and public administration still contains many loanwords from German, all reflecting the powerful economic hegemony of the Hanseatic League during the 13th, 14th and 15th centuries. Since this was a rather unheroic period for Sweden, detailed knowledge of it is limited to the scholars. Every school-child, however, is familiar with Albrecht of Mecklenburg. His name seems indissolubly linked with oppression, a trait that is always easier to impute to an outsider. Actually, the election of this German prince to rule Sweden changed very little.

The need for a counterweight to Germany was certainly a

Gustav Vasa, founder of the Swedish nation-state. He gave his support to the Reformation for domestic political reasons. His reign marks the end of late medieval attempts to unify Scandinavia under one sovereign. More than any other Swedish king he has come to be celebrated as a patriotic champion of freedom.

compelling force in the formation of the Kalmar Union in 1397, linking the crowns of Sweden, Denmark and Norway. However, the genesis of the Kalmar Union is less well remembered than the many fights which took place while it lasted. The patriotic historiography of the 19th century has portrayed an enduring picture, in black and white, of a Sweden struggling to throw off the foreign yoke. As a result our annals have been enriched with the names of Engelbrekt, Sten Sture, Gustav Vasa and other champions of liberty who can hold their own with William Tell. Oppression is symbolized by the Danish kings, especially during the last phase of the union. Thus Christian II (1481–1559) is forever doomed to bear the surname of "Tyrant"; the Swedes bestowed it on him after a wholesale massacre of nobles and clergy in 1520, known as the "Bloodbath of Stockholm". The incident was certainly made to order for the new regent, Gustav Vasa, whose skills as a propagandist have largely withstood the attempts of scholars to introduce a subtler picture of the 16th century. It is to Gustav Vasa that we largely owe the conception of Denmark as Sweden's natural arch-enemy. Actually, the head-on conflicts of the two countries came after his death, towards the end of the 16th and during the 17th centuries, when Swedish expansionism challenged the supremacy of Denmark in the Baltic.

Gustav Vasa's other claim to fame in international relations comes from his support of the Reformation, though he did so for domestic reasons. An opinion-moulding Protestant clergy has since found nothing but good in the severance of ties with the Catholic cultural world.

A period of major expansion begins towards the end of the 16th century. Its initial thrusts, made in the old go-east tradition, brought in large slices of territory on the other side of the Baltic. Attention was then shifted toward the south, the more or less avowed objective being to make the Baltic a Swedish lake so as to control its trade. Sweden's emergence as a first-rate military power, which lasted for about 100 years, is known in our history books as the Age of Greatness and is most brilliantly represented by Gustavus II Adolphus. Patriotic historians have tried to add "the Great" after his name, but without conspicuous success.

Because the expansive wars of Gustavus Adolphus happened to coincide with the Thirty Years' War, giving him the excuse to intervene in this conflict of Protestants and Catholics, his military fame has always carried a religious aura. To further the Protestant cause, however, Sweden saw fit to enter into alliance with Catholic France. The two countries thus began a close relationship, one of whose results was to replace German with French cultural influence.

Many of the possessions gained by Sweden during the Age of Greatness were eventually lost, though the economically important provinces of Skåne, Blekinge and Halland still belong to us. The biggest losses were suffered by Denmark. And looming menacingly on the horizon was Russia, which cared little for a Swedish presence on its side of the Baltic. Most of our disdain may have been heaped upon Denmark, but Russia turned out to be a much more dangerous adversary.

In the closing decades of the 17th century and the beginning

The Swedish Age of Empire was ushered in by Gustavus Adolphus with his military campaign in Germany during the Thirty Years' War. At the same time his intervention in the struggle between Catholics and Protestants touched off nearly a century of Swedish involvement in Continental wars. This period ended with the defeat of Charles XII by the Russians at Poltava in 1709.

of the 18th, Sweden was an embattled land trying to preserve its empire. Around 1720, after some 20 years of exhausting wars, the effort proved futile, but not without another brief outburst of heroics under Charles XII. After a series of brilliant victories in Eastern Europe, Charles was decisively defeated by Peter the Great in 1709 at the battle of Poltava. Its aftermath does not cut much ice historically but ought to commend itself to a librettist. Charles fled to Turkey, where he spent several years vainly trying to whip up a coalition against Russia and making himself a nuisance in the process. The ending is in true operatic style: A whole Turkish army was sent to Bender in Bessarabia

Jean Baptiste Bernadotte was a marshal of France. After incurring the disfavor of Napoleon, he was appointed successor to the Swedish throne in 1810. He reigned under the name of Charles XIV John from 1818 to 1844.

to eject him from his house, which Charles fiercely defended with a handful of men, only to be driven out by fire. With only one man left to accompany him, he made his escape to Sweden. He was killed in 1718 during a campaign against Norway.

After 1720 Sweden was no longer the scourge of Europe and lost her rank as a great power. She then adapted herself to a second-class role, with peace and neutrality as her objectives.

Subsequent history is fairly devoid of excitement, providing little fuel to fire patriotic zeal. The further we come from the 17th century, the more history becomes the exclusive province of scholars, at least up to the events which can be reinforced by living memory. Still, it is characteristic that more people can fix the date of the battle of Lützen (November 6, 1632) than the year of our first pension law. But if forced to choose between the two, they would doubtlessly prefer their pensions to the Swedish victory at Lützen (which was a Pyrrhic one, anyway).

It should be pointed out that Sweden took a long time getting used to her less determining role in European affairs. The series of wars waged against Russia during the 18th century were unsuccessful attempts to recapture past glories; a modern historian might use the less flattering epithet of "revanchist policy". These struggles culminated in the Napoleonic Wars, when Russia forced Sweden to cede Finland; Swedish interests in that country had been of very long standing and were the product of colonization rather than warfare.

The revanchist spirit was probably decisive in the election of a new regent in 1810. He was a Marshal of France, Jean Baptiste Bernadotte, who founded the present dynasty. Under his leadership Sweden entered the war against Napoleon and was compensated in 1814 for the loss of Finland. Denmark was forced to cede Norway, which was joined with Sweden in a personal union. The union was dissolved in 1905, "peacefully" say the history books, though martial rumblings were distinctly audible for a time.

The conquest of Norway was Sweden's last warlike exploit, achieved, it must be admitted, at the cost of no more than token support to the campaign against Napoleon. By the 19th century, Sweden had not only developed a more active desire for peace, but also took a more realistic view of her military potential. The effective war machine of the 17th century had been allowed to obsolesce as proposals for modernization were defeated time and again in the Riksdag.

In spite of relative stagnation in foreign affairs, Sweden made great forward strides at the end of the 19th and beginning of the 20th centuries. This was a completely different kind of expansion than its predecessors, though of no lesser scope. Social and religious discontent, and the mobility which accompanied industrialization, produced many consequences, among them a mass emigration from Sweden to North America.

Towards the end of the 19th century, the traditional ties with France gave way to closer relations with Germany, the new first-rank power on the Continent. Sympathies were divided during World War I, with the pro-Germans arrayed against those who identified the Western powers with the new ideals of democracy and parliamentary rule. During World War II Swedish sympathies were so overwhelmingly pro-Allied that there wasn't any other side to speak of. However, neutrality was maintained in both World Wars: though in the latter conflict, Sweden had to make rather far-reaching concessions to one of the belligerents, Germany, in order to preserve her desire for peace.

The first visible manifestations of neutrality as a policy go back to the end of the 18th century, when alliances were formed with Prussia and Russia to safeguard non-belligerent shipping. In more recent times, declarations of neutrality have been issued only on the basis of understandings with our Scandinavian neighbors. For instance, the Scandinavian prime ministers met for this purpose after the outbreak of both world wars. The formation of a defence pact was considered after World War II between Sweden, Norway and Denmark; the latter two, however, elected to join NATO while Sweden continued her policy of non-alignment.

The Road to Democracy

The struggle for political power in Sweden obeys democratic and parliamentary rules. There is nothing remarkable about democracy as such in the political and cultural sphere to which Sweden belongs. But though the world's democracies have a lowest common denominator, they have reached it in different ways.

The history of democratic evolution is therefore important in order to understand how a people regard their form of government.

In Sweden, as in the rest of Europe, the chief contenders for political power in the past were kings and nobles. Towards the end of the 18th century, when Sweden experienced her last period of absolute monarchy, some clever propaganda was built up against the nobility and its aspirations. The anti-nobility bias was swallowed, though not whole, by later historians, with the result that the popular sympathies of an older day are usually made out to be pro-monarchy.

These sympathies have been reinforced by the picture, lingering from the historiography of the 19th century, of a close and trusting relationship between the king and his people (read peasants). The role assigned to nobility in this idyll is that of the interloper gnawing between the bark and the tree.

ʻTo take one example: At the end of the 17th century large parts of the alienated estates were coercively restored to the Crown to help fill a depleted national treasury. In the conventional history, however, this repossession is portrayed as an act by Karl XI to save from tyranny the peasants who worked the nobles' estates.

Another impetus to democratic growth alleged in the conventional history is that the Swedish peasants were never serfs. However, the freedom to leave one's farm and to have some discretion over one's personal property is a far cry from the exercise of political influence. Rival political groups might vie with one another for agrarian favor, but it was more usual to disregard the will of the peasantry. Besides, this will could be shaped to suit those in power. And closer to our own time, at the beginning of this century, most of the men who campaigned for the enlargement of democratic rights did not come from the land but from other sections of the community. Nevertheless, the ancient picture of an unenslaved peasantry did carry weight in the arguments for a broader-based democracy.

The period from 1397 to 1520, when the crowns of Denmark, Norway and Sweden were united in the Kalmar Union, shows the opposition of monarchy and nobility at its most illuminating. In this struggle the peasants were also involved and exploited. Their objectives, however, could hardly be called political: most of them could be boiled down to the much less subtler question of reduced taxation. From the Swedish horizon, the turbulent strife which marked the Kalmar Union has come to be known as an unrelenting war of liberation. In the end a nobleman emerged the victor: he was Gustav Eriksson Vasa, who in 1523 founded a new dynasty under the name of Gustav I.

There was never any doubt during his reign as to where the central authority lay. Where it had formerly been the practice to elect rulers, Gustav I made the kingship hereditary in his dynasty. The once so mighty church aristocracy was stripped of almost all political power by the property confiscations which followed in the wake of the Reformation. A similar loss of influence befell the secular aristocracy as the king surrounded himself with untitled advisers and officials, many of them from abroad. The decline of the nobility might be thought to have ushered in a flourishing period for the peasantry. Not at all. The peasants fared even worse; among other things, taxes were increased, which led to a number of abortive uprisings.

The struggle for power gained new momentum under Gustav I's three sons, who each succeeded him on the throne. During this period the opposing nobles championed new political ideas calling

The struggle for power between monarchy and nobility was for centuries a recurring feature of Swedish history.

for a division of authority. The "divine right of kings" ultimately carried the day, at least temporarily, under Karl IX, the last of the three sons. His triumph was bloodily rubbed in at Linköping in 1600 with a mass execution of leading nobles. In his fight against them Karl IX found it convenient to invoke the support of the commoner estates, in which the peasants were of course the most numerous.

When Karl IX died in 1611 his son, Gustav II Adolf (Gustavus Adolphus) was still too young to assume full powers. This gave the aristocracy a splendid opportunity to put forth new claims. It was also seized under the leadership of Axel Oxenstierna, best known in Swedish history for his statesmanly defense of the national interest. As an able defender of the aristocracy, however, Oxenstierna is decidedly less well known.

Later in the 17th century there were two fairly long periods of minority-age rule, again enabling the nobles to expand and consolidate their power. The regents who ruled in between, Kristina and Karl X Gustav, strove energetically to uphold the monarchy. For this purpose Kristina exploited the disaffection of the peasantry—a source of support which had been heavily drawn on during the war years. However, aversion to the aristocracy did not stem from the commoner estates alone; much of it came from the "distressed gentlefolk", the poorer ranks of the aristocracy itself.

The coup engineered by the close associates of Karl XI at the end of the 17th century, which again made Sweden an absolute monarchy, can be explained in part by unrest in different classes of society.

At his death Karl XI could bequeath the royal power intact to his son, Karl XII, but it was swept away by the wars which in effect brought Sweden's Age of Greatness to a close. But before his death in 1718, Karl XII had developed absolutism to a degree which in our time would be called military dictatorship.

In the ensuing period chief authority lay with the Riksdag, or Swedish parliament, where it was mostly vested in the nobility, still pre-eminent among the country's four estates. The other three were the clergy, burghers and peasants. According to some scholars, the emergence of present-day parliamentary rule may be traced to this prototype, since it supposedly foreshadowed the dissolution of a system in which privileged classes of society were vested with distinct political powers. But if the seeds of such a development did exist 200 years ago, they were effectively quashed by the coup d'etat of Gustav III in 1772.

The period from 1720 to 1772 is popularly called the Age cf Liberty. It is a name that obviously reflects the evaluations of those in power at the time. Contemporary historians, with more fitting examples to draw on, have been inclined to put "liberty" as then used in quotation marks. The word "license" would seem to have been apter, and the period is regarded as a depressing episode in Swedish history. In any case, the propaganda of the man who put an end to it, Gustav III, continues to carry weight.

Under the pressure of hostility from the nobles, poorly planned wars and wretched government finances, Gustav III staged a new coup d'etat which made him an absolute monarch. In 1792 he was assassinated at an opera ball, the victim of a conspiracy by his nobles. However, his son, Gustav IV Adolf, assumed a strong royal power.

Gustavus III was assassinated in 1792 at a masked ball in the Royal Opera House, the victim of a conspiracy among the nobles. Few events in Swedish history have so intrigued posterity as this act of regicide. Gustavus was an ardent patron of literature and the theater.

Absolute rule from the closing years of the 17th century had foundered in a war which caused Sweden to lose much of her foreign possessions. Its later manifestation was likewise eroded by war, the one which separated Finland from Sweden. Gustav IV Adolf was deposed in favor of his uncle, Karl XIII, who had no heirs. A successor had to be elected outside the dynasty, but not before steps were taken to lay down rules for conduct of the government under constitutional forms.

The result was an Instrument of Government, a Riksdag Act, a law regulating succession to the throne, and a Freedom of the Press Act. "Swedish Flag Day", celebrated on June 6 as a sort of national holiday, traces its origin to the adoption of the Instrument of Government on this date in 1809.

Its adoption did not of course signify the immediate advent of democracy or parliamentary rule. Instead an evolutionary process was set in train which gradually shifted power from the Crown to the Riksdag, with the original Instrument of Government left unamended.

The old four-estates Riksdag persisted until 1866, by which time it had long outlived itself. Socially and economically important sections of the community were more or less without political influence because this rigid stratification of classes operated to give them only a limited say, if at all.

In 1866 the Riksdag was reformed by a government under Prime Minister Louis de Geer. The four estates were replaced by a two-chamber parliament. But this change did not signify a democratic breakthrough, either. The overwhelming majority of Swedes were still debarred from political influence by restrictions of one kind or another on the right to vote; in this respect the general restrictions were of greater significance than the special rules on eligibility and suffrage, which operated to make the First Chamber more exclusive than the Second.

However, the new system did favor landowners, giving rise to a compact agrarian majority in the Second Chamber. The Swedish farmer, whose freedom had long been paeaned in the popular folklore, was now finally asserting himself through the sheer counting of heads at the polls. But the agrarian way of life was even then in decline, yielding ground to an industrialism which was swiftly forming new social groups with their own demands for political influence. In the spread of liberal and later of socialist ideas, farmers were conspicuously absent from the vanguard.

During the latter part of the 19th century, when the most controversial issues were concerned with national defense, tariffs, the suffrage, and the personal union with Norway, the king occasionally tried to intervene.

Later historians have professed to detect either full or partial parliamentary hegemony in late 19th century politics. However, the first Prime Minister to adopt parliamentarianism as an explicit part of his program was the liberal statesman, Karl Staaff, at the beginning of the 20th century.

In 1914 the Staaff government resigned because the king had personally intervened in a defense question without consulting his ministers. The resignation was precipitated by a massive, well-organized Conservative demonstration, the "March of the Peasants" in support of the king. It was the last time that any great number of Swedes have endorsed an anti-parliamentary act.

The election laws were amended several times between 1900 and 1920 to make them more democratic. A final push was given to the process by the warning examples of revolutions abroad in the wake of World War I, and in 1921 the Riksdag enacted universal suffrage.

By and large, the definite emergence of modern democracy in Sweden was a subdued process. The most severe conflicts involved the rights of workmen to strike and organize.

Pär-Erik Back

Born in 1920. Professor of political science at Umeå University. The history of ideas, Swedish parties and interest organizations are among his specialties.

How Sweden Is Governed

The manner in which Sweden is governed is quite different from that of a few decades ago. Indeed, so great is the contrast between 1900, when only a small minority enjoyed the suffrage, and the mid-20th century, by which time Social Democracy had held sway for almost 20 years, that it might at times appear overwhelming. What must be borne in mind, however, is the continuity of the change itself, though its pace was at first unusually slow and from the 1930's onward unusually swift. Moreover, the Swedish form of government has been remolded without abrogation of the two centrally important fundamental laws: the Instrument of Government, 1809, and the Organic Law of the Riksdag (Parliament), 1866. Although both have been amended at many points, the most essential reforms have taken place apart from or in conflict with their constitutional provisions. Two examples may be mentioned. The Instrument of Government is worded to give great influence to the monarchy and it prescribes a true separation of powers between Crown and Riksdag. In practice, however, the parliamentary authority has not been challenged since 1917. Similarly, the constitutional powers of the Riksdag to raise and appropriate money cannot be fully applied in a modern society, where the government budget performs the function of economic regulator. The drafting of budgets follows a procedure which has evolved on its own in the absence of specific written rules.

Sweden has had a bicameral Riksdag since 1866, with powers equally divided between its two chambers or houses. Since 1921 a system of universal suffrage has been in force for both general and local elections. Members of the Second Chamber are elected directly by the voters, while members of the First Chamber are elected indirectly by county councils and representatives of cities having autonomous status. First Chamber M.P.'s serve for eight years and one-eighth of their number is elected every year; the term in the Second Chamber is for four years. All citizens who have reached their 20th birthday the year before an election are entitled to vote; the suffrage is withheld only from persons who have been placed under legal guardianship because they are incapable of managing their own affairs.

Election to both chambers is based on proportional representation. The distribution of seats in the First Chamber follows the d'Hondt method, which consistently favors the largest party. In the Second Chamber, seats have been distributed since 1952 after the "adjusted" Sainte-Laguë method, which is much more favorable to the smaller parties yet at the same time prevents splintering. The Cabinet is entitled to dissolve the Riksdag and call for new elections to one or both chambers. This right has been invoked only once during the postwar period: in 1958, when all Second Chamber members stood for re-election to resolve the fierce controversy over supplementary retirement pensions.

Sweden has no legislation relating to the nomination of candidates at general elections. In practice, however, the parties have completely filled this vacuum. Although a voter is within his rights to strike out the names of candidates on the ballots distributed by the parties and substitute his own selections, any such acts of rugged individualism are unavailing. To all intents and purposes, a candidate who isn't listed on an "official" ballot stands no chance of being elected to the Riksdag.

The Political Parties

The Swedish multi-party system has long presented a picture of rare stability, reflecting a society of homogeneous population and few serious conflicts. From 1945 to 1964 parliamentary representation was confined to five parties: Conservative, Liberal, Center, Social Democratic and Communist. Other parties have wooed the voters from time to time (and one did so successfully in the 1964 election; see below), and some have even won seats at local elections, but their significance has never been more than marginal. In terms of popular votes, the Social Democrats have usually amassed somewhat less than half and the Communists around five percent, while the other parties have more or less fraternally shared the remainder. The 1960's show striking similarities with the 1930's in the distribution of votes and seats.

The parties form one of the two main channels for resolving the wide diversity of popular concerns into patterns where the essential differences of attitudes and opinions clearly stand out. The other main channel is represented by the powerful groups organized to foster specific interests of one kind or another; these will be discussed separately.

Channelizing the opinions of citizens is only one of a party's functions. By shaping the minds of a politically conscious and initiated elite, it also exerts a long-range influence on the opinions and attitudes of the "man in the street". The kind of influence sought may be partially ascertained from a reading of the party platforms. However, these are incomplete and some of their planks have faded with age. The platform of a party sometimes brings to mind the written constitution of a country: what may have had the force of imperatives when first set down on paper receives no more than lip service today. To find out where a party really stands on an issue one often has to analyze its actions over a period of time. The following brief survey of Swedish party platforms is accordingly couched in terms of "Let's look at the record".

The *Conservative* party has always regarded the sanctity of private property as indispensable to sound national growth. In this scheme of things there is no place for State regimentation or nationalization of industries. The country must have a strong defense and its integrity safeguarded. Our primary institutions are the family and the church, and instruction in Christianity must be maintained in the schools.

Within the scope of these generalizations certain shifts of party outlook have become discernible. One example concerns the objectives of Swedish foreign policy. While continuing to agree with other parties that Sweden should continue to avoid association with any great-power alliance, the Conservatives have increasingly emphasized that non-alignment must not lead to isolation. Sweden, they argue, should enter into a limited measure

of defense collaboration with her Scandinavian neighbors. The Conservatives have warmly endorsed the latter-day movement to unify Europe economically and politically.

The planned-economy school of thought receives short shrift from the Conservatives, who regard expansion of the public sector as a menace to individual liberties and to the continuance of political democracy. Their charges of State paternalism were particularly withering in the 1950's. Taxes should be kept within reasonable bounds and the private citizen be given greater discretion over his purse. Insistence on government economies ultimately took on the guise of a thrift creed.

Conservative attitudes to social welfare have been somewhat ambivalent. Towards the end of the 1940's the party was decidedly pro-reform, but in the following decade it applied the brakes. The 1956 platform declared that the legitimate task of social welfare is to prevent and alleviate hardship, as well as to provide maximum security with due regard for the individual's economic and personal liberty.

The *Center* party was originally formed to look after the interests of farmers as a class—hence its earlier name, the Agrarian party. Collaboration with the Social Democrats in the 1930's forced the party to abandon much of its former resistance to social and economic reforms. Since then the party has largely retained its more radical approach to issues. It has accepted the pro-labor policies of Social Democratic government in return for favorable consideration of measures on behalf of agriculture.

Large-scale migration from the countryside confronted the Center party with difficult tactical decisions during the 1940's. Its 1946 platform continued to stress a fair deal for farmers, but new planks were built in whose purport could be taken to include all rural Swedes. When the party lost heavily at the polls in consequence of the coalition government it shared with the Social Democrats from 1951 to 1957, internal demands for modernization and a broadened appeal became stronger. In 1958 the name of the party was changed from Agrarian to Center, and that same year it campaigned on a platform which deliberately catered to different sections of the community. Farmers and other rural interests no longer dictate the party philosophy. Approaches to issues are guided instead with reference to the impact that technological advance, with its tendencies towards concentration, has on the individual. The party endorses government incentives to industrial location and rural development, public support of small business, and private ownership of forest and farmland.

As a matter of practical politics, the Center party has sought to gain adherence in the cities. There it struck a responsive chord in 1960, especially among small businessmen, for its stand against a compulsory retirement pension scheme. However, agricultural interests continue to remain uppermost in the party's actions.

The *Liberal* party was formed in 1934 by the merger of two liberal groups. From the beginning it espoused a middle-of-the-road function dedicated to mediating between extremes. This role came natural to a party which contains not only representatives of all the social classes, but also a whole spectrum of minority interests ranging from nonconformists to radicals in the spiritual and cultural sphere, and from urban merchants to rural small-scale farmers in the economic world. The resulting common denominator works out at a minimum value, and has tended to point up tolerance and freedom of thought as the party's sustaining elements.

Under the inspiration of Bertil Ohlin, a professor of economics, the Liberal party adopted a program in the 1930's which eventually won wide appeal, not least among the newly emergent white-collar middle class. Ohlin was influenced by British liberal thinking, in particular the theories of John Maynard Keynes, on the contracyclical uses of economic policy. Social liberalism, as Ohlin called the new philosophy, demands an active economic policy, as opposed to the reliance of "old-time liberals" on the self-healing powers of a free market in times of depression. At the same time, however, clear lines of separation from both socialism and conservatism were drawn. There must still be primary emphasis on a free market, but safeguards would have to be built into its operation. Supply and demand must remain the determinants of production, and there should be no interference with the right of private enterprise to set prices, but these two factors must be combined with a recognition of "public trust". Ownership of property was viewed as an obligation to manage companies and assets in the interests of the community as a whole. On the other hand, unavoidable State encroachment on the independence of entrepreneurs must be kept to a minimum.

Social liberalism has been the chief lodestone of Liberal party policy in the past three decades. Strong advocacy of social welfare goes hand in hand with criticism of "the queue society", a phrase which alludes to the long waiting lists for housing, higher education, and other perquisites of the good life. According to the Liberals, there would be no queues if the Social Democrats were less fond of regimentation and more confident in the ability of private enterprise to create prosperity. The Liberal party has always shown great interest in legal and constitutional questions. Its latest platforms explicitly call for the introduction of a unicameral Riksdag.

As late as the 1930's the *Social Democrats* imparted a distinctly Marxist flavor to their platforms, in which the sins of capitalism were enumerated in detail. Long before then, however, the party had accepted ideas and acts that could not possibly be reconciled with the image of Karl Marx. The party had gone on record as supporting democracy and parliamentary rule without reservation. Universal nationalization of the means of production was no longer regarded as a panacea for capitalist ills.

Developments have continued along this path. The Social Democrats were also influenced by Keynes, being particularly keen to apply his ideas towards realization of the "People's Home", as Swedes call their welfare state. Differences in income were to be levelled out and prosperity achieved by means of progressive taxes and welfare programs, and by the conduct of an active government economic policy, reinforced by real or potential intervention against private enterprise as soon as signs of inefficiency became apparent in any sector.

This welfare policy remains the chief determinant of Social Democratic actions, though different parts of it have been stressed at different times. More remnants of Marxism were purged from the party platforms of 1944 and 1960, with correspondingly greater commitments to welfare ideology. Full employment has been fixed as the primary end, and the most creditable means to achieve it is a planned economy under State direction. In relation to this, high priority is given to reforms intended to make business and education more democratic.

During the 1950's and 1960's there has been increasing concern with problems of production and capital formation. A stable financial basis is required to further the work of social reform and to sponsor greater public commitments to science and technology. It is against this background that the party's favoring of higher indirect taxes should be viewed. The Social Democrats found a theoretical justification for giving the public sector a larger slice of the resources pie in J. K. Galbraith's analysis of the disparity between public squalor and private affluence.

Anti-militarism, which used to be one of the party's hallmarks, has faded with the years. The Social Democrats have become pro-defense in principle and have helped to put the issue of national security above the level of partisan politics.

An increasingly important party concern is to stimulate industrial production by resort to measures of employment policy and plant location, with emphasis on flexibility to facilitate adjustment to rapidly changing needs.

The *Communist* party long professed to expound the cause of "scientific socialism", that is, the doctrines of Marx and Lenin as interpreted by Soviet ideologists. However, that hasn't stopped the party from reversing direction in strategy and tactics at different times in its history. Up to 1960 the party adhered rigidly to the Moscow line. After that some new discordant notes were heard, chiefly in response to "de-Stalinization" and the emerging signs of disarray in the world communist movement. In its 1964 platform the party contended that socialism can be achieved by peaceful means to break the power of monopoly capitalism. Under the leadership of C. H. Hermansson the Communists have come around to sharing the other parties' acceptance of parliamentarism and democracy. They also reserve to themselves complete freedom of action vis-a-vis their fellow parties in other countries. To all appearances, however, the degree to which Western interpretations of democracy should be adopted is a matter of continuing internal controversy. In any event the Communists have exerted no more than negligible influence in Swedish politics. Although Mr. Hermansson's new course has undoubtedly increased party popularity, there is no reason to believe that a trend towards greater Communist influence is in the making.

The stability of Sweden's multi-party system up to 1964 was

mentioned above by way of introduction. In that year, however, the ferment of other forces began to manifest itself when two new parties ran in the general election: the Christian Democratic Union (KDS) and the Citizens' Front (MbS). The votes cast for them betokened earnest attempts to break up a long-standing pattern. Campaigning in 16 electoral districts, KDS polled more than 70,000 votes but failed to win a seat. MbS confined itself to a single district, in southern Sweden, where it received about 65,000 votes or almost 28 percent of the total cast. This feat entitled MbS to three seats beginning with the 1965 session of the Riksdag.

Two factors may be singled out in trying to explain the relative success of the new parties. First of all, the political parties have recruited the bulk of their voters from certain well-defined social or occupational groups. As many people see it, the consequence has been for M.P.'s to be elected on overly narrow grounds. It cannot be taken for granted that the views of legislators on a particular issue, for instance one with a strong moral tinge, represent the spectrum of opinion within the electorate as a whole. Thus the formation of the Christian Democratic Union may be taken to signify the dissatisfaction of many voters with what they regard as an overly secular-minded Riksdag.

The other factor concerns the effects of many years of rule by the Social Democrats. Trying to dislodge them from power by conventional methods is regarded by many as of formidable difficulty. The opposition parties, it is argued, are their own worst enemies because of fighting among themselves. Why can't the Conservatives, Liberals and Center party join forces instead? The Citizens' Front was frankly organized as an attempt to effect a change of government, on the ground that the opposition's only hopes of doing so lies in unity.

It is still too early to say whether a definite tendency toward splintering of parties is asserting itself. The forces working for stability are very strong. Paradoxically, the longer-range prospects that KDS and MbS may have for effecting change is impeded by the limitation of their initial triumph. Since the Social Democrats, contrary to wide expectations, failed to carve out a larger share of the total vote, the ground was cut from under one of the leading arguments on behalf of change: the danger that Sweden was on her way towards one-party rule. As far as KDS is concerned, its success has probably had another stabilizing effect. The votes it amassed will compel the parliamentary parties to pay greater heed to the interests of active Christians in the electorate.

Lack of space does not permit a detailed treatment of party organization and development of the actual power structure. By and large, the Swedish parties cope ably with their role as vehicles of opinion in an era of mass communication. They have been criticized for falling victim to the bureaucratic virus; indeed, a tendency may be discerned towards the concentration of power in the hands of a few. The rank and file note that a handful of leaders and officials are looking after their interests, to all appearances with great efficiency, and then let matters rest at that. The voters (say the critics) duly cast their ballots on election days, but in between devote themselves to activities other than politics.

Perhaps the critics should pause to consider that times have changed. Nowadays, it can scarcely be a democratic ideal to have all citizens give most of their leisure time to public affairs. A more legitimate target of criticism would appear to be party finances or, more specifically, getting exact information as to where the parties get their money from. The more that parties take on the guise of semi-official bodies, as elements in a quasi-legal power structure, the more reasonable is the demand for insight into the principles under which they obtain their funds. The financing question has indeed become a hot potato, but for another reason. Costs have consistently moved in an unfavorable direction. Present-day election campaigns incur big outlays, with television appearances adding greatly to the expense. If it is held that the political parties perform a useful function in society, it follows that their resources should not only pass an audit but that they should also be adequate.

The idea of having the State contribute to party finances came to the fore in the present decade. It was related in part to the question of the economic conditions under which newspapers operate. The issue of party support generated a vehement debate. According to spokesmen for the non-socialist camp, the award of State subsidies would pose a threat to the independence of parties. Such subsidies, they also argued, would tend to make rigid the present party system and impede the formation of new parties. The Social Democrats stressed a different kind of risk: for lack of money, the parties would have to reduce their activities to a minimum. In the Social Democratic view, the work of political enlightenment carried on by the parties was essential to preserve and strengthen the "formation of democratic opinion".

In 1965 the Cabinet submitted a bill on party support which the Riksdag passed. State subsidies will be awarded to every party represented in the Riksdag which is regularly engaged in shaping the opinions of its members and the general public. To qualify, a party must have gained at least one seat in the most recent general election and received at least two percent of the national popular vote. Every eligible party gets an annual subsidy prorated at Swedish kronor (SKr) 60,000 per parliamentary seat. For 1966 total subsidies were to be distributed approximately as follows: Conservatives, SKr 3,500,000; Liberals, SKr 4,000,000; Center party, SKr 3,000,000; Social Democrats, SKr 11,500,000; and Communists, SKr 600,000.

Parliamentarism

Brief reference has already been made in the foregoing account to the form that parliamentary government has taken in Sweden. It is now relevant to call attention to some other of its characteristics. The long period of power enjoyed by the Social Democrats has been due in part to their majority in the First Chamber. Even at times when the non-socialist parties have outnumbered the Social Democrats in the Second Chamber, the Center Party chairman, at any rate, has held back from a coalition government with the Conservatives and Liberals because of the situation in the First Chamber. In addition, the fairly equal division of strength between the socialist and non-socialist camps has often enabled the Communists to tip the scales; for practical purposes, however, the Social Democrats have usually been able to count on Communist support to pass legislation whenever critical deadlocks have threatened. Majority parliamentarism as practiced in Sweden has thus become pretty blurred at the edges. Indeed, it is not a little strange that a party can muster 50 percent of the popular vote only on rare occasions and still run the show so thoroughly, as the Social Democrats have done throughout the postwar period.

Another aspect of Swedish parliamentarism is the role of the opposition. It has been molded in part by the system of proportional voting and in part by national tradition, which considers it "fair" for all parties to have a say in the making of decisions. As the role has developed in this country, one might say it has imparted a curious split personality to the opposition parties. At elections they comport themselves as if a classical British-style parliamentarism held true: their sole concern is to win enough votes to oust the party in power. But once they occupy the opposition benches in parliament, they abstain from the role which regularly befalls the opposition under a classical two-party system where power changes hands regularly: to concentrate on criticizing the party in power and gain the electorate's support for its stand. Instead the Swedish opposition parties are willing, in proportion to their strength, to take part in the decisions made by the ruling party, and in so doing share responsibility for implementing much of the policy with which the Cabinet ministers are largely identified.

Although the split personality of the opposition can be both explained and defended, there are clear indications that the parties concerned are beginning to feel it more and more like a millstone around their necks. This feeling is reinforced by another circumstance, namely the enhanced prestige of the executive over the legislative branch of government. This is not solely or even chiefly due to the continuity which comes from the long period of Social Democratic rule. A similar inability of parliaments to assert their traditional authority is observable in most of today's highly industrialized welfare states, and Sweden is no exception. The need for an effective economic policy which permits swift public action in crises has given the executive branch an advantage. And when policy is specifically aimed to counteract fluctuations in the business cycle, it becomes natural for the executive to act directly on behalf of the State. By virtue of its budget-making powers, the executive is enabled to direct public financial policy.

In addition, the accelerated pace of publicly sponsored reforms must proceed on the basis of supporting facts and data, which means inquiries. Since the investigating machinery is in the hands of the executive, that too has added to its prestige. Parliament has been neither able nor willing to exploit its formal authority to create a competing organization. It is pertinent here to call attention to the growth of the Swedish civil service. The number of persons employed in central and local government offices has increased sharply during the past few decades. This development reflects the expansion of the public sector. The authorities penetrate the lives of Sweden's citizens more and more often and to greater depth. In their efforts to control economic events as they happen, to plan for the long run, and to act as a primary impetus to continuing prosperity, the men in power have built up a far-reaching executive apparatus. At the apex of this pyramid-like structure stands the Cabinet or the King in Council. To find its counterpart in terms of flourishing bureaucracy, one would have to go back to the middle of the 19th century. Over and above the prestige accruing to the Cabinet members as ultimate trustees for the majority electorate, they can add the prestige which comes from their direction of a widely ramified public administration.

It follows from the foregoing that Sweden has evolved a form of parliamentary government which in no small measure is distinctively indigenous. The system does pose its problems, even though it has functioned without major conflicts. Most of the skepticism expressed in public debate as to its viability concerns the opposition's chances of continuing to operate as an effective force. Can the parties really content themselves with the role of eternal opponents, in spite of the fact that they are given a say in executive decision-making between elections? Doesn't it have bearing on the vitality of a party in power to know that it must always reckon with a change at the helm? Doesn't it need to be on the outside looking in from time to time in order to renew itself?

The Organized Interests

It was noted above that the parties comprise one of the two main vehicles for channeling public opinion. The other main vehicle consists of powerful interest groups. Scarcely in any other country have privately formed organizations achieved as much power and exert as much influence over political decisions as they do in Sweden. This is true both of those which primarily "represent an interest" and those which chiefly "propagandize a point of view". Trade unions, organized management, cooperatives, temperance societies, church groups—all are successfully engaged in fostering the interests of their members.

The present-day significance of organized interests in Sweden derives from many causes. A more important one can be found in the fundamental structure of the modern economy. The preservation of free enterprise, together with the unimpaired right of individuals to promote mutual concerns in association, is nowadays supposed to go hand in hand with far-reaching measures by the community at large to safeguard the prosperity and security already attained. The organized interests occupy an ideological halfway house between individual liberalism and traditional socialism. As such they are widely believed, and no doubt reasonably so, to have a legitimate function to perform in public life and to share responsibility for shaping the future of Sweden's welfare state.

The organized interests draw on a formidable arsenal to make known their views to other people in power. Two methods of applying pressure have long since become classical: submissions, that is, rendering opinion and comment on proposed legislation; and membership of the government committees whose inquiries precede such legislation. Many of the interests have set up secretariats for the special purpose of keeping an eye on any initial moves the authorities may take. The larger organizations, moreover, have their own men in the Riksdag, who propose motions that have already been drafted in their essentials at headquarters. And if any of these means are unavailing, an organized interest can always ask to send one or more of its representatives for face-to-face talks with Cabinet ministers.

Then there are other ways and means of establishing influential ties where presenting information or applying pressure is not explicit but nevertheless implied. Representatives of organized interests have been given seats on the boards of civil service departments and public trading agencies. In some cases the organizations more or less voluntarily undertake duties of a public nature in order to prevent the passage of inconvenient legislation.

What we have said so far essentially applies to the decision-making powers of government itself irrespective of their source or motivation. However, any attempt to portray a realistic picture of the power structure in present-day Sweden must also take into account the important decisions reached outside the government chancelleries. Thus the top labor and management groups bargain collectively without government interference, and the decisions involved vitally affect the lives of most Swedes. Not only that, but they have virtually the same binding effect on the individual as those emanating from government. The more powerful organized interests command an armory of sanctions scarcely less effective than those of the State, which of course has ultimate resort to police power.

The consequences of power vested in these interests pose some intractable problems. Such power diminishes the stature of political parties—in certain situations they tend to behave as pressure groups vis-a-vis the special interests. Direct contacts between government and organized interests sometimes put the opposition parties in a predicament, worsening a position that prolonged majority parliamentarism has already made inferior. The State's collective agreements with civil servants on salaries, or with agricultural interests on farm prices, can push the Riksdag aside. The scope within which a long-range and rational economic policy can be conducted is curtailed as the special pleadings of group interests carry the day at the expense of the larger community. It is relevant here to note that the organized interests are also afflicted with an "elite problem". The risk is that many of their stances will reflect the views of a submission-writing bureaucracy than those of their general membership.

Arguments in defense of the niche carved out by the organized interests for themselves have not been lacking. One of them is that the individual should be enabled to identify himself with more than one type of collective. At a time when technical and economic forces are generating strong centralizing tendencies and the State keeps encroaching on individual liberties, it is important to have several centers of power, even if each of these appears to strike the homely eye as a colossus. A pluralistic society serves to maintain a balance of power. Negotiations between groups on a more or less equal footing take the place of unilateral diktats and help to guarantee the continuance of political democracy.

Central and Local Government

We have already had several occasions in this essay to refer to the expansion of the public sector. In the ideal society envisioned by liberals of the old school, private enterprise was to be left strictly alone; however, that thesis holds true no longer. The State does not, as it once did, limit its purview to looking after the country's defenses against possible agression from the outside, and ensuring law and order for its citizens on the inside. Instead, it is actively committed to reform and stimulate. The local authorities have been increasingly enlisted in this wider concept of government, either by sponsoring activities of their own or by executing programs imposed on them from Stockholm. Both central and local government have assumed many functions which used to be private concerns.

  Although the central government is an entrepreneur in its own right, having taken over or started several undertakings, the control it exercises over business is essentially indirect. Sweden's welfare state is marked by a condition of equilibrium between "government" and "business". The balance is precarious at any given moment, yet gives the impression of indefinite stability. "Government" derives its strength from lush tax revenues, access to an ever-growing administrative arm, the triumph of welfare ideology and a long period of homogeneous political leadership. "Business" has not a few advantages on its side, too: a prolonged economic boom, rapid urbanization, the headlong surge of technology, and the incentive (originally regarded as a liability) to modernize plant and cut costs to avert threats of nationalization. To be sure, there are frictions between the two and sometimes the old ideological differences are aired anew, especially in election and after-dinner speeches. On the other hand, many observers profess at times to discern a distinctive bond of fellowship; the sense of common interest is manifested in more or less explicitly worded agreements between "big business" and the ruling party, which would appear to circumvent the normal democratic procedures for decision-making.

As indicated earlier, much of the public sector's expansion is at the local level. In 1962 the primary communes (all units of local government below the county level) spent more than SKr 11,000 million, as compared with around 3,000 million in 1949—a tremendous increase even when allowance is made for depreciated money. Local authorities are accelerating their outlays faster than the national government: from 1913 to 1958 local consumption increased from 4.3 percent to 12.6 percent of the total spending; the corresponding increase for central government was from 2.4 percent to 6.1 percent. One of the impelling reasons was the new Local Government Act of 1953, which permitted the local authorities to diversify their activities much more than before.

Great changes have been wrought in the status of Swedes as local citizens and on their potentialities for bringing political influence to bear on municipal affairs. Here again one detects the forces at work in the larger society: the business of government has become increasingly professional and sophisticated, favoring the influence of experts at the expense of laymen; and service functions have had to be centralized and formed into larger units to make them operate efficiently. In addition, the policies formulated in Stockholm have the effect of curtailing local freedom to maneuver. The continuing process of realigning local boundaries provides a ready barometer of the change. In 1952 the number of primary communes was reduced by amalgamation from about 2,500 to a little over 1,000. But the reduction soon proved to be inadequate; far too many of the new units were too small to discharge the many tasks assigned them by the central government. A new realignment is now in progress: although the communes are theoretically free to amalgamate or not as they wish, Stockholm is pressing hard and it is expected that their number will fall to 282.

Critical voices have been raised against this reform. Among other things, it allegedly endangers "local democracy". What good does it do to vote when you can't have a say in local affairs anyway? Is there any kind of debate that can be made to keep officialdom in check? Can accountability be demanded or does an elite run the township's affairs as it sees fit? Many take a pessimistic view of the situation. Others contend that the criticism is based on partly untenable premises. According to the apologists, expectations of paragon democratic behavior on the part of local governments must be weighed against the necessity for them to function effectively as administrative units within the overall democratic pattern.

Legislation, Budget Work, Taxation

The rules governing elections and the make-up of parliament were described above by way of introduction. Our subsequent discourse has been chiefly concerned with institutions and relationships which receive either cursory treatment in the written constitution or none at all: the political parties, parliamentarism, organized interests, and the division of authority between central and local government. It remains to describe briefly the central administrative boards and the decision-making procedures in which they are involved. As already indicated, much of what the fundamental laws have to say about their regulation is obsolete. Custom and practice play the major role, and in this regard the differences between Sweden and Britain are less than one might think.

According to the Instrument of Government, the authority to enact most types of laws is vested jointly in the King (the King in Council or Cabinet) and Riksdag. The usual procedure in respect of a civil or social law is generally as follows. At the request of an organization or through initiation by some other means, the Cabinet will introduce a bill submitted in the Riksdag. If the question is of more than average importance, the Cabinet in all probability will appoint a committee to conduct an inquiry beforehand. Even though parliamentary debate on a matter occurs at an early stage, it is rare nowadays for a private member's motion or a party motion to contain a complete legal draft. As a rule the motion will conclude by calling on the Riksdag to ask the Cabinet to appoint a committee. If the Riksdag agrees with the motioner's aims, a request to this effect generally covers the action it takes.

The system of official investigation is exceptionally important in Sweden. A tremendous amount of work already goes into formulating the terms of reference that guide the work of a

Local government is strongly entrenched in Sweden. Responsibility for the hospital system is vested in the county council. Shown here is a part of Danderyd Hospital north of Stockholm. Architect: Folke Löfström Photo: Hans Hammarskiöld.

committee of inquiry. Apart from the limitations imposed by these directives, the committee has a relatively free hand. If the question is political dynamite, the committee will often be composed of M.P.'s, with particular care given to having different shades of opinion represented. Depending on the issue, a committee may include officials from the large organized interests. Or it may have a heavy admixture of expertise, especially if intricate points of law are involved. The target of every committee is to frame a unanimous final report of recommendations. In the last few decades the target has been hit often enough to permit political compromise to be reached by the time a committee finishes its work. The finest legal scholarship in Sweden goes into the writing of committee reports.

The final report is turned over to the Cabinet minister in his

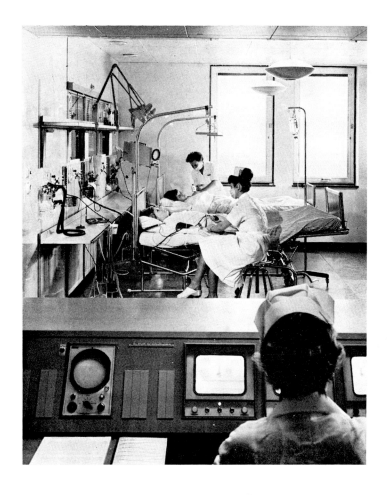

Danderyd Hospital. Newly operated patients are kept under close surveillance with the help of TV. Photo: Sune Sundahl.

capacity as head of the department concerned. Together, department and committee draw up a list of the authorities, institutions and private associations who are to comment on the report. A deadline is fixed for the return of submissions and after studying these, the minister determines whether the committee's recommendations can underlie a government bill. If so, the next step is to prepare the bill in detail. In due course the King in Council formally decides on presenting the bill to the Riksdag.

One of the parliamentary judiciary committees then gets to work on it, eventuating in a statement of opinion which both chambers of the Riksdag consider simultaneously. If the two chambers reach a concerted decision, the bill becomes law. Upon notification thereof, the King in Council issues a promulgation order. In the event of disagreement between the two chambers which cannot be ironed out, the question falls by the board until another legislative session.

Certain legislation of an economic or administrative nature is for the Cabinet alone to enact. Taxation laws, on the other hand, are the Riksdag's exclusive prerogative, since the raising and expenditure of public money have always been parliamentary functions. In practice, however, the Cabinet has acquired continually increasing influence over State finances. This is because of the great importance attached to its annual budget proposal and to its long having been able to count on a parliamentary majority, which accepts the ministerial draft with extremely small modifications.

In Sweden the fiscal year runs from July 1 of one year to June 30 of the next. Work on a new budget gets under way about 18 months before the fiscal year starts. Lower-level officials make known early their budget requests to superiors. The central administrative boards have until September 1 to submit their requests to the ministries (departments). After that date the ministries get down to work in earnest. A key position in the process is occupied by the Ministry of Finance, which has come to acquire the character of overseer in relation to the other, more specialized ministries. After the latter perform a severe weeding-out of the many requests they have received, a tabulated specification is given to the Finance Minister. He consults his Cabinet colleagues and arrives at a general appraisal of the budget situation. In this process regard is paid to what the Cabinet considers politically crucial, the reforms that are going to be backed, the likely objects for tax increases, and so on. The specialized ministries will then usually be told to prune their demands further. The Finance Ministry's examination of budget requests from the other ministries is extremely painstaking. The outlay side of the budget is supposed to be in finished form by the beginning of December. The estimates made by the central administrative boards are generally accepted with only minor modifications. When the Riksdag is formally convoked on January 11, it is presented with the complete draft budget together with all its elaborate appendices.

The Riksdag goes through the draft with a fine tooth comb. Most of the outlay side is examined by the Select Committee on Estimates, while the Ways and Means Committee takes charge of the income side. The ministries are represented in the operating budget by separate estimates, each of which is dealt with in turn during the spring on the basis of committee statements of opinion. The budget draft regularly gives rise to a number of motions, but only a very few of them are ever accepted. By and large, the Cabinet has its way. At the end of May the sequence of decisions on the estimates is summarized, as well as other budget rulings. The budget is now all worked out and is presented to the Cabinet signed by the Speakers of both chambers.

A New Constitution?

The 1809 Instrument of Government remains the oldest fundamental law in Europe still in existence. But because of its many obsolete provisions there has long been a clamor for sweeping constitutional reform. In 1954 the Cabinet appointed a special committee to study the problems of democracy in action and to recommend proposals for bringing the constitution up to date. The committee went about its task in thoroughgoing fashion. Since its members were sharply divided on many points, a final report did not appear until 1963. As a starting point for its recommendations, the committee favored adaptation of the old constitutional text to bring it in line with current usages. Thus parliamentarism was to be spelled out where it had only been adumbrated previously; the budgeting clauses were to reflect the development that had taken place since the adoption of modern contracyclical economic policy; and the operation of government was to be geared to the system that had actually evolved and which gave the individual Cabinet member much greater power than the constitution envisioned.

These recommendations generated little controversy between the parties, nor did the committee's view that all legislative authority be vested in the Riksdag. However, political toes were pinched by what the committee had to say about how the Riksdag should be composed. In regard to the electoral system, a majority of the committee had originally favored a shift to majority voting in single-member constituencies, largely after the British pattern. According to several of the committee's Social Democratic members, such an arrangement would compel a desired reorganization of the Swedish party system; in due course, they argued, a two-party system would emerge under which power could be alternated. As the inquiry proceeded, however, these members realized that not even their own party stood behind them. The idea of majority voting was therefore dropped and the committee went on record for maintaining proportional representation.

The more detailed design of the electoral system depended in part on how many chambers the future Riksdag would have. Most of the committeemen wanted a unicameral legislature, tentatively consisting of 290 members. Of these, 230 would be elected in the present Second Chamber constituenceis and under the present method of distributing seats between the parties. The other 60 members would be elected at the same time, but in six regions each having jurisdiction over 10 members. Seats would be apportioned by the d'Hondt method, the aim being to make parliamentarism function better because majorities would be easier to form. The committee also suggested a measure of voting for personalities rather than party in the constituency elections. However, the wording of this recommendation floundered in technicalities and immediately encountered strong opposition.

Other recommendations met with a lukewarm reception at best. It is worth emphasizing, however, that two far-reaching and important sections were treated kindlier: first, the provisions relating to financial powers; and second, the recommendations on parliamentary procedures and legislation. The criticism levelled at the other sections of the committee report may be conveniently divided into two classes. The first class of objections comes from the political scientists and is often more concerned with legal scholarship. It is held that the catalogue of rights and freedoms is incomplete. Further, several passages in the clauses dealing with monarchy are alleged to be unfortunately worded: they serve to strengthen the king's influence although the committee's intentions were quite the opposite.

The second class of objections is for the most part politically motivated and comes from parties and individual politicians. No party was happy after figuring out the seats that would accrue to it from a combination of constituency and regional elections. The non-socialist camp, and in particular the Liberal and Center parties, demanded a unicameral system and exact proportionality between votes and seats. For their part, the Social Democrats stress an electoral system which makes it easier to form a strong Cabinet—in other words, an executive branch able to count on a stable parliamentary underpinning between elections that will permit it to govern forcefully.

In the years that have passed since the committee's final report was published, party officials have convened in a series of attempts to hammer out a compromise. New aspects have been introduced into the debate. Especially important is the Social Democratic demand for preserving a link between national and local elections.

Postscript

Two important events have occurred since the above lines were written. First, the local elections in September 1966 inflicted heavy losses on the Social Democratic party, whose proportion of the electorate fell from 50.5% to only 42.3%. After some hesitation the party decided to continue in office, in the hope of regaining voter confidence before the next general election takes place in 1968.

Second, opposition successes helped to pave the way for a partial solution of the constitutional problem. According to a binding agreement reached between Conservative, Liberal, Center and Social Democratic leaders, in March 1967, a unicameral Riksdag will be introduced in 1971. It will have 350 seats, to be proportionally distributed between those parties which poll at least 4% of all the votes cast. However, parties of local strength will be able to gain seats if they obtain at least 12% of the votes in a constituency. Parliamentary terms of office will run for three years, and local and general elections will be held at the same time.

Nils Andrén

Born in 1918. Associate professor of political science at Stockholm
University 1958–67, now professor at the University of Copenhagen.
From 1951 to 1967 director of studies at the Institute for English-
speaking Students in Stockholm. Publications include *Modern Swedish
Government* (1961), *Government and Politics in the Nordic Countries*
(1965), and *Power-Balance and Non-Alignment* (1967).

National Security and International Solidarity

Swedish Foreign Policy after World War II

From War to Peace

With the end of the Napoleonic Wars in 1815, Sweden entered into a period of peace that has lasted up to the present day. During the early part of this period, however, foreign policy was not marked by a conscious quest for neutrality. Sweden attempted to safeguard her national security by orienting herself in turn to different great powers: first, Russia, later Britain, and—towards the end of the 19th century—Germany. Only once was this orientation bound by treaty. During the Crimean War Sweden actually prepared to join Britain and France against Russia. However, peace was concluded before Sweden was ready to intervene.

Under the influence of pan-Scandinavianism—the growing sense of community between Norway, Denmark and Sweden which developed during the 19th century—Sweden made attempts to help Denmark in her dispute with Germany over Schleswig-Holstein. In 1848 Swedish troops were stationed on the Danish island of Fyn. In 1864 Sweden was restrained only by her own military weakness from helping Denmark against Prussia and Austria.

These episodes did not indicate a deliberate striving for neutrality. It was not until World War I that neutrality emerged as a full-blown doctrine of foreign policy. Swedish policy during this conflict was largely construed as being pro-German. In fact, it bore the strong personal stamp of the then Prime Minister, Hjalmar Hammarskjöld, who firmly espoused neutrality as a concept of international law.

The transformation of Swedish foreign policy derives from a number of causes, some of which here merit particular attention.

73

An altered international balance of power had undermined the basis for any *Machtpolitik* on Sweden's part. At the same time the course taken by events abroad had served to build up a position of relative security. Sweden did not represent a point of friction between rival great-power interests. On the home front, developments moved more or less smoothly in the direction of greater prosperity, which meant that Sweden was not tempted to enlarge her resources for economic growth by embarking on foreign expansionist ventures. As for the political leadership, the checks which constitutional law imposed on its powers ruled out attempts to divert attention from internal difficulties by conduct of an aggressive external policy. The long period of peace, marked by increasing prosperity, helped to instill a change of attitude, which can be described by saying that the Swedes have become a peaceful, indeed a "peace-loving" people. It is thus to favorable external and internal circumstances that we must look for the causes, and not to any intrinsic trait of the Swedish character.

The Interwar Period and World War II

The interwar years and the second World War had several important bearings on Sweden's foreign policy and international outlook. Simply expressed, Swedish thinking on foreign affairs may be said to have moved by tradition within a magnetic field. The one pole is represented by a nationalistic, largely isolationist and suspicious view of the outside world, marked by a wish to maintain a strong defense. This view is traditionally conservative, rooted as it is in the country's martial past. The other pole is internationalistic, marked by an optimistic belief in cooperation between peoples as a means to achieve a lasting peace. In Sweden this is the traditionally "leftist-tinged" view. It often has purely pacifist undertones. During the interwar years the two differences of outlook were particularly manifested on two occasions: when Sweden was to enter the League of Nations, and when it was decided in 1925 to reduce the defense establishment.

The tensions between these two attitudes have been greatly diminished by developments that have taken place since the latter part of the 1930's. At first the conservative-pessimistic school of thought appeared to have gained justification. Sweden began to rearm in 1936 in response to the deteriorating international situation. The impotence of the League of Nations, underlined with special force when Italy attacked Ethiopia, resulted in a declaration—issued jointly with other European countries outside the great-power sphere—that Sweden no longer felt bound by the League's sanction rules.

Although this change of posture was dictated by external circumstances, it had evidently been facilitated by economic and social levelling-out processes on the home front, which among other things weakened the former socialist conception that armed forces exclusively served the interests of the privileged classes. Stalin's non-aggression pact with Hitler, followed by Soviet attacks on Finland and the Baltic countries, further undermined the traditional socialist view of armed might and warfare as the political instruments of capitalism. Hence it became possible for Sweden to rearm quickly during World War II under general agreement on pursuing a policy of neutrality in order to keep the country out of the conflict.

The war imposed great strains on the leadership responsible for Sweden's foreign relations. Major departures from the requirements of strict neutrality had to be made from time to time. Germany's initial successes led to the complete encirclement of Sweden. The country felt compelled to make concessions, especially on transit rights for German troops and materiel over Swedish soil both between Germany and Norway and between southern and northern Norway. In the closing phase of the war concessions were made to the other side, albeit with less reluctance.

At the beginning of the war all the Nordic countries[1] had declared themselves neutral, but in trying to implement this policy they proceeded separately rather than in joint solidarity. The effort was frustrated by Russia's attack on Finland and the German occupation of Denmark and Norway. With the Nordic area now split up by force of arms, Sweden was confronted with

---

[1] As used here the "Nordic countries" refer to Sweden, Norway, Denmark and Finland. The term "Nordic area" will also be used where applicable to include these four countries together with Iceland. "Scandinavia" is understood to embrace Sweden, Norway and Denmark.

political and emotional problems that could not be wholly overcome. Sweden's feeling of shared destiny with her ravished
neighbors was most strikingly demonstrated by large-scale programs
of humanitarian aid. These also helped to lay the groundwork
for the increasingly extensive cooperation of the Nordic countries
during the postwar period.

Before the war ended, leading delegates of the Western powers
had met in San Francisco to form the beginnings of a new
peace-promoting world organization. Most sections of the
Swedish community welcomed the initiative. Not having taken
part in the war against the Axis powers, Sweden could not
qualify as a charter member of the United Nations, but it was
unanimously agreed that she ought to apply for membership.

By the end of the war little substance was left to the former
dichotomy of attitudes on foreign policy. The basis was laid for
the remarkable national unity that has imbued Swedish activity
on the postwar international scene. This unity has rested on
certain guiding principles: neutrality in relation to great-power
conflicts, a strong defense, active participation in international
organizations and international cooperation in general, and greater
integration with the other Nordic countries. In the following,
Swedish foreign policy during the postwar period will be chiefly
explained in terms of these aspects. They can be summarized
with reference to the main title of this essay: national security
and international solidarity. The sequence of the two is not
arbitrary, since demands of national security have always been
given the highest priority.

The Affirmation of Non-Alignment

Both aspects came to the fore when Sweden first declared
herself for the UN. The question of joining the new security
organization was discussed in characteristic tandem: on the one
hand, a resolve to help promote the newly won peace; on the
other hand, an illusionless view of the UN's importance for
Swedish security. Sweden wanted to contribute towards securing
the international rule of law and peaceful conditions throughout
the world. In 1946 the parliamentary Foreign Affairs Committee
described the UN as a renewed expression of concerted inter-

national endeavor for this purpose, based on the experiences of World War II. In the Committee's words, Sweden should, "without exaggerated hopes or distrust, seek to support the new organization and help to make of it a workable instrument for peace".

Sweden joined the UN in full awareness that, in so doing, she shouldered the broad commitment to support sanctions, even of military import, if the great-power members of the Security Council were unanimous. At the same time it was emphasized that the veto right of these Council members debarred Sweden from taking part against her will in a concerted action aimed at one of the great powers. In other words, a policy of neutrality was incompatible with membership of the UN as long as the world body functioned. In the event of a great-power conflict, on the other hand, there would be "no objection of principle to the pursuit of Sweden's policy of neutrality". Hence neutrality would be impossible only in situations when it would not be necessary in order to pursue the traditional aims of Swedish foreign policy.

Events soon justified the cautious pessimism on great-power relations expressed by Sweden when she joined the UN. Differences between the Soviet Union and the Western powers turned increasingly acrimonious. The Marshall plan, though intended to embrace all European states when first promulgated in 1947, worked out in practice to promote the economic recovery of Western Europe as a bulwark against Communist pressure from the east. However, no political strings were attached to Marshall aid, and Sweden therefore felt she could take part in the program with tangible benefits for her own economy.

In 1948 the Communist seizure of power in Czechoslovakia definitely alarmed the West to look after its defenses. The result was the North Atlantic Treaty Organization, followed by consolidation of the Eastern bloc in the Warsaw Pact. The efforts to form an Atlantic defense community exerted a great attraction for Norway. Finland, burdened by the payment of huge reparations to the Soviet Union, became more closely associated with the Russian system of collective security by a treaty of mutual friendship and assistance.

These extensions of rival great-power interests to the far north of Europe were perceived as a threat by Sweden, which accordingly sought to counter it by asking Denmark and Norway to join in a Scandinavian defense alliance. Negotiations for this purpose were held from the autumn of 1948 to the beginning of 1949. As envisioned by Sweden, the three allies would pursue a common neutrality completely detached from the power blocs of East and West. The negotiations broke down, chiefly because Norway wanted a link with the Atlantic security system that Sweden could not accept. Norway was primarily concerned to make sure of really effective outside aid in the event of aggression. She was also dependent on American arms shipments for her own defense forces.

From the viewpoint of the Nordic area, the essential failure of the defense alliance talks was that it removed a vital political sector from the wider associations its member countries were in process of developing. Both Norway and Sweden (Denmark played a secondary role in the negotiations) put principal emphasis on their own security. If this objective could be accommodated within a Nordic framework, all well and good. Neither country, however, was prepared to sacrifice the primary objective for the sake of wider Nordic cooperation resulting from military integration. This could not be accepted as an end in itself, but only as an alternative for the furtherance of national policy.

As it turned out, certain advantages eventually accrued to Sweden from the failure. Denmark and Norway joined NATO on what might be called minimum terms. They have managed to avoid making their membership provocative in Soviet eyes. In peacetime they will not permit the stationing of allied troops or nuclear warheads on their territories. Finland has come to enjoy a similar status on the other side: she does not belong to the Warsaw Pact, has preserved her democratic system, and has come to be accepted by both blocs as a neutral. The practical operation of this political pattern has clearly served to reduce East-West frictions in northern Europe. And in the bargain it has helped to ease Sweden's own international position. By excising the controversies of bloc politics from its purview, Nordic cooperation has been able to embrace not only Denmark, Norway and Sweden, but also Finland and Iceland. These countries have since continually enlarged the breadth and depth of their cooperative endeavors outside the military sphere.

When nothing came of the attempt to extend neutrality to Denmark and Norway, Sweden definitely committed herself to non-alignment. In the main the Western bloc has accepted this policy. The Soviet Union was at first distrustful, as witnessed by a number of incidents in the Baltic Sea. The makings of a changed attitude from this quarter became apparent after the death of Stalin. Growing Soviet trust—or perhaps we should say relaxed Soviet suspicion—of Swedish non-alignment may stem from a more realistic view of the outside world. Another explanation may also be ventured: non-alignment, having proved its value as a conducer of Swedish interests, has developed over the years into a fairly rigid doctrine, and as such belief in its credibility has been strengthened.

An Armed Neutrality

Foreign policy and defense policy are intertwined. When Sweden preferred non-alignment to the security that would come from membership of a great-power pact, she was not making the less expensive choice. A strong defense has been regarded throughout the postwar period as a necessary buttress of non-alignment. In order that national defense may be as effective as possible— complete security has never been regarded as attainable—it shall be "so well prepared for war that it serves to maintain peace". The Swedish armed forces must therefore have "such strength, composition and readiness that an attack on Sweden will demand such great resources, and take such a long time, that the advantages to be gained from the attack cannot reasonably be deemed worth the effort involved". The quoted passages are taken from the official government statement on defense policy.

A state that wishes to be truly non-aligned cannot be dependent on military supplies from the outside. The existence of an efficient Swedish armaments industry (represented in particular by the Bofors and SAAB companies) strengthens confidence in Sweden's ability to uphold a foreign policy marked by non-alignment in peace for the purpose of maintaining neutrality in war. Actually, Sweden has imported weapons to a certain extent, but such purchases are not held to be incompatible with the policy of neutrality. They have not had any political strings tied to them. Only one class of weapons is considered prejudicial to non-alignment if obtained from abroad. These are the nuclear weapons, but as long as Sweden abstains from incorporating them in her arsenal, the question lacks practical significance.

Be that as it may, Sweden's position on nuclear weapons has mattered a great deal for her actions in international affairs. Ever since the mid-1950's debate has been raging as to whether or not the country should acquire nuclear weapons. Differences of opinion on this issue have cut across party lines, not least within the governing Social Democratic party. However, it has been possible to subdue the controversy up to now by a decision to postpone definite commitment. This decision, reached in 1959, was acceptable because it has only been in very recent years that Swedish nuclear research has reached the point where further postponement would delay production of a domestic nuclear armory.

The 1959 decision also reflected considerations of foreign policy. At that time the great powers were negotiating for a test ban treaty. On the one hand, Sweden did not want to impede an international agreement by being a party to the proliferation of nuclear weapons. On the other hand, Sweden was of no mind to renounce the acquisition of such weapons for herself. As one of several states lacking nuclear weapons but technically capable of producing them, Sweden could scarcely exert pressure on the nuclear powers other than by means of a more or less explicit threat to acquire them should these powers fail to reach agreement at least on a test ban treaty.

It is against this background that one should view the various positions and initiatives taken by Sweden on the issue. The Undén plan of 1961 pledged the non-nuclear states to sign a test ban treaty if it were brought about. Its purpose of exerting pressure was clearly spelled out: The nuclear powers "might find it easier to agree on a test ban if they were confronted with a concerted manifesto from a considerable number of states". Although nothing directly came of the Swedish initiative, the United States, the Soviet Union and Great Britain eventually agreed, in 1963, on a nuclear test ban. Sweden signed the treaty, together with a great many other states. The two other nuclear powers, China and France, did not. It was nevertheless hoped that the test ban would pave the way for wider accord.

Sweden has come to take a very active part in the disarmament talks which opened in Geneva in 1962. The Swedish proposals on nuclear weapons were put forth in the form of a three-point "package deal": a complete ban on nuclear tests of all kinds; discontinued production of fissionables for weapons use; and a non-proliferation treaty. The package is worded so as to prevent any disruption of the power balance between the nuclear powers. In principle, its sets of proposals are technically and politically impartial. To help in solving the knotty question of controls, Sweden has announced plans to build a seismic observation station, whose readings will be available for the international flow of data.

Sweden and the United Nations

Sweden's policy of neutrality has had great bearing on her role in the UN. On the one hand, difficult considerations of non-alignment and international solidarity have had to be weighed against one another whenever certain situations of wide import have arisen within the UN (the Korean War and Lebanese crisis are two examples). As a rule these problems have been resolved in clear favor of non-alignment. On the other hand, the consistent application of this policy has gained acceptance for Sweden as an uncommitted state, with no axe to grind in bloc-infected conflicts. She has therefore been considered especially useful for mediating tasks ever since Folke Bernadotte was sent to Palestine in 1948, for holding offices in the world body (most notably Dag Hammarskjöld as Secretary General), and for peace-keeping (especially in Gaza, the Congo and Cyprus).

When Sweden joined the UN, she did so in the conviction that membership could not force her into a military conflict between great powers. A prior condition, of course, was that all authentically great powers would be represented on the Security Council. This was in actual fact the case until Mao Tse-tung won control of China in 1949. When the pro-West majority of the Security Council voted under American prompting to keep

China's seat for the nationalist regime of Chiang Kai-shek on Formosa, the Soviet delegate absented himself in protest. Hence a new and unfamiliar situation obtruded itself: one great power was not even a member of the world organization, while another great power was not deliberating in its most important assembly. From the Swedish point of view, here was an anomaly fraught with dangers. Sweden has always maintained that the UN must be universal in order to be able to perform its tasks.

It was at this juncture that North Korea attacked South Korea. Russia's continued boycott of the Security Council made it possible, under America's resolute lead, to authorize military action which could be expected to violate the wishes of an absent member entitled to cast a veto. Effective military support of South Korea was hurriedly organized. The Korean conflict thrust Swedish policy-makers into a serious dilemma. However, Sweden did not try to take advantage of the possibility offered by the situation to avoid taking a stand. The North Korean attack was branded as an attempt to violate by force a provisional solution of the Korean question that the UN had helped to work out. Accordingly, Sweden could support the UN action both morally and materially.

The Swedish Government, however, was not prepared to contribute combat units to the UN forces. Restraint was presumably called for by the dual nature of the Korean War: as a UN operation against an aggressor, and as a limited conflict between the two power blocs. Sweden resolved her dilemma by despatching a field hospital to South Korea. This contribution was in line with the country's humanitarian traditions, and as such constituted tangible support of the UN in its reaction to the North Korean aggression. It was officially emphasized that no departure from neutrality was implied. Should the Korean War develop into "a war between the great powers, we shall strive, on the strength of our defense, to keep Swedish territory out of the war, in keeping with the policy of armed neutrality", said the then foreign minister, Östen Undén.

The Korean War took on a new dimension when China openly intervened on behalf of North Korea. Sweden found the time ripe to make it plain that the enlarged conflict must be prevented from developing into a direct great-power war, and that she must dissociate herself from a course of action which could bring such calamity in its train. This position was soon made manifest: the Swedish UN delegation abstained from voting when the General Assembly adopted an American draft resolution branding China as aggressor; the draft had left open the contingency of imposing direct sanctions against China.

For Sweden, the course of the Korean War entailed a precarious act of balancing between solidarity towards the UN and a desire to reconcile this with the basic principle of foreign policy: non-alignment aimed at preserving neutrality in time of war. This attitude also found expression when the "uniting for peace" resolution (Acheson plan) came up in 1951. Sweden endorsed the proposal entitling the General Assembly to recommend to member states the adoption of collective security measures if the Security Council should be unable to discharge its duties. At the same time, however, Sweden said she could not undertake to support future sanctions if that "should embroil the country in a world war".

Opposing considerations of non-alignment and UN solidarity have also had to be weighed in other international situations involving the UN. The Lebanese crisis of 1958 can serve as another example. Lebanon had complained of unlawful infiltration from Syria, and the Security Council passed a Swedish resolution for sending a UN team of observers to the border between the two countries. Shortly thereafter the United States landed troops at the request of the Lebanese government, and Britain did likewise for the protection of Jordan. Sweden felt that these moves so far vitiated the terms of reference under which the observers operated that they should be recalled. The help requested by Lebanon was thought to have turned the crisis into an affair outside the UN's jurisdiction. Her proposal to this effect was rejected. None the less the Swedish proposal, accompanied at the same time by an appeal to the Western powers to accede to a Soviet request for a summit conference, reflected not only concern over the course of events but also the desire to mark out a position of aloofness from the Anglo-American intervention.

It is beyond the scope of this essay to elaborate on Sweden's usefulness as a non-aligned state in various mediating tasks. Several examples have already been given. It can be pointed out that Sweden is very much aware of her unique position in this respect. Participation in the UN's peace-keeping forces is considered to be in full accord with Sweden's traditional foreign and defense policies. The purpose of her defense establishment is to maintain the country's peace. Whether or not she can do so depends on what happens in the rest of the world. The ability to lend ready and effective support to the UN's peace-keeping actions is therefore regarded as naturally relevant to the purview of Swedish national defense. No differences between the great powers are affected, and it has therefore been possible to proceed on these matters in close contact and collaboration with the other Nordic countries.

Sweden and the Developing Countries

When Dag Hammarskjöld became Secretary General of the UN in 1953, one of the reasons for his election was that he came from a neutral country which represented a kind of balancing force within the world body. By the time of his death in 1961 he was no longer accepted by the Soviet Union, and he had increasingly tended to look on himself as a spokesman for the many new member states from Asia and Africa which had won their independence during the 1950's. Hammarskjöld was succeeded by U Thant, a genuine representative of the ex-colonial Afro-Asian states. His appointment marked an altered balance within the United Nations. The large group of new and uncommitted states presented new challenges as well as new scope for maneuver between power blocs for a non-aligned country like Sweden. At the same time the changes brought new problems of foreign-policy adjustment in their train.

In common with other "rich countries" in the world, Sweden has begun to pay increasing attention to the needs of developing countries for assistance. The provision of this assistance fits in very well with Sweden's best humanitarian traditions. It has also been held to accord with another objective of Swedish foreign policy, which is to help achieve equality between peoples and thereby foster international solidarity and continued peaceful development. Neutrality plus the absence of an embarrassing colonial past give Sweden a good springboard for gaining the confidence of developing countries. This heightens her responsibilities and opportunities for providing assistance.

Some of the assistance programs sponsored by the great powers are devised to promote their own general strategic interests. Sweden has no such interests in the power-political sense. But Sweden's natural basic concern to contribute to relaxed international tensions does not rule out preoccupation with the political effects of her aid programs in the recipient countries.

Even if it is conceded that Sweden's social and political system may be unsuitable or unattainable for all developing countries, it has been emphasized that aid should be of the kind which promotes political and social equality. Aid programs can also take on long-range significance by establishing economic ties between donor and recipient. However, Sweden has largely avoided making her help conditional on the placing of orders with Swedish industry. The point here is that Sweden, though she lacks power-political ambitions and refrains from attaching strings to her assistance programs, may still want her efforts in this field to serve the cause of improved relations with the new states; the one consideration does not exclude the other.

The motives behind aid influence its shape. As a matter of principle, Sweden has long maintained that multilateral assistance should take precedence over the bilateral form. Coordinated resources can be deployed more efficiently: if international organizations distribute the aid, their authority is strengthened. For various reasons, however, the bilateral form has assumed growing importance. An intermediate form is the regionally based aid supplied by several countries in partnership; an example is joint Scandinavian aid to Tanzania.

As is true of many other donor countries, aid rendered to the developing countries has not yet reached a level equivalent to the declared objective. The target set by Sweden is one percent of the gross national product, which has long been criticized as inadequate.

Political behavior toward the new states includes an aspect which may be vaguely described as commitment to the liberation of colored peoples. Expressions of opinion on South Africa and other countries, most recently on the United States over Vietnam, should be viewed in this context. Here a strong and vociferous public opinion, representing the ideological legacy of an earlier pacifism and anti-militarism, has long stood far ahead of official foreign policy. In recent years the latter, too, has gone on record in words which underline awareness of the actual, and even more so the potential, significance of the new states. At the same time, however, these postures have been nicely adjusted so as to make clear Sweden's determination to avoid siding with or against the great powers.

Sweden and the European Movement

The policy of non-alignment is reflected in the stands taken by Sweden on all international matters of any consequence. This also holds true in regard to regional cooperation in Europe. When the Council of Europe was formed in 1949 Sweden did not hesitate to join. Membership offered an opportunity to demonstrate affinity with the democracies west of the Iron Curtain. Sweden's firm refusal to join their military security system, NATO, did not detract from this affinity. The character of the Council of Europe, as an organization limited to economic, social, cultural, scientific, legal and administrative duties, enabled Sweden to become a member. Questions of military and security policy lay outside the Council's purview. The Council was empowered only to advise, not to make binding decisions.

The Council of Europe was therefore well suited to states who did not want to commit themselves to far-reaching European integration or to accept the authority of supranational bodies. Frictions arose at the very outset between these states—Sweden among them—and those which advocated more extensive integration. The latter group, known as "The Six", adopted a "functional approach" towards the avowed goal of unification. Their endeavors bore initial fruit in the Coal and Steel Community. The project for a European Defense Community failed, but further efforts in the economic sphere eventually culminated in the Common Market, or EEC.

From time to time Sweden has been confronted with situations where her policy of non-alignment has compelled her to say no to the European Movement. Thus she could not accept the Eden plan of 1952, which sought to incorporate into the Council of Europe the representative bodies not only of the Coal and Steel Community, but also of the projected European Defense Community, which of course was to consist of states already bound to NATO. However, the Swedish threat to withdraw from the Council of Europe never had to be implemented, since the EDC project fell because of lingering French fear of Germany.

The efforts to integrate Europe economically have occasionally actualized the same set of problems. Of the two solutions that have presented themselves since the middle of the 20th century, a European free trade area without common external tariffs and a protected common European market, Sweden and the other Scandinavian countries came out for the former. Considerations of trade policy could be cited in support of this stand, especially the trade with Great Britain. In addition, extensive integration with NATO-affiliated states could prejudice the country's freedom of action in foreign affairs. When the Six resolutely proceeded with their plans anyway, the result was the formation of two trade blocs, EEC in 1957 and EFTA (the European Free Trade Association) in 1959. For Sweden and the other EFTA states, their association was meant not only to promote their mutual trade but also to pave the way for a future merger with EEC. As admittedly the stronger of the two blocs, the Common Market exerted powerful attraction for the EFTA states.

Could membership of the EEC be reconciled with Swedish non-alignment? This question was brought to a head when Britain, in 1961, announced her intention to open negotiations with the EEC for membership. On grounds of trade policy, there appeared to be compelling reasons for Sweden to do likewise. If so, should she ask to become a full or associate member? After thinking the matter over, the Government concluded that associate status alone was compatible with Swedish foreign policy. The case was made out by the Prime Minister, Tage Erlander, in a noted speech given before the metalworkers' congress in August 1961. This was in effect an important statement of foreign policy, and several of its points warrant special attention. One condition of Swedish policy was a certain measure of "freedom of movement both in practice and as laid down by formal agreements". Non-alignment formed a part of this, "but it must be supplemented by a consistent endeavor to avoid commitments, even outside the sphere of military affairs, which make it difficult for Sweden to choose a neutral course if faced with a conflict, and which would make the rest of the world less confident that Sweden really wishes to choose such a course". Non-alignment, in other words, must be credible. Other reasons related to important policy objectives were also advanced against full membership. The Common Market could be interpreted as a protectionist bloc of rich, highly industrialized states discriminating against the less favored nations. Deference to the wishes of Sweden's neighbors, especially Finland, also dictated restraint.

Considering the obvious fact that a close relationship with the EEC was thought as very important on grounds of trade policy, the stand taken by Sweden may be said to show that the country's economic interests are subordinated to those of national security. As was true earlier of the talks for a Scandinavian defense pact, non-alignment set the framework within which all other problems of foreign policy must be solved.

Since 1961 a cautious reappraisal of membership in the EEC has taken place. Even if Government spokesmen still maintain the absolute need to safeguard the policy of non-alignment, full membership is now talked of as a possible and even desirable goal for Sweden's European policy.

Sweden and the Nordic Area

The Nordic countries share a common culture and, except for the Finnish majority in Finland, speak cognate languages. From the outside, the Nordic area probably tends to be viewed as a composite whose members do not always emerge with separate and distinct national images. Indeed, awareness of a close affinity has also grown within the area itself during the past decades. The conceptual and practical bases from which this sense of community springs will not be discussed here. Enough to say that it exists, and that it plays an important role in the relations of these countries.

Nordic cooperation is very pragmatic. Inasmuch as Sweden, Norway, Denmark, Finland and Iceland form a homogeneous area in many respects, it should be possible to use the presence of a large common environment to the advantage of all parties concerned. The most successful example to date is SAS, the Scandinavian Airlines System, though it affects only three of the five Nordic countries: Denmark, Norway and Sweden. As was noted earlier, the Nordic countries have found different solutions for their problems of national security; their cooperative endeavors are therefore concerned with other sectors.

During the postwar period Nordic cooperation has been cast in an ever firmer institutional mold. Government ministers regularly consult one another. Intergovernmental bodies of various kinds have been formed, many of them being in the nature of permanent committees of experts. Most important of these is the Nordic Council, established in 1952 for consultation between the legislatures and governments of member countries in matters where joint action by all or some of them is being considered.

The different sectors of Nordic cooperation were codified in a convention signed in 1962. One of its purposes was to give binding legality to previous achievements as a safeguard in relation to the further development of European integration. The convention dwells particularly on matters of law, culture, social welfare, economics and transportation. Although foreign policy does not come under a separate heading, the convention touches on trade policy, international organizations and the developing countries. It obligates the Nordic countries to consult and pay regard to one another in a number of specified situations "whenever this is deemed possible and appropriate". In plainer language, any undertakings they subscribe to are conditional. The five signatory countries are not formally bound and their sovereignty remains unimpaired.

When dealing with issues of major significance, the Nordic countries have found it difficult to arrive at solutions which could essentially broaden their cooperation. Nothing has come of the two biggest joint projects conceived so far. Both would ultimately be bound to impair sovereignty, or at least would be capable of doing so, yet Sweden was greatly interested in their realization. The one project, already discussed above, called for Denmark, Norway and Sweden to form a defense alliance with a common outward posture of neutrality. The other project, which sought to set up a common Nordic market, bogged down for various reasons. Many Norwegian manufacturers feared competition with the more efficient industries of Denmark and Sweden. Swedish and Norwegian farmers demanded exemptions to protect them against Danish agriculture, which is highly geared to export marketing. In spite of prolonged efforts not even a limited market could be established. Yet in the end such a market did evolve, within the wider framework of EFTA.

Cooperation with the other Nordic countries has developed into a primary concern for Sweden during the postwar period. It seems to be increasingly recognized that such cooperation has come to occupy a special position. Its objective is to fuse as many aspects as possible into a common Nordic milieu, where all people are to be on an equal footing regardless of their nationality. Sweden is the party in this association which commands the largest and best-developed resources of the five Nordic countries. She has therefore had to impose a certain self-restraint, because the weaker members of a team tend to regard the stronger with a distrust that isn't always necessarily unfounded. In an extreme sense, the position of Sweden vis-a-vis her neighbors may be likened to that of the United States in relation to her allied countries in different parts of the world.

Conditions of Non-Alignment

The preceding survey illustrates the various ways in which non-alignment has affected the positions taken by Sweden on different postwar problems. The overall picture that emerges is of a policy carried out with remarkable consistency. Even when dealing with intractable situations, Swedish policy-makers have sought to preserve the measure of latitude needed to realize non-alignment in peace so as to make possible neutrality in war.

It should be emphasized that, by contrast with Switzerland, Swedish neutrality is not guaranteed; nor is it imposed by a peace treaty, as in the case of Austria. Neutrality has been freely chosen to serve Sweden's own interests. It has been officially declared in Parliament that neutrality should not be restricted by foreign guarantees which can reduce the country's freedom of action in foreign affairs. Non-alignment bears reference to Sweden's relations with constellations of great powers. The project for a Scandinavian defense alliance was not considered in 1948–49 to prejudice Swedish foreign policy, and the same view would presumably hold if the question were reopened.

For all that has been said above about Sweden's freedom to act in principle, her postwar postures have been just as restricted as if the neutrality she pursued were guaranteed or imposed by treaty. The chief explanation here is to be sought in the "Cold War", which so completely dominated the international picture until the last few years. Sweden has continually had to make clear that her non-alignment is meant in earnest. To make it credible she must proceed with great restraint in enunciating political stands and statements of opinion. But even official restraint has its limits, especially when public opinion is aroused by certain events abroad. In 1956 there was general indignation, reflected in official statements strongly criticizing the Soviet Union, when the popular Hungarian uprising was bloodily suppressed. The same applies to reactions to certain cases of Soviet espionage in Sweden, and not least to Russian unwillingness to help shed light on the fate of Raoul Wallenberg, the Swedish diplomat who vanished in 1945 when the Red Army captured Budapest.

Self-restraint has had to be observed not only by Cabinet ministers, but also by representative spokesmen for the opposition. "Intemperate attacks by influential politicians against the policies of other states tend to counteract the policy of neutrality to which we officially adhere". These words were once used by Prime Minister Erlander in a showdown in 1959 with the Conservative party leader, who had been excluded from the Swedish UN delegation because of his persistent criticism of the Soviet Union; the delegation regularly includes representatives of the democratic opposition parties: Conservative, Liberal and Center (formerly Agrarian).

During the acute phases of the Cold War most of the Swedish press levelled its critical sights at the Soviet Union. This bias may have hampered official efforts to gain universal credence in non-alignment. Active Swedish participation in the European Movement and in Marshall aid may have had the same effect. From time to time political correctives have been thought necessary to keep Swedish policy from leaning too much in a westward direction. These have found expression in postures and statements that sometimes must have appeared as harsh displays of anti-West attitudes.

From the beginning, the chief objective of non-alignment has been to preserve the country's freedom of action in foreign affairs so that neutrality will not be vitiated in advance in the event of war. As will have emerged from the foregoing account, the intermediate position this policy has conferred on Sweden has enhanced her potential for playing an active, mediating role on the international stage. Indeed, the role seems so vital at the present juncture of world events that one may safely say that this very result of non-alignment has become one of its primary purposes.

A change of outlook has occurred in the process. Swedish foreign policy, once so passive ("The foreign policy of Sweden is not to have any policy.") has become more active and extrovert.

In this transformed guise, foreign policy demands a new kind of realism and probably even greater insight into the outermost limits of Sweden's ability to act as an international performer. New choices will have to be carefully weighed to decide on courses of action to take in international organizations and negotiations—courses that will fit in with the non-alignment which also underlies the conduct of an active foreign policy in peacetime. Some indication of the new straws in the wind may be gleaned from the growing Swedish interest in research concerned with the material and psychological conditions of foreign policy.

Stig Strömholm

Born in 1931. Lecturer in Comparative Law, Uppsala University. Has
written on private international law, copyright and comparative law. His
principal works, *Torts in the Conflict of Laws*, *Legal Values in Modern
Sweden* (in collaboration with F. Schmidt), *Das Veröffentlichungsrecht
des Urhebers*, *Le droit moral de l'auteur,* are written in foreign
languages. Also writes for the press on literature, with a predilection for
old French.

The Law and Its Administration

The legal system of a given community may be envisaged as a
set of technical solutions given to problems which recur, in one
form or another, in all communities with the same basic economic
and social structure. However, the technical approach will not be
adopted here, since a description of the rules involved will
hardly be able to give a satisfactory idea of the actual operation
of a legal system. It is impossible to overlook the institutional
framework, the general ideas and attitudes, the economic
background and the social philosophy which make up the
"climate" of the legal system under consideration.

A second possible approach, which may be called "institutional",
would seem more satisfactory from many points of view: it
consists in giving an outline of the sources of law, the way in
which they are used and interpreted, and of the bodies entrusted
with the administration of the law. These features, being more
permanent, are likely to give a more faithful picture of the actual
life of the law and of its role in the community.

There is also a third approach. Legal rules, apart from their
obvious functions as solutions to practical problems, *express
something:* envisaged as sociological data they are characteristic
features which contribute to make up the likeness of the
community as a whole. This point of view would seem to be
most helpful for our present purposes: it provides a principle for
picking out a number of specific legal rules which are likely to
interest the foreign reader not only—nor, indeed, chiefly—because
they constitute solutions to problems of particular practical
importance, but because they are particularly characteristic for the
community which framed them. Since legal rules have impact on
a great number of widely different social situations, they accordingly

reveal prevailing ideas and attitudes on topics of widely different character and importance. Thus matrimonial law, or family law in general, is likely to express a country's notions of the good life. Other enactments express deep-rooted notions of right and wrong and of the basic elements of personal liberty. The best example embraces the rules on serious crimes and on criminal proceedings. Then, too, the very status ascribed to legal rules as problem-solving instruments expresses a social philosophy. It is commonly claimed that the "rule of law" characterizes Anglo-American social thinking. In the Swedish legal system, one particular field is apt to illustrate prevailing attitudes: administrative law. In modern states based on the principles of private property and freedom of contract, such as the United States, Britain, Germany and Sweden, there exist many shades between laissez-faire and State control. Another topic which would be examined is the extent to which Swedish rules in these fields of law express a conscious social philosophy or at least reasonably clear-cut prevailing attitudes.

Finally, two more features likely to contribute to the likeness of today's Swedish community may be taken from its legal system. One is the slowness or quickness of change in the more important fields of law. The other is more difficult to define. There are, basically, two different views of the law, envisaged as a body of technical solutions. The one is scientific and systematic: the law is an edifice of perfect logic and coherence. According to the other view, the law is no more than the sum of solutions given to a number of specific problems; it is incomplete and not necessarily coherent, each solution being invented to meet the needs of a given situation.

Historical Background

The earliest phases of Swedish legal development have left scanty direct evidence. For all practical purposes the earliest authoritative sources are the provincial codes written down in the course of the 13th and 14th centuries. These codes constituted a relatively uniform body of private law, reflecting a static rural community essentially made up of free landowners, living in villages and politically organized in "hundreds". The "thing", or meeting of the hundred, was at the same time a court of justice and political body. Above the hundred was the province or "land", which also had its "thing", presided by a "lawman", a local landowner of high descent, chief justice of the land and guardian of its law. Above the lands and the hundreds was the Kingdom of Sweden, but its influence meant little to the everyday life of the community. From the yeoman's horizon—which is also that of private law—the two basic cells of the community were village and kin. Land, the only kind of property with real economic importance, was always part of a village; it could only be exploited within that framework, which implied a far-reaching community of work. Nor could land be freely sold, since kinsmen held the first option to buy.

It would be little short of a romantic lie to pretend that anything of this community has survived, but it is worth pointing out that a continuous line of descent can be traced from the early medieval hundreds and their "things" down to the present-day rural district courts, which are still called "courts of the hundred" (*häradsrätt*). The president of such a court still bears the title of *häradshövding,* "chieftain of a hundred".

With the 13th century, the monarchy becomes the active element in Swedish public life. Uniform legal codes—one for the boroughs and one for the countryside—were promulgated by the King, with the consent of the provincial "things", about 1350. The modern type of legislation slowly came into existence in the course of the 16th and 17th centuries. Apart from minor enactments, the King now took the consent of a Riksdag or parliament. After many attempts, a new legal code for the whole Kingdom (including Finland) was enacted in 1734 and promulgated two years later. It embodied private, criminal and procedural law; systematically it followed the pattern of the medieval codes. Its language, laconic or picturesque but never abstract or learned, also drew heavily on the medieval inheritance.

Officially, the Code of 1734 remains the law of the land (it is also still in force in Finland). This only means, however, that it has never been superseded by a new code and that its titles and systematic framework have been retained. Of the original contents, only a handful of sections remains; the rest have been amended. The code is divided into "books" (Book of Marriage, of Succession, of Commerce, of Crime and Punishment, of Procedure, etc.), and most of these have been completely redrafted in the course of the present century. Thus a new Book of Marriage was adopted in 1920 and a new Book of Procedure in 1942. Besides the work of redrafting the books, numerous minor amendments and an ever-increasing mass of legislation outside the systematic frame of the old code have been introduced.

Although Swedish law has been deeply influenced in the course of history by foreign legal systems—the Roman in particular—it forms part of an independent family of Scandinavian law alongside the common law family, that of "civil law" as prevailing in France, Germany and most Latin countries, the Socialist systems, etc.

It follows from the foregoing that Swedish law is essentially codified law, not case-law. It is no exaggeration to state that in no other country are statutes prepared with such care, the reasons for the adoption of each single rule laid down so fully in published documents and each single word in a proposed enactment enlarged upon in such detail by the experts who drafted the bill. The "legislative material" (Swedish: förarbeten), i.e. the documents drafted and published in the course of pre-paring a statute of any consequence—containing, say, a hundred short sections—will often amount to a thousand printed pages or more. Among these documents, moreover, the records of the usually laconic parliamentary debates, some twenty pages or so, are the only elements which are not composed of cogently written expert opinions. The actual statute text is often drafted, wherever technical reasons do not prevent it—as in the case of fiscal law—in a brief, incisive style which is a cherished tradition going back to 1734 and beyond.

The Swedish technique of legislative preparation obviously has considerable impact on the way in which statutes are used. The brevity of the text—and the absence of any pretension by lawgivers to cover every imaginable case with sweeping generalizations—gives the judge a great amount of liberty. At the same time, the very extensive "legislative material", which is more or less readily acknowledged as "subsidiary" sources with rather more than persuasive authority, reduces that liberty in fact if not in principle, for more often than not the judge will find that the case put before him has been foreseen by the Royal Commission or the responsible Ministry in their comments on the proposed enactment and that a certain solution has been suggested to the problem he is facing.

The statement that Swedish law is essentially statute law does not tell the whole truth. There are vast and important fields where the existing statutes are so old and so laconic that the "living law" is really a body of precedents. In private law, this is particularly true in regard to torts. Administrative law is another field where large areas are not covered by provisions of a general scope and where many important rules are based on precedents rather than enactments.

Even where written law prevails, the role of judicial or administrative case-law is of considerable importance. The statute texts are seldom such as to impose clear solutions to doubtful issues; the body of "legislative material", however important in fact, is not absolutely binding, and as the years pass by, expert opinions put forward in connection with the drafting and passing of a statute may lose weight because the social facts concerned are no longer the same. This is where precedents—in the first place the decisions of the Supreme Court—come in to keep the law alive, as it were. Occasionally, the Supreme Court, in construing a statute, may disregard opinions in the "legislative material" which seem inacceptable because they imply a strained interpretation of the text or for some other reason. Precedents are not formally binding either, but for obvious reasons, the principles adopted by the Supreme Court and—to a lesser extent —the courts of appeal enjoy high authority.

Organization of Justice

We have already mentioned the stages of the Swedish judicial hierarchy; both the specialized tribunals and the numerous agencies which handle the ever-increasing mass of administrative law must be left outside with few exceptions. At the bottom, there are the courts of first instance, with full jurisdiction in all civil and criminal matters. Their organization reflects a traditional difference between town and country. The rural district court— the "court of the hundred"—is presided by the "chieftain of the hundred" or one of his assistant judges. Offences punishable by fines are tried by the judge alone; whenever the sanction may amount to a term of imprisonment, he is assisted by a panel of lay assessors (*nämndemän*), from three to nine according to the seriousness of the crime. Civil actions are always tried before a panel of seven to nine assessors. Since 1948 the only difference between rural and urban district courts is that in the latter, (called *rådhusrätter,* "Town hall courts"), civil actions are heard by three judges without any panel of laymen. Before that year the institution of lay assessors existed only in rural courts.

It is important to stress the fundamental difference between the lay element in Swedish courts of first instance and the Anglo-American jury. The latter does not sit on the bench; its function is to evaluate the evidence and to give its verdict. The cooperation of lay assessors in the Swedish ordinary rural courts of first instance goes back to the Middle Ages and has always been justly considered a democratic element in Swedish public life, since the assessors were originally required to be farmers and the rural district courts transacted much administrative business of considerable importance for the whole population of the district. The laymen are members of the court and as such take part in its deliberations even where points of law are concerned. They are elected for a period of six years by the local borough or district councils. Their position is not equal to that of the presiding judge; in principle, he can be overruled only if all the lay assessors agree on an opinion different from his.

The six courts of appeal (*hovrätter*), the largest and oldest being that of Stockholm, founded in 1614, present less original features. They are entirely composed of career judges, assigned to divisions, who hear civil and criminal appeals without any restrictions as to the importance of the case. Each division is composed of five judges, but four are enough to make a quorum. Incidentally, the courts of appeal—which have been justly called Sweden's "civil staff colleges"—have long been a source of recruits for senior posts in the civil service as a whole. The secretaries of important Royal Commissions, the heads and members of the legislation departments existing in all Ministries and—where politicians are not preferred—the Secretaries of State in charge of the Ministries immediately under the Cabinet

Ministers are almost regularly taken from among the junior judges of the courts of appeal.

At the top of the judicial hierarchy is the King's Supreme Court (*Konungens Högsta Domstol*), composed of twenty-four Justices assigned to three divisions. While the right to challenge the decision of a court of appeal before the Supreme Court is limited in various respects, the limitations are fairly liberal, and most cases of any importance may be brought through all the three instances.

As already mentioned, the ordinary courts of justice do not handle administrative law. Nor can the decisions of administrative agencies or bodies of local government be challenged before the courts, although the limits of their competence are vague and there is at least a tendency to extend them in the interest of the citizens. Administrative appeals are normally brought either before the next instance in the civil service hierarchy or before a specialized tribunal. Jurisdiction in the last instance is divided between the King in Council (*Kunglig Majestät*) and the Supreme Administrative Court (*Regeringsrätten*). Generally speaking, administrative appeals where the legal element prevails—such as taxation cases—are tried by the Supreme Administrative Court, whereas the King in Council decides in matters involving a stronger element of policy-making.

In certain actions concerning land and the expropriation of property for public purposes, the district courts are specially constituted, with one or several experts sitting on the bench instead of or beside the lay assessors. The exploitation of water and waterpower—a cornerstone of the modern Swedish economy—raises particular problems, since most coastal waters, lakes and rivers are privately owned and a planned engineering project may interfere with the rights of hundreds or thousands of parties. In principle, therefore, such exploitation requires special permission which is granted upon conditions determined by a judicial decision. Six special courts of the first instance and one court of appeal hear petitions to exploit waterpower and all actions pertaining to this field of law.

Lastly, mention should be made of a highly specialized tribunal, the Labor Court (*Arbetsdomstolen*). Founded in 1928 and composed of one president (invariably a former Supreme Court

Justice), two other senior officials, and two representatives each from organized labor and management, this court tries, in the first and last instance, all cases relating to the application of collective agreements on the labor market. An important point to be noted, however, is that the Court is limited in its competence to the interpretation of contracts which already exist. It does not mediate between disputants or offer them equitable solutions for acceptance, nor is it involved in any of the other public machinery of conciliation for resolving differences between labor and management. Its sole purpose is to enforce the law of contract within its domain.

After this survey of the principal judicial institutions, a few words should be devoted to the people who make them work. The common legal education and training of judges—as well as of public prosecutors, attorneys and, indeed, of the majority of civil servants in responsible positions—starts with four or five years of study at one of the three State faculties of law. All the future judges and a decreasing but still very large proportion of other graduates from the law schools then serve for some two-and-a-half years as clerks and assistant judges in the courts of first instance. Specialization normally begins only after this term of basic practical training is completed. The future judge goes on to a court of appeal, serves for about a year as a qualified clerk and then submits to a final test.

A reasonably successful judicial career will lead to an ordinary judgeship in a court of appeal or to the office of district court president. The future prosecution official also undergoes special training, the would-be attorney goes into practice, the civil servant starts at the bottom of the ladder for academically trained officials, and a number of young lawyers enter the service of trade, industry or local government.

The public prosecutors are organized in a hierarchy composed of district prosecutors and their assistants, chief prosecutors responsible for a number of districts and, at the top of the ladder, the Chief Prosecutor of the Realm (*Riksåklagaren*). Until recently, most district prosecutors were also local chiefs of police and charged with the execution of judgments. In 1965 these three functions were divided into three distinct public services. Senior positions in the police forces and the authorities for the execution of judgments (and collecting of taxes) are generally held by officials of legal training.

The Bar, or Association of Attorneys (*Sveriges Advokatsamfund*), was organized as a semi-official body—acting, in certain respects, under the supervision of the Chancellor of Justice—as late as 1948. It has no exclusive right to appear or represent parties in court; in fact, anyone may plead his case for himself, or through a friend, even before the Supreme Court. However, only members of the Bar are appointed as public defenders, briefs under the statutes on legal aid are hardly given to others than attorneys (or at least legally trained persons), and generally speaking, little civil litigation of any importance is conducted without Bar assistance.

Little need be said about court proceedings in Sweden. Apart from technical details which are of small interest here, the pattern comes near to that adopted in common law courts. In the courts of first instance the final hearing in civil actions is normally preceded by pre-trial hearings held by the judge alone in chambers. The trial itself proceeds in very much the same way in all the three instances, for both the courts of appeal and the Supreme Court normally try the whole action—including the evaluation of evidence—and do not confine themselves to the points of law at issue. There are certain restrictions on the right to produce new evidence before the superior courts.

By and large, the costs of litigation in Sweden are low in comparison with those incurred in common law countries. Legal aid is granted not only for actual litigation, but also for certain non-contentious and administrative actions. In criminal actions of any seriousness, the accused is assisted by a public defender, whose fee is forwarded from public moneys. In case of a verdict against the accused, he is sentenced to pay costs, but for obvious reasons this obligation generally remains platonic.

Before leaving the organization of justice, three public offices characteristic of the Swedish legal system should be mentioned. In 1809, the year Sweden received her present Constitution, an original invention was made: this was the "ombudsman", or Parliamentary Commissioner for the Judiciary and Civil Administration. In 1914 he was joined by a similar Commissioner for the Armed Forces. These two officials, invariably prominent judges, are appointed by the Riksdag for a short term of office (but usually re-elected for several terms). Assisted by a growing staff of specialists from various branches of public administration, they work wholly outside the State hierarchy. Their task is to redress wrongs committed by the authorities against citizens and they are vested with far-reaching powers to inspect all public authorities, including courts and municipal institutions. The two ombudsmen are free to investigate any case brought to their attention by a formal complaint, by the press or in any other manner. All public officials are bound to give them the assistance they need. One point should be stressed emphatically, however: the ombudsmen have neither the right to decide in what way wrongs should be redressed nor to pass judgments on the doings of the authorities. Technically, they act as prosecutors. If they find that a complaint is justified, they institute an action before the competent court of justice.

The ombudsmen are regarded as citizens' defenders. The Crown's rights and the public interest in strict observance of the rule of law in the courts and civil service are safeguarded in very much the same way by the Chancellor of Justice; the holder of this office is appointed by the King, also invariably from among the judiciary élite.

Some Aspects of Swedish Substantive Law

When the reform of Swedish matrimonial law was being prepared at the beginning of this century, there was agreement on at least one point: future legislation would have to be based on the principle of equality between the spouses in economic as well as personal respects. This principle (which originally suffered certain exceptions, now abolished, in favor of the husband) raised a problem: in case of complete disagreement between husband and wife on important questions, how could a decision be reached? In some Latin countries the ultimate decision lies with the husband as "head of the family"; other legal systems provide for recourse to the courts. The Swedish lawgivers refrained from laying down rules. If, for example, married couples disagreed on choice of residence, no legal formula could offer a solution of lasting value: the spouses would have to thrash it out for themselves. There may be some pessimism in this outlook, but it certainly reveals insight into the facts of life and awareness that fixed principles have limited use in personal matters. Lastly, the principle is based on profound respect for personal liberty: the law does not cross the threshold of the home.

Under the Swedish system the only way out of complete and lasting disagreement between spouses is divorce. There are basically two ways to put an end to marriage under Swedish law. A decree can be obtained immediately by the aggrieved spouse if his or her consort is proved guilty of certain kinds of gross misconduct; this principle, more or less liberally realized, is found in most countries. But Swedish law also knows another way, by far the most frequently traveled on: if the spouses agree that there is deep and lasting disruption in their union (and if they have submitted to at least an attempt at mediation), they are entitled to judicial separation; the court suspends their right and duty of cohabitation, but the marriage as such and all other matrimonial rights and obligations survive. One year after the separation decree becomes effective, each of the spouses may obtain divorce, provided he or she can prove that the couple's matrimonial life has not been resumed in the meanwhile. This system expresses the same refusal to keep personal relations going by any form of constraint that we have noted above. The spouses have to think the matter over for one year; after all, they are the best judges of the chances of successful conciliation. If they find their union doomed, the law can only draw the same conclusion, and in so doing take care to ensure proper safeguards for any offspring. On this latter point the law no longer leaves matters up to the spouses. Irrespective of any agreement they may have made, the court investigates which of them, if any, is to be entrusted with the responsibility for the personal and economic interests of the children.

If the Swedish lawgiver has refrained from any attempt to realize ethical ideals in matrimonial law and accepted things the way they are, penal law makes moral evaluations inevitable. There is not much point here in discussing where the line between forbidden and permitted acts has been drawn and why, for although ethical considerations are certainly involved, and such

Friherre L A Mannerheim
"Riksens Ständers Ombudsman"

ℒ.ℋ.Roos. 1823.

features of Swedish penal law as the criminalization of malicious propaganda directed against ethnical and cultural minorities, lenient treatment of women guilty of abortion, or severity on drunken driving and tax evasion certainly say something about the community where such features are found, there is nevertheless a high degree of uniformity between most Western nations on these matters. It seems more rewarding to put the emphasis on certain guiding principles for the treatment of offenders. The term "treatment" is not chosen at random: after decades of animated and even acrimonious public discussion and expert work, the new Penal Code which came into force in 1965—formally it constituted the "Book of Crime" of the General Code of 1734—upholds that school of thought which contended that crimes shall not be considered as evil deeds calling for revenge and repression, but rather as indications for the use of individual curative treatment. There is by no means agreement about this and the Swedish Penal Code is certainly a compromise rather than a clear victory, but it is important to stress that such sanctions as probation or the surrender of culprits to social or medical authorities for treatment are resorted to almost as often as the classical forms of punishment, fines or imprisonment. Juvenile delinquents below 18 are sentenced to prison only rarely, as for serious acts of violence. There is, obviously, a conflict between the traditional outlook—revenge, or repression, should be proportionate to the seriousness of the deed—and the curative approach: the need for treatment should determine the sanction. The "curative" approach does not render the rule of law inoperative in criminal procedure: a person may be kept in arrest or questioned by the police only for a limited number of hours; the public prosecutor may order a further detention for a couple of days, after which the accused must be released or an order of arrest secured from the competent court.

In short, modern Swedish penal law reveals—like that of most Occidental countries—hesitation between two approaches: the one firmly rooted in a time-honored legal tradition, to which the defense of individual liberty was paramount and which put the emphasis on equal sanctions for equal crime; the other based upon more recent ideas of the relations between a community and its members. It may perhaps be stated that the conflict is clearly seen and understood, and that the actually prevailing attitude is to find an acceptable equilibrium.

The fundamental importance of the rule of law in Swedish public life is even more obvious in the field of administrative law. Basically the civil service, as opposed on the one hand to the courts of justice and on the other to political (i.e., policy-making) bodies, may be envisaged in two different ways. It may be considered as the Sovereign's arm, acting upon his orders and intended to carry his policy into effect by means which are essentially measured in terms of efficiency.

The choice of means being thus free (within a framework of general legal principles), the most characteristic feature of this conception is the wide latitude left for what has been called "administrative discretion". Conversely, the civil service may be considered chiefly as an institution entrusted with the administration of legal rules and bound, with regard both to the forms in which it operates and to the substance of its decisions, by rules of law almost as strict as those which govern the operation of courts.

There is no doubt that the latter conception prevails in Sweden. The administration, both local and central, is bound to follow written or (more often) unwritten rules of law both in transacting petty business such as the issuance of driver's licenses or pass-ports and in matters of greater weight, such as town and country planning. Administrative appeals are handled, by the superior authorities or special tribunals with which they are lodged, in very much the same way as challenged court decisions; the principal point is whether the law has been correctly applied to the case at issue. In fact, with few exceptions the Ministers, who are technically only the King's Councillors, cannot give an order *ad hoc* to an administrative agency: each case must be decided by the competent service on its own responsibility according to the applicable general rules.

The traditional conception is countered by another and more recent tendency. Obviously, the sovereignty of law in civil administration is best suited to a static community, or rather to a community where public authorities do not interfere with economic life beyond narrow limits. The modern Welfare State, particularly a State under socialist leadership, aspires to guide economic development, to plan the community as a whole, and to interfere where necessary in order to secure conformity with its plans. This presents a grave problem which has yet to be resolved. On balance, however, it is justified to conclude that Swedish administration remains more bound by the rule of law than in most other States; further, the tradition opposed to public authorities acting as the instruments of discretionary political power is so firmly established that it is likely to survive.

The basic principles of Swedish private law are still private property and freedom of contract. Exceptions from these principles must be specifically provided for by law. Nevertheless, the modern evolution has brought decisive changes in the application of these principles. A striking example may be found in the law of landlord and tenant. An Act of 1907 regulates the relationship between these two parties. For the purposes of that Act in its original drafting, houses and flats may be described as goods subject to the economic laws of a free market. The legislature imposed no more than a few indispensable rules on the form of contracts and on their validity against third parties; apart from that, the provisions of the Act were interpretative and thus could be set aside by a contract between the parties. After a number of years an amendment was added, signifying the arrival of a new policy: the courts were allowed to set aside or modify contract conditions which were manifestly unfair when applied. The State had stepped in to restrict freedom of contract in the interest of the weaker party. Similar provisions have now been introduced into numerous statutes on specified contracts. The next step was taken during World War II: to cope with a housing shortage which is still acute, rent control was introduced. The landlord's right to end his tenant's lease was radically reduced by statutes that were not incorporated with the basic provisions of private law. Public authorities also interfere with the housing market in other ways: loans of public money to construction work on favorable terms are granted only if the landowner undertakes to offer the flats thus produced to a public housing agency which distributes them to families in need of housing. In short, the provisions of the 1907 Act can tell no more than a fraction of the truth about the complicated network of legal rules actually governing the housing market.

As in all other Western countries, expropriation of land for public purposes can be effected only in accordance with clearly defined legal provisions; compensation is fixed by a court of justice. However, property is by no means illimited. In particular, the owner is increasingly prevented from doing what he likes with his land by a growing body of administrative law: statutes on the protection of forests, on keeping arable land in cultivation, on town and country planning, building regulations, etc. Farm land can be bought only by persons authorized by local boards of agriculture; estates cannot be divided into smaller plots without the consent of the competent authorities; construction work cannot be undertaken without permission, at least in urban areas; and local authorities are entitled to prescribe in detail the dimensions and exteriors of buildings. At present a bill intended to give local councils an unconditional right of pre-emption in all land sales is being considered.

Traditional versus Functional Concepts of the Law

It should be apparent from the preceding description of selected aspects of Swedish law that it presents a curious "peaceful coexistence" of new ideas and ideals and a traditional framework. However, the future of the present equilibrium between old and new is far from assured. What is important to state in this context is that the Swedish legislative, judicial and executive apparatus has proved capable not only of surviving but also of working smoothly in the ideological climate of the Welfare State. The pace of reform and change in all fields of public and private law is high; in fact, the Swedish State now considers it an obligation to keep the legislative process in continuous motion. The traditional concept of the law as an edifice of established principles venerable by virtue of age has given way to a "functional" approach: the law is a piece of social machinery rather than a temple; it must be oiled and kept in repair in order to work. One of the most interesting aspects of continuous law reform is the regular collaboration between Sweden and her Scandinavian neighbors. Ever since the 1870's, uniform legislation on important matters is traditional, and a great number of statutes in various branches of private law, such as the formation of contracts, sale of goods, insurance, copyright, patents and succession have their origin in inter-Nordic legislative cooperation. Since the end of World War II, the Nordic Council has been pursuing this work as one of its most important tasks.

Scandinavian lawyers have much in common, not only specific rules of law, but also habits of legal thinking. It is characteristic of them to take a pragmatic rather than abstract view of the law. Politicians are not the only ones who prefer to look on the legal system as a unit of working machinery rather than a temple; this view is shared by the lawyers themselves.

Under the influence of various elements—one of them being the ideas of a group of internationally known legal philosophers working from the 1910's onwards—Scandinavian legal thinking has moved towards a strictly matter-of-fact attitude which rejects both the conceptualistic system-building dear to 19th century lawyers and the traditional concepts of natural justice or the "law of nature" resorted to for centuries as the ultimate test of legal rules and decisions. Instead, various tests of social utility are proposed. However, this change of theoretical outlook has hardly brought changes in actual practice. The basic notions of justice and equity seem to recur as frequently in legal reasoning based upon social considerations as where traditional concepts are at the bottom of judicial thinking. The stern and venerable Goddess of Justice may seem a displaced person in the ideological vacuum of the demo-bureaucratic Welfare State, and displaced she is indeed, after having moved from a temple to a machine, a construct of social engineering. The essential thing, however, is that she still has an altar where she is worshipped, though sometimes as an unknown deity or under strange names.

Bengt Rydén

Born in 1936, Master of Business Administration. Attached to the staff of the Federation of Swedish Industries. Does research for the Industrial Institute for Economic and Social Research. Has published works on structural changes in industry, with particular reference to corporate mergers.

The Swedish Economy

In Sweden as in other industrial countries, the economy has undergone continuous changes from the beginning of industrialization. This process, however, got off to a much later start in Sweden because our society was so long predominantly agrarian. The Industrial Revolution did not really take hold until the mid-19th century, when the first sawmills were erected along the Bothnian coast.

Since then the changes have been nothing if not dramatic. Where 80 percent of the population used to be attached to farms, the proportion is now less than ten percent. Similarly, agriculture's share of the national production has fallen from twenty to four percent. As for the sawmills, their halcyon days have already become ancient history. New products, enterprises and industries have sprung up, while others have faded into complete insignificance. An extensive services sector has developed, especially in the field of government. This shift of emphasis between different sectors of the economy is the most important thing that has happened in the past hundred years. During this period the changes have been particularly rapid in agriculture. In the rest of the economy, on the other hand, the truly big changes have taken place within the sectors rather than between them. Manufacturing provides the most impressive illustration: though its share of total production and employment has held fairly level over a long period of time, the relative contribution of its component industries differ greatly from those of a former day.

In terms of any criteria one chooses, mining and manufacturing have long been the sturdy twin pillars of the Swedish economy. Manufacturing alone accounts for one-third of the total production of goods and services (GNP), and its share of employment is

113

just as large. Inasmuch as so much of its output is exported, manufacturing also makes a substantial contribution to Sweden's earnings of foreign exchange. Agriculture and lumbering each account for four percent of the GNP, but the former employs eight percent of the labor force and the latter only two percent. More than half the value of the GNP derives from the production of goods and energy.

In the services sector, the largest component is trade with a GNP and employment share of 14 percent. The public services, which embrace education, medical care, national defense, administration and the like, contribute 12 percent to total production but employ 15 percent of the labor force; the latter proportion was at ten percent in 1950 and the long-term trend points to a continued increase. Of the remaining services, communications account for nine percent of the GNP, and private services and housing for seven and six percent, respectively. All told, the services sector turns out to be as large as the goods sector, which in its own way indicates a relatively

Production and Employment in the Swedish Economy, 1950 and 1965

	Share of value added, in percent		Share of employment, in percent	
	1950	1965	1950	1965
Agriculture	8	4	18	8
Lumbering	4	4	2	2
Mining and manufacturing	35	33	32	33
Power (electricity, gas, etc.)	2	3	1	1
Building and construction	8	8	8	10
Total production, goods and power	*57*	*52*	*61*	*54*
Communications	9	9	8	8
Trade	13	14	12	14
Private services	6	7	9	9
Housing, etc.	5	6		
Public services	10	12	9	15
Total production, services	*43*	*48*	*38*	*46*
Totals	100	100	100	100

high degree of economic development in Sweden. Only the United States and Canada have relatively larger services sectors, while the British and Swedish are about equal.

Pattern of Ownership

Sweden seems to be widely pictured abroad as a socialist state, with all that this implies in the way of regimentation, a managed economy and public ownership. To be sure, the Social Democratic party has been in power ever since the beginning of the thirties, but it can scarcely be said to have espoused socialism as this term is commonly understood. Private enterprise is and always has been the mainspring of the Swedish economy. Actually, a far less proportion of business is in government hands as compared with such industrial countries as Italy, France and Britain. And out of a total labor force of about 3,500,000 persons, only 200,000 or six percent are employed by State companies.

Where the government has seen fit to enter the business domain its motivations have been employment-creating, strategic and fiscal rather than ideological. As in many other countries, the postal, telephone and broadcasting services are run as State or State-controlled monopolies. The government owns the largest railway company, which in turn operates a major road haulage enterprise. About 40 percent of the ownership of Scandinavia's leading airline, SAS, is divided in equal shares between the Swedish government and private Swedish interests, while the remainder is in the hands of the Danish and Norwegian governments. The government has also set up a commercial banking system—third largest in Sweden—and is a co-owner with private business interests of a few special credit-granting agencies. It owns a chain of popular restaurants. The tobacco industry and the trade in wine and liquor were made State monopolies in order to raise tax revenues and promote temperance. As far as tobacco is concerned, however, the monopoly is being phased out, since manufacture will no longer be profitable when import duties are completely abolished under the tariff reduction program of the European Free Trade Association. The State monopoly on imports of foreign tobacco products was already abolished a few years ago.

Most of the government's industrial interests are in mining, metalworking and forestry. In the far north, the great Kiruna iron ore mine used to be jointly owned by the government and a private company under an agreement dating from 1907. This enterprise, LKAB, became a State company in 1957 when the government exercised its option to take over all of the stock after 50 years. The original agreement was primarily formed for strategic reasons. Be that as it may, LKAB has proved to be a very profitable venture for the government in spite of the present downward tendency of prices in the international market for iron ore.

The government also runs some smaller iron mines in central Sweden, though with less satisfactory results. Their chief purpose is to provide employment, as is also true of several timber-working plants, which in 1950 were merged into one State company. The problem of creating employment in the far north also lay behind the establishment of a State ironworks at Luleå. It is fulfilling this function effectively, though as yet the enterprise is barely breaking even, let alone returning a profit.

Since the end of World War II a large-scale program of research and experimentation has been in force to develop the civilian uses of nuclear energy. The government has invested huge sums in the company it has formed for this purpose. From time to time there has been lively debate in Sweden as to whether a small country of limited resources is justified in committing itself to an undertaking that devours so much capital. To judge from the achievements to date, the skeptics are having the better of the argument.

The distributive trades are exclusively a private concern, though here the word "private" should be qualified to take into account the strong role played by the cooperative movement. Local consumer cooperatives account for about 15 percent of all retail sales, and 25 percent in food alone. The cooperative movement also owns important manufacturing interests, especially in the production of consumer goods. Local producer cooperatives predominate in the supply of prepared meats and dairy products. The largest cooperative enterprise, KF, owns some 30 plants which manufacture margarine, vegetable oils and other food products, wearing apparel, and products of wood and metals.

The Size Structure of Industry

Although a day hardly passes without report of a new merger on the business scene, Sweden is still a long way from being a nation of truly large-scale production. By international yardsticks Swedish firms are pretty small. Thus none of our giants, including SKF, Volvo, ASEA and LM Ericsson, will be found on a list of the world's 100 largest corporations even though each of the four named transacts a big volume of business. If the list is enlarged to 200, only one Swedish firm makes the grade: SKF (AB Svenska Kullagerfabriken), the well-known manufacturer of ball and roller bearings, which employs more than 50,000 people throughout the world.

The advantages of large-scale operation will no doubt become increasingly evident as international competition promises to become even keener than it is today. A powerful spur has already been provided by the European Free Trade Association in that it has widened a home market of 7.5 million people into a seven-nation market of 90 million. This, in combination with steadily rising wage costs and other factors, has persuaded more and more firms to merge or otherwise pool their interests, the better to concentrate their resources and to rationalize their production, distribution and management. At the same time this tendency has augmented facilities for research and development. Larger scale, moreover, makes it possible to get more efficient use out of the very expensive machinery which technology is making available to the industrial community at an ever faster rate.

An inevitable consequence of business concentration has been to reduce the number of small firms. Since 1950 alone, the number of establishments employing less than 50 workers has declined from 40,000 to 34,000, or by 15 percent. At the same time, the number of medium-sized and large firms has increased. As a result, of course, the average size of firms has continually grown, whether this is measured by number of employees, production value or any other yardstick.

None the less, Sweden is still predominantly a nation of small business. Firms with less than five employees account for 60 percent of the total number of manufacturing plants. 75 percent of the manufacturing plants have less than ten employees and 93 percent less than fifty. There are only about 250 firms with more than 500 people on their payrolls, and they comprise no more than one-half percent of all the manufacturing firms in Sweden. In terms of manual workers employed or the value of production, the larger firms naturally take on a completely different aspect. Establishments with less than 50 workers employ only 25 percent of the manual workers in manufacturing, while the very small proportion of big firms employs about one-third.

A similar concentration into larger units has been taking place in other fields of economic activity during the postwar period. The number of farms has declined rapidly, though without an appreciable increase in average size of acreage. Retail trade is undergoing comprehensive structural change, affecting the number of stores, their location, and ways of doing business. The emergence of new distribution methods has taken a particularly heavy toll of food stores. Virtually all the new stores built in the past 15 years emphasize self-service. Present-day competition in wholesaling and retailing is dominated by powerful chains. An independent store owner who wants to "go it alone" finds that the cards are increasingly stacked against his chances of success.

Industry[1]

Industry undoubtedly constitutes the basis of Sweden's economic well-being. Amply endowed with three key natural resources— iron ore, forests and water power—Swedish industry has made extraordinary progress in the 20th century. This trend has been given a decisive forward push by the demand of other countries for our products. Industrial exports are now running at the rate of Swedish kronor 20,000 million annually, equal to 20 percent of the GNP and almost half the value of all industrial production. Products of wood and metal make up an overwhelming share of the exports—about 90 percent.

Industry's heavy dependence on economic trends in other countries is for both good and ill. Sometimes it imposes strains

---

[1] "Industry" is understood here to embrace manufacturing activity as a whole. In the Swedish industrial classification, mining is paired with manufacturing to comprise industry. The term will also be used to refer to organizations that have a similar technological structure of production, such as electrical engineering industry, textile industry and so on.

and tensions on the economy, at other times it is the chief generator of rising business activity. On balance, however, the good definitely outweighs the bad. Dependence on foreign trade has compelled Swedish firms to cut costs and improve their efficiency. Without foreign trade they simply would not have had the incentive to better their performance.

By contrast with many other countries, Swedish factories do not cluster in enclaves. There is nothing in Stockholm's industrial life to suggest any resemblance with cities such as London, Milan and Hamburg. The dispersion of industry derives primarily from historical reasons, more specifically the peculiarly Swedish manufacturing estates known as "bruk", which were originally formed to combine agriculture and forestry with one or several kinds of industrial enterprise, such as mining. The "bruk" were located in rural areas so as to be near sources of raw materials or water power, or because they enjoyed special advantages in transportation. A number of these "bruk" are to be found at the mouths of Sweden's northern rivers.

The largest industrial concentrations are in Göteborg and Malmö. Göteborg, besides being a chief shipbuilding center, is the home of SKF and Volvo. However, it is typical for these and other large-scale enterprises to decentralize their productive activities. Thus L M Ericsson, the manufacturers of telecommunications equipment, have their headquarters and one factory in Stockholm, but their systematic policy has been to set up other factories in regions of weak industrial development with an ample supply of labor. It was such a factory which helped reverse the threatened depopulation of Gotland, Sweden's largest island in the Baltic.

Mining and Metalworking

Iron, the most valuable of all metals, has long played a salient role in the Swedish economy. Indeed, if it weren't for her vast resources of iron ore and her ability to process it, Sweden would probably never have achieved her brief period of military greatness during the 17th century. At that time Sweden accounted for an estimated one-third of the world's iron output, roughly equivalent to the share now held by the United States. Sweden's share today is barely more than one percent.

By far the greater part of present-day mining relates to iron. Orefields are concentrated in two limited areas: Lapland in the far north and Bergslagen in central Sweden; the former is unusually rich in iron, and the latter unusually low in phosphorus content. Two State companies, LKAB and AB Statsgruvor, bulk large in production. Out of an annual yield of more than 20 million tons, 85 percent is exported, most of it to West Germany. Sweden's share of world export trade in iron ore runs to between 15 and 20 percent. At the present rate of extraction the country's proved resources of iron ore are predicted to last for 200 years. For various reasons, among them a slow increase in world consumption of steel, the likelihood is that the extraction rate will not increase very much in the coming years.

Despite the absence of native coal resources, Sweden has a large and highly developed iron and steel industry. Production is spread out over many establishments, of which the largest manufacture steel for ordinary commercial uses. Preeminent among them is Domnarfvet, owned by Stora Kopparberg, the oldest chartered company in the world still in existence (it was founded in 1347); among other things, Domnarfvet has provided the track steel for virtually the whole Swedish railway system. Of greater interest, however, is the production of quality steels—a specialty for which Sweden has become well known abroad. Quality steels for razor blades and watch springs are only two of many examples. Another specialty is stainless steel, whose manufacture dates from 1921.

High-grade steel plus availability of cheap electric power help to explain the supremacy of metalworking on the current industrial scene. It contributes more than one-third to the value of both production and exports. This sector also includes the internationally known firms. In addition to those already mentioned, there are Alfa-Laval (dairy equipment), AGA (light-house beacons, etc.), Electrolux (vacuum cleaners, refrigerators), Atlas Copco (compressed air equipment), SAAB (passenger cars, aircraft) and Scania-Vabis (trucks). Other distinguished products under this head include business machines, cameras, turbines, cannon, locomotives and ships. Sweden ranks with the world's top shipbuilders, a position carved out by the application of industrial engineering on an advanced scale. A good example is the new Arendal yard near

ASEA's high-tension laboratory at Ludvika. The company has long pioneered in the transmission of electric power at high voltages, and its special designs for long-distance D.C. transmission are known the world over. Photo: K. W. Gullers.

Göteborg, where ships are built on land in accordance with factory-based techniques of the assembly line and conveyor belt. This new method of shipbuilding has proved so effective that foreign interests, among them the United States Navy, have asked to try it out under licensing arrangements.

The metalworking industries have grown fast in the past few decades. To meet foreign competition they put their chief relianc on quality, engineering and new products rather than mass production. It seems likely that Sweden's economy will become even more dependent on the metalworking industries in the years ahead. Their share of the export trade is increasing constantly and future prospects look brighter than for most of the other industries. Two persistent problems cloud the horizon, however: one is the rapid rise of wages, which hits the "labor-intensive" factories especially hard; the other is a chronic shortage of labor in the metropolitan areas, where most of the exporting firms are located.

Employment and Production in the Metalworking Industries, 1963

	Employment		Value added	
	Number	Percent of ind. total	Million SKr	Percent of ind. total
Metal fabrication	78,900	9	2,046	8
Mechanical engineering	156,200	17	4,347	16
Electrical engineering	65,900	7	1,877	7
Transportation equipment	48,800	5	1,571	6
Totals	349,800	38	9,841	37

The Forest Industries

Sweden's most important natural resource is timber. Forests cover more than half the total land area. One-fourth of the forest acreage is owned by government, one-fourth by private enterprise, and the rest by individuals. Owing to mismanagement and overcutting, companies were debarred from acquiring forest properties at the beginning of this century. The ban was lifted in 1965, and it is expected that companies will increase their acreage through the purchase of individual holdings.

Thanks in large part to the many rivers which flow through them, Swedish forests are relatively easy of access. The timber is felled in winter, taken out to the ice-covered rivers, and then carried by the spring thaw down to the lumbering districts which are particularly concentrated at the river mouths of northern Sweden. This method of transportation has its drawbacks, however. For one thing, floating the logs takes too much time; besides, there is a great deal of wastage en route. The job of transporting logs is therefore rapidly being transferred from water to trucks.

Exploitation of timber resources in the mid-19th century was the generator that got Swedish industrialization rolling. Between 1850 and 1870 more than one hundred steam sawmills were built along the Bothnian coast, and lumber became the country's export commodity Number One. Today, the sawmills contribute only a minor share to industrial production and exports, though their output still comprises 15 percent of the world lumber trade. The 1920's and 1930's witnessed the shutdown of many small sawmills which could no longer compete with the larger, highly mechanized units.

Although lumber itself has declined in importance, other products of Swedish forests have filled in the export gap, though not to the same extent as in the interwar years, when between 40 and 50 percent of the export total regularly stemmed from timber sources. Today's proportion is about 30 percent, somewhat less than that of the mining and metalworking sector. The forest industries contribute about 13 percent to the value added by manufacture, and they employ the same proportion of the labor force.

Most of the large sawmills in northern Sweden are owned by vertically integrated enterprises, which embrace all the stages of operation from management of forest properties to logging to production of lumber, joineries, pulp and paper. This integration illustrates the structural change that Sweden's forest industries have undergone. The shift towards a higher degree of processed output began at the turn of the century, and the end is not yet in sight.

Sweden is the world's leading exporter and third largest producer of pulp. Manufacture is distributed among a hundred-odd plants in the central and northern areas. Pulp first became an important commodity between the wars, but the swiftest post-1945 expansion has been shown by paper. It is now common for pulp and paper mills to operate in directly adjoining facilities. Sweden also holds a first-rank position in the production and export of paper, and per capita consumption of paper is among the world's highest.

A further example of the continuing growth in the manufacture of more highly processed products is provided by wallboard. It is chiefly used for heat and sound insulation, wall coverings and joineries. The annual consumption of wallboard, amounting to about 77 pounds per head, puts Sweden at the top of the list. Sweden is exceeded only by the United States as a producer of wallboard and by no other country as an exporter.

Latter-day developments in the forest industries have proceeded along three main lines. First of all, technology has penetrated the forests themselves. The work of floating, barking and trimming logs, once done by human muscle, is now almost entirely taken over by machines. This has led to the displacement of many lumberjacks in the interior of northern Sweden. Wherever possible, these men are retrained for other occupations, thus helping to alleviate labor shortages elsewhere.

Secondly, the forest industries have been vigorously pushing the trend towards concentration. This is especially true of the pulp industry, where many mills have proved to be far too small and unmodern to cope with toughening foreign competition. Shutdowns and mergers have already taken place on a large scale and are sure to take on even greater importance in the coming years.

Thirdly, these industries have gone international in a big way. Several of the largest companies, such as Svenska Cellulosa AB and Mo och Domsjö AB, have bought paper goods factories in Europe. Others have joined with foreign interests in launching new production ventures abroad; so far new factories have been set up in Canada and Portugal.

Other Industries

The wearing-apparel sector, comprising textiles, ready-made clothing and shoes, is the industry group that has attracted most of the mass-media publicity in Sweden in the past years. It is in the throes of a crisis, which has caused a wave of mergers and shutdowns as one plant after the other has been unable to meet the lower prices of apparel coming from "low-wage" countries, especially in southern and eastern Europe and the Far East. The present crisis, however, is only the latest in a recurring series. All have originated in competition from imports, which present considerable difficulties for a country where industrial tariffs have traditionally been very low. About half the textiles consumed in Sweden today are imported.

The rapid readjustment that postwar events have forced on the textile industry can be illuminated by a few figures. Its work force has fallen by 50 percent, while volume of production has increased slightly and value of output somewhat more. During the same period the metalworking and chemical industries have doubled their work force. Since 1950 one-fourth of all the textile factories have shut down. Two firms now produce two-thirds of the woollen fabrics and two other firms produce two-thirds of the women's hosiery. In the production of cotton fabrics, the largest segment of the textile industry, three firms now completely dominate the picture.

For all the intensity of this transformation, it has been possible to respond with a minimum of pain. Most of the released workers have moved over to jobs in expanding industries and occupations, often after retraining and change of residence. Since the end of the 1950's the government has gone to great expense to facilitate these structural changes and to soften their negative impact on the labor market. About one percent of the labor force is enrolled each year in government-sponsored retraining courses.

The government's employment programs have become an essential component of national economic policy. Here, too, lies the explanation for organized labor's support of present trends. Indeed, Swedish trade unions prefer to accelerate structural change and industrial modernization rather than deter them— an attitude that is probably unique by international comparisons.

To the chemical industry goes the distinction of showing the lustiest growth during the postwar period. Production has more than doubled in volume since 1950. When measured by the international yardstick, however, the Swedish chemical industry is still a baby. Its share of total industrial production is five percent, which is pretty low for a country with an otherwise highly developed economy. The present decade has witnessed a faster rate of progress, and the outlook for chemical products appears to be exceptionally bright in the next few years.

The economies of scale particularly recommend themselves to the chemical industry, but achieving them requires an enormous capital investment as well as massive research and development outlays. Here we have at least a partial explanation for the special characteristics of this industry in Sweden, at least as far as the production of basic chemicals is concerned. It is largely dominated by big corporations, which have expanded in collaboration with or at the initiative of foreign entrepreneurs. This is particularly true of the petrochemical industry at Stenungsund on the west coast north of Göteborg.

Included in the chemical classification are some other industries which are fairly well known abroad. One of them, the match industry, has more than a century of history behind it. Sweden used to figure high in the international match statistics, with an annual production of 50,000 tons in some years of the 1920's and 1930's; present-day output is 20,000 tons. Where about 150 match factories once operated in Sweden, there are now only six, and before long even these will probably dwindle to two or three. Since 1917 all the match factories have been owned by STAB (Svenska Tändsticks Aktiebolaget), which also transacts a sizable international business. In recent years STAB has greatly diversified its operations to make up for the decline in its match output.

The inventions of Alfred Nobel in the mid-19th century gave rise to an important explosives industry in Sweden. Nobelkrut at Bofors, founded in 1894 by Nobel, is the largest and best-known company. Lastly, no description of the Swedish chemical industry would be complete without mention of pharmaceuticals. The manufacture of drugs and medicines has expanded at record speed during the postwar period. Since 1950 the average rate of growth has been ten percent, as compared with eight percent for the chemical industry as a whole and five percent for all of industry. The largest pharmaceutical houses are Astra and Pharmacia.

Fuel and Power

Sweden's consumption of energy per head of population has increased rapidly in recent years. At the same time the relative importance of different energy sources has changed: domestic fuels, coal and coke have declined, while oil and hydro-generated power have moved ahead. The influence of prices has favored an increasing shift to the use of electricity, which is relatively cheap in Sweden.

The most important domestic source of energy is water power, whose potential has yet to be fully realized. Out of a developable capacity of 80,000 million kilowatt hours, only half has been harnessed. It is highly uncertain, however, whether anything will be done about the other half: in the past few years the competitive appeal of water power has fallen off vis-a-vis thermal and nuclear power.

A major impediment to the extension of hydroelectric capacity in Sweden is the irregularity of terrain. The rivers do not flow in a neat staircase sequence of horizontal stretches and precipitous falls; instead, they rush ahead in long rapids interrupted by segments of placid water. Engineers therefore build underground stations, in which the whole vertical drop of a low river stretch is concentrated. This system permits a more or less complete utilization of a river's total drop with a small number of power stations. Sweden is well qualified to perform this kind of civil engineering thanks to the existence of primary rock, the domestic production of tungsten carbide drills and compressed air equipment, and the development of home-researched blasting methods.

75 percent of the harnessed water power is in northern Sweden, but only 30 percent of it is used there. Electricity is transmitted from the north by high tension lines for alternating current. The main grid, with voltages of 380,000 and 220,000, has a total transmission length of about 5,000 miles. Gotland is connected to the mainland by an underwater d.c. cable. The long-distance transmission of high-voltage d.c. is a specialty developed by the ASEA company, which has been awarded contracts to install it in other parts of the world: across the English Channel, on the Pacific coast of North America, between the two main islands of New Zealand, etc.

Svenska Cellulosa Aktiebolaget (SCA) exports its products on custom-made ships, equipped with deck cranes which permit loading and unloading in record time. Photo: IBA industribild.

About half the electric power is supplied by private companies and the other half by the national government and local authorities. 20 percent of the power is fed directly to industrial plants, which produce electricity mostly for their own needs, but with a good deal left over to cater for other consumers.

Agriculture

This is the branch of economic activity that has experienced the most radical structural change in Sweden in our time. The population of farmers was at its highest in 1880, and since then

A high degree of mechanization has entered into the logging industry, with increasing use made of electronic techniques. Photo: IBA industribild.

has fallen by more than half. Although the "flight from the farm" is by no means unique to Sweden, it has proceeded at an exceptionally swift pace during the postwar period. Where farmers comprised 30 percent of the gainfully employed in 1940, the proportion declined to 20 percent in 1950, to 14 percent in 1960, and less than 10 percent today.

During the 1930's 25,000 people abandoned agriculture each year; the number swelled to an annual 35,000 during the 1940's and 1950's and the exodus in the present decade is even greater.

The rural depopulation has been paralleled by rapid mechanization. In 1945 there were 600,000 horses as compared with 150,000 today. During the same period the number of tractors has soared from 25,000 to 250,000. In 1900 there were more than 200,000 oxen in Sweden. Today it would take a good eye to spot a single one.

For all this sweeping transformation, Sweden continues to be a nation of small farmers. Almost one-third of the holdings have less than five hectares of arable land, and another one-third are between five and ten hectares. (One hectare equals 2.471 acres.) A mere one percent, comprising about 200 farms, exceed 100 hectares. However, they aggregate more than ten percent of the total acreage as compared with 20 percent for the two-thirds of the farms with less than 10 hectares. The vast majority of farms are run as family operations, which explains the preponderance of small holdings. 90 percent of the total acreage is individually owned.

Since 1947 the chief objective of national agricultural policy has been to ensure that persons employed on farms of up to 20 hectares earn the same real income as the average of industrial workers. The principal instrument of this policy (which of course has served to slow down the structural change) is the maintenance of high food prices by protective tariffs. Another policy aim has been to achieve a high level of national self-sufficiency in foodstuffs. At the present time it is estimated that Sweden can meet nearly all her food requirements from domestic sources.

However, a new agricultural bill has just been passed by the Parliament (June 1967). The new agricultural policy will undoubtedly speed up the rate of the structural change in agriculture even more. Among the objectives are to increase efficiency by introducing cost-reduction measures and exposing Swedish farm products to more foreign competition, to reduce the number of farms and increase their average size, and to lower the degree of self-sufficiency. It is hoped that the closure of inefficient farms will release people for employment in other sectors of the economy, manufacturing industry in particular, which have long been plagued by labor shortages.

Agriculture earns 80 percent of its income from raising livestock. Milk is the leading market product, followed by meat. Virtually all the processing of these products is handled by producer cooperatives, to which the farmers are required to deliver their output. Of the various cereals, oats take up the biggest acreage, while wheat is the leading grain. Most of the wheat is grown on the fertile plains of southern Sweden. There is also large-scale cultivation of potatoes, oil crops and sugar beets. However, the production of sugar is favored by restrictive quotas on imports, which will partly be abolished when the new agricultural policy goes into effect.

The Services Sector

The shift of emphasis away from production of goods to rendering of service is common to the economies of industrial countries. Its primary impetus comes from increasing incomes, which generate a sharply growing demand for private and public services. Another important fact is the less favorable movement of prices in the services sector as compared with industry. It is for this reason that industry can cash in more quickly on the improvements in productivity which result from cost-reduction measures.

Trade is the largest component of the services sector. Wholesaling and retailing employ more than a half-million people, equal to 14 percent of the gainfully employed. Employment in trade has more than doubled since the mid-1930's. It would appear, however, that the peak has now been reached. As far as retailing is concerned, the outlook is for declining employment in the next few years.

Transformation, closures and concentration are terms that well describe postwar developments in trade. Food retailing provides the most telling example: 20 years ago half the country's 83,000 retail establishments were food stores; of the slightly more than 70,000 in operation today, food stores account for no more than 40 percent. Although small over-the-counter stores have been the chief victims, they still dominate the scene by force of sheer numbers. Stores employing up to ten persons comprise 97 percent of the total retail outlets, while stores employing more than 25 comprise less than one percent.

Sweden's first self-service store opened its doors in 1947. Since then the dam has burst in the food trade, and other lines of business are finding it harder to resist the tide. About 70 percent of the retail food business is transacted by 9,000 self-service stores. On a per capita basis the system of self-service is more widespread in Sweden than in any other European country.

The past decade has also witnessed a proliferation of department stores, from a mere dozen or so to about 200. They now gross 20 percent of the total retail trade business. These stores are owned by a handful of competing chains, all of which are vigorously expanding their empires. A big factor in promoting the growth of department and self-service stores was the abolition of resale price maintenance in 1954, since it meant that retailers could add price to their competitive arsenal. The ability to sell brand-name merchandise at low prices and without service has also stimulated the advent of discount houses.

An important element of the Swedish trade scene is the rapid expansion of chains and variety stores. More than half the food stores are chain-owned and they handle two-thirds of the retail trade in food. The independents are increasingly caught in a position of sink or swim. In other lines of business, such as wearing apparel, toiletries, radio and TV appliances, hardware and home furnishings, various forms of cooperation between independent enterprises have been established.

The pattern of distribution has also been significantly affected by the trend towards segregated shopping districts. These have sprung up both in the redeveloped hearts of cities and amidst the giant new housing developments on the urban fringe. In either case, the result is a compact cluster of shops selling all kinds of products. Typical examples of such districts may be found in downtown Stockholm and in the Vällingby and Farsta suburbs.

Another growing type of outlet might be described as the "multi-owned department store", which resembles the ordinary type except for the fact that each department represents one firm.

The cooperative movement is of major importance in Swedish trade. It operates nearly 5,000 stores, of which more than half are built for self-service. Cooperatives also own a hundred department stores all over the country, as well as two of the three self-service, full-line discount houses which have been established to date. However, more discount houses can be expected before long.

Foreign Trade

We have already mentioned that Sweden carries on an extensive foreign trade. As of 1966 exports were valued at SKr 22,100 million and imports at nearly SKr 23,700 million. It was also noted that the most important exports are products of iron and timber. Raw materials and semi-manufactures such as iron ore and paper pulp used to dominate, but have now been surpassed in value by machinery, cars, ships and other finished goods turned out by the metalworking industries. Food products are also exported to a certain extent. The crafted products of our furniture and ceramics industries are well known abroad, but do not figure prominently as earners of foreign exchange. A not insignificant export of textiles has been developed in recent years.

Machinery and instruments bulk large on the import side. A conspicuous import item is cars, which make up 70 percent of the cars sold in Sweden today. Thirty percent of the imports consist of petroleum products, food products, and textiles-apparels, each at values in excess of SKr 2,000 million.

Sweden's biggest customer is West Germany, which buys one-sixth of our exports, closely followed by Britain. Norway, Denmark and the United States come next, though they are much farther down on the list. Intra-Scandinavian trade has increased sharply in the present decade, chiefly in consequence of EFTA's tariff reductions. In 1966 the EFTA countries absorbed 42 percent of Sweden's exports, the EEC countries 30, the United States seven, and Eastern Europe four percent.

West Germany contributes the biggest portion of imports, followed by Britain, the United States, Denmark, Norway and Holland. A regional breakdown of the statistics shows that 36 percent of Sweden's imports come from the EEC area, 34 percent from EFTA, 9 percent from the United States, and five percent from Eastern Europe. The United States evidently plays a significant role in Swedish foreign trade, while commercial ties with the Eastern bloc are not as extensive as many people seem to believe.

Kurt Samuelsson

Born in 1921. Docent of economic history at Stockholm University in 1951, of sociology in 1966. Has a notable record of achievement as controversial political journalist, most recently as editor-in-chief of the Stockholm daily, *Aftonbladet*, from 1961 to 1965. Appointed president of the Graduate School of Social Work and Public Administration in Stockholm 1966. *Religion and Economic Action* (Eng. trans. 1961) is his bestknown work of scholarship.

Patterns of Postwar Economic Debate

Gunnar Sträng, a member of the Social Democratic party, became Minister of Finance in 1955. Economic policy is but one of the fields in which he has exercised great influence. In the picture, he is sitting on the "government bench" in the Riksdag. Photo: Folke Hellberg.

As a non-belligerent in World War II, Sweden emerged from the conflict with her industrial plant intact and a standard of living that was relatively high. The ensuing years witnessed a fairly rapid succession of social reforms which, at least initially, greatly equalized income levels in the sense that extensive purchasing power was put into the hands of large sections of the community: the retired aged, families with many children, and students in higher education. At the same time, "regular" incomes were rising swiftly, partly in consequence of fattened pay envelopes and partly because a policy of full employment made wage earners of everyone who was able-bodied and willing to work. Given the tolerably decent standard of living to start off with, the result was to increase not only effective demand but also to generate new needs; in other words, the economic expectations of many people began to take a completely different turn. In the field of private consumption, interest focused on such things as cars and houses (we would have preferred to write "houses and cars", but that would be misrepresenting the priorities). Over in public consumption, there was greater need for such "heavyweights" as improved medical care, expanded education, and enlarged municipal services to take care of the large-scale population inflows into the towns.

We have here the Galbraithian dilemma, but in a different guise, for Sweden has been deliberately seeking to give the public sector its due in real terms, but, as Galbraith contends for the United States, to some extent starving it of funds. The problems are crucial: How shall the authorities of central and local government acquire the resources to meet the new demands of a welfare economy? And since a larger slice of the cake for the public sector inevitably

135

infringes on private consumption, how can a fair share of resources be allocated to the business community for spending on plant and equipment? It certainly cannot be said that Sweden has managed to resolve these difficulties more rationally than other countries. Instead, an irrational solution has obtruded: an upward spiral of prices, continuously moving and fairly steep, and in any event so headlong as to justify use of the word, "inflation".

As is only to be expected, this situation has greatly affected the course of debate on economic policy throughout virtually the whole postwar period. It has done so somewhat confusingly, according to the various lights of those in power. One might say that the holders of political responsibility have been playing both ends against the middle. On the one hand, they have insisted on vigorous anti-inflationary action, chiefly by resort to tax devices to balance the budget, accompanied since the late 'fifties by restrictions on credit at high interest rates and by certain physical controls; on the other hand, they have tried to play down the size and importance of inflation in their propaganda. The opposition parties have long been following the opposite tack: to emphasize the iniquity of price increases and at the same time criticize the heavy burden of taxation. However, there has been a shift of targets and, as far as can be determined, 1960 was the turning point. The growth of the public sector is no longer inveighed against and the tax bite is accepted for the time being, though a different sharing of the burden is urged.

To understand the pattern of inflation in Sweden, reference must also be made to the system of rent control that was introduced during the war. Rent control has undoubtedly done much to deflect purchasing power from houses to other consumer goods, such as cars. This system has been combined with government subsidies of housing construction to hold down rents, with the added result of increasing the demand for roomier accommodation beyond the available supply. A considerable shortage of housing has arisen in consequence. In a society of rapid migration from countryside to small towns, and from the small towns to the cities a certain degree of housing shortage would have been unavoidable in any case. Naturally, the avoidance has not been made easier by price reductions plus controls on housebuilding itself, which have allotted the cities a quota smaller than what is needed to cater for their growing share of the population.

And here we come to another anomaly: for years the opposition parties, especially the Conservatives and Liberals, have used the housing queues as a political bludgeon, but they have never vigorously attacked rent control. Its critics must be sought elsewhere, among scientists and publicists, as well as several members of the ruling Social Democratic party itself. The explanation, of course, is that rent control has been far too well-favored by far too many: by the existing holders of leases, especially in houses of older vintage, where the rents fall particularly short of the level that would obtain in a free-market "equilibrium".

The difficulty of debating such an issue may be peculiar to the Welfare State, which from a sociologist's point of view might explain why it is so much easier to talk about inflation in general terms than to do anything about it. If the debate were ever to pass much beyond the stage of general complaints and criticism, and thus serve as a harbinger of forceful action, it would have to recognize the necessity of eroding the perquisites that so many Swedes already enjoy.

Indeed, a system of direct privileges is embedded in the formulation of Swedish housing policy. The lucky people with leases are favored at the expense of those who don't have them, but the latter still have to help foot the bill for subsidies, while the occupants of older dwellings get better treatment than those who live in more recently built housing. To the extent that middle-aged and old people, who are generally favored by this policy, have a stronger political say than the younger generation, who are generally disfavored, the policy readily tends to become rigid. A process of modification is bound to be very slow and gradual. It would appear to be imminent for two reasons: the strains of trying to keep within the limit of available economic resources are becoming too vexatious; and the bulge in the youth population is beginning to make its influence felt at the polls. An official plan has already been adopted which calls for the decontrol of rents in successive steps. The 1968 election campaign promises to be very interesting in this respect.

While on subject of "welfare queues", housing is far from being the only field where they are evident. The subsidizing of education

—or perhaps it would be more correct ideologically to speak of its democratization—has given rise to overflows for the schools and universities. No better evidence of the thoroughgoing ferment of change in Sweden can be had than to look at these queues. As late as the 'forties educational debate was centered on the problem of how parents in the "lower classes" could be persuaded to get their children to study; it was assumed that social lags would be more difficult to overcome than the economic. The educators and university authorities were the first to be caught napping, and some time elapsed before the truth dawned on government officials as well. A veritable educational explosion took place, and the supply of qualified teachers and physical plant was soon outstripped by the demand.

The difficulties here are of a different nature than where housing is concerned. Nobody wants to staunch the flow of knowledge-seekers by charging prohibitive prices; on the contrary, it is generally accepted that education shall not only be free, but that pupils and students are entitled to various forms of public financial aid. In its most recent platform, however, the Conservative party has favored restricting public support to the scholastically gifted; those of poorer intellectual endowments should be required to pay for their studies out of their own pockets. Apart from this digression, however, the fundamental problem is a different one: Can educational expansion be given sufficient priority so as to be assured of the necessary resources? This would presumably have to come out of taxes, but is it politically feasible to raise them if that means putting a damper on private consumption? Which brings us back to the Galbraithian dilemma we mentioned earlier.

The issue is all the more controversial because it involves not only the overall burden of taxation, but also the distribution of incomes. Thus at the end of the 'fifties the Liberal party wanted to call a halt to the pace of social reforms to permit the exchequer to catch up with expenditures without having to resort to tax increases; according to one of the party's arguments, the level of taxation was such that large groups of people were financing their own social benefits in any case, and hence had nothing to gain from a policy of income distribution. A heated discussion on the rates of surtax has pretty much followed the same lines. According to one school of thought, a progressively higher tax bite acts as a disincentive to hard work; the opposite school contends that the surtax is an "equitable" means of sharing the burden; in other words, it helps to distribute incomes.

Actually, surtax and social security are not at all that decisive in their effects on income distribution: most people are presumably able to compensate for the former by negotiating higher pay for themselves; as for the latter, the value of benefits is determined not by income level but by the insurance risk involved. The market trend in wages and salaries is far more important. And there can be no doubt that those who pay tribute to the principle of income equalization in a welfare economy with a rapid rate of growth have had to see their ideal sorely squeezed by reality.

In the first place, the gaps in income and wealth have widened during the 1950's and 1960's. The play of market forces is ultimately decisive here, but an important marginal force has been at work also: all large sections of the community have formed powerful organizations, which in effect has meant that the better-paid have been well able to maintain their income differentials, the more so in view of the extra premium which skilled manpower can command in an expanding technological society.

In the second place, the postwar wave of structural economic changes has inflicted special hardships on certain industries which have either long lagged behind in their pay levels or been recently put into this predicament. This situation has preoccupied collective bargaining in the past few years. The unions have been consistently, and to some extent successfully, pushing claims for their low-paid members. However, these efforts to apply a sort of catch-up formula are largely frustrated by the ability of the better-paid to secure increases above the negotiated rates.

The debate has since shifted from the conference tables of labor and management towards the corridors of political power. Has the government done enough to check the new income gaps? Hasn't it been too complaisant in its acceptance of the situation? Indeed, hasn't it missed the boat by not bringing its social policy to bear as an equilizer? When social benefits are related to income (social insurance makes allowance for loss of income and scales its charges by income level; the higher the income, the higher the benefits), they exert virtually no income-equalizing effect once the subsistence minimum is exceeded. Here a new "left wing" has entered the stage by taking a "radical" stand against the government's "bourgeois" policies. While the significance of this criticism to date should not be overestimated, it does point up a likely source of increased future tension in our Welfare State. The conflict between demands of large groups of people for greater equality and the continued widening of the income gap, which is perhaps an unavoidable concomitant of desired economic growth, may well set the tone of future political debate in this sphere.

The need for economic growth has another aspect, too, and it conflicts with other ideals represented by the ruling Social Democratic party. This is the integration movement in Western Europe.

The question of a greater commitment by Sweden to this movement was not seriously considered until Britain tried in 1961 and 1962 to gain admission to the EEC. Debate on the subject eventually sorted out into two factions: the one, Conservative-Liberal, favored Swedish entry into the Common Market as a full member; the other, Social Democratic-Center, recommended the looser or associate form of membership. The latter faction holds that full membership conflicts, or could conflict, with Swedish neutrality in foreign affairs. The arguments pro and con are more fully set forth by Nils Andrén in his essay for this book; the discussion here will be confined to the special aspect of economic policy.

Actually, the Swedish debate was not fully conclusive. This was natural enough, since all the parties agreed not to commit themselves too firmly to possible negotiations. None the less, two main lines of reasoning may be discerned. The advocates of full membership, backed by the business community, stressed the handicaps that would befall Sweden if she were to become the only member of EFTA to stay outside. The other side held that full-fledged economic association would, in addition to inflicting political disabilities, tie Sweden's hands in domestic economic policy. In this way the debate on Sweden and the EEC also came to reflect a collision of economic philosophies: between "free enterprise" in its Liberal-Conservative version and the "planned economy" of the Social Democrats, with support from the Center party in certain aspects relating to agriculture and forestry.

As far as the Social Democratic party is concerned, however, the controversy had less to do with economic expansion than with allegiance to ideology—in this case, the principle of full employment. Foreign observers often tend to view the practice of full employment in Sweden as primarily motivated by production technology, as an integral part of a policy of economic growth. That is true enough so far as it goes. But as the architects of this policy, the Social Democrats were primarily moved by ethical considerations. For them, everyone's right to a job and the right to pick a job of one's choice were paramount. If productivity improved in consequence, all well and good, but that was of secondary importance.

In this ideological structure, the concepts of freedom and equality became vital cornerstones. Moreover, it is no doubt correct to regard the Social Democratic view of inflation in this light. If the party were forced to choose between inflation and stable prices with less-than-full employment, it would plump for inflation. In Social Democratic eyes, full employment is a higher moral commandment than, say, price stability. In return, the party may well find itself in the position of having to "sell" other parts of the policy it wants to pursue to the European market, which would presumably mean sacrificing the demand for income equalization.

The parties have yet to debate these problems in the sharp, specific terms that they deserve. It takes listening of near-electronic sensitivity to make out the finer shades of meaning in the statements that are made from time to time. A conjuncture of new circumstances, however, may well force the calling of a spade by its right name. After all, not even the Promised Land of the Middle Way can go on tolerating ideological dichotomies forever. Sooner or later, priorities will have to be sorted out along a fairly clear-cut scale of preferences.

Siv Thorsell

Born in 1937, Master of Arts. Staff researcher at the Industrial Council for Social and Economic Studies (SNS), an organization founded by the business community to promote a constructive debate on the relations of private enterprise to the community at large. Co-editor of the English version of *The Changing Roles of Men and Women* (1967).

Swedish Women Today

Wire being tested for quality at a steel mill. An increasing number of women are entering the industrial labor force, and it is also becoming more common for them to perform physically demanding tasks. Photo: Wolf Krabel.

Evolution of the Feminist Issue

Towards the end of the 19th century and at the beginning of the 20th, the feminist movement was concerned with removing legal, political and social discriminations against women. In due course Swedish women gained their objectives as then defined, as have women in a number of other countries. Since then, however, new dimensions have been added to the question of women's rights by major social and economic changes. In a country like Sweden, with a high standard of living and the existence of widespread opportunity for individual self-fulfillment, such factors as sex, social class and residence pattern continue to be determining. They affect not only the choice of education and career, but also the very style of life.

To describe the position of women in present-day Sweden, their roles must be compared with those of men in education, employment and the home. What changes have taken place? It is revealing that only ten years ago or so, the debate was still mostly concerned with the issue of feminism as such, but now the emphasis is on the roles of both sexes. That more than mere change of labels is involved is shown by the contributions of sociological and psychological research to the debate. The issue has been framed in broader terms to give it the character of a *social problem.* In consequence the debate is being argued with more consistency and in greater depth. It is appreciated that women cannot improve their status on the labor market and at the same time have their status as dependent housewives strengthened. A new and deeper interpretation has been put on equalitarianism with the realization that the man's role cannot remain unaffected by a change in the woman's role.

143

The Debate on Sex Roles

Two main approaches may be distinguished under this heading, the one usually designated as moderate and the other as radical. The former tends to stress limited, short-range objectives, while the latter focuses on the longer term and is more explicit in its demands for equality. However, this is not to suggest that the radical wing lacks roots in today's real world; indeed, it is very much characterized by immediate experience of realities.

The moderates are less disposed to assume that a change in the woman's role will entail a change in the man's role. They are not conservative in the sense of insisting that woman's only place is in the home, but aim rather to enable her to cope with both family and occupational roles. This can be achieved either by dividing her career into a sequence (typically, from paid job to homemaking back again to paid job) or by providing community services that will permit her to perform both roles at the same time.

According to the radicals, the principle of strict equality admits of only one logical deduction: both men and women have two roles, a vocational and a familistic. The moderates, they contend, offer no more than compromises and expedients. Far from improving woman's status in the home and on the labor market, these solutions put her on "parole", that is, in a kind of halfway house where she is entitled to participate in paid employment only if this does not encroach on her traditional family duties. Nor do the radicals have much use for the "options", frequently cited in political debate, whereby women should be free to choose between home and job. Why restrict the options to women? And what about the barriers, external and internal, that make all talk of options so much poppycock? Among the external barriers is a system of taxation which dissuades many married women from working because the take-home pay isn't worth the trouble of earning it. The difficulty of arranging day care for children is another. The internal barriers comprise the deep-seated sexual prejudices which are inculcated in the child-rearing years and later reinforced by the mass-media stereotypes. As a result, the radicals contend, both men and women come under strong environmental pressures to live up to the roles traditionally expected of them.

An Altered Situation

The familistic and vocational roles of men and women may be regarded as an adjustment to a fairly regular yet changeable pattern, which is largely dependent on the family's traditional functions. It becomes relevant here to ask: To what extent are these functions influenced by other developments in society—by technological advance, conditions on the labor market, social welfare measures, etc.? Male and female roles in the family must also be viewed against the background of a changing life pattern brought about by prolonged education, a higher incidence of marriages, lowered marrying ages, dwindling family size, earlier child-bearing ages, and increased longevity. All these factors have affected women's opportunities for gainful employment, some negatively and others positively.

Women in Employment

At the beginning of the 1960's a far higher proportion of men were gainfully employed as compared with unmarried women. The disparity is especially wide in the highest age bracket: 90 percent of the men as against only 50 percent of the women.
Poorer employment opportunities for women are probably the chief explanation.

There are striking differences between those married women who have children below the age of seven (the school-starting year) and those who didn't. None the less, it is relatively common for married women to hold jobs even when they have children of

Participation Rates in Different Age Groups among Men and Single Women 1961–1965[1]

Age group	Men, percent	Single women, percent
20–24	79	77
25–54	96	80
55–64	89	54

Source: National Central Bureau of Statistics; Statistical Reports V, 1965:16.
[1] An average of the data from the labour force surveys in 1961–1965.

Participation Rates among Married Women in Different Age Groups with and without Children under 7 Years[1]

Married women in age group	Participation rates according to labor force surveys 1961–65	Activity rates according to the 1960 census
20–24 years		
With children under 7 years	29.4	17.0
Without children under 7 years	79.4	71.3
Total	46.1	34.2
25–34 years		
With children under 7 years	33.4	17.1
Without children under 7 years	70.9	55.0
Total	45.0	28.8
35–44 years		
With children under 7 years	34.2	14.6
Without children under 7 years	58.6	35.8
Total	51.1	28.6
45–54 years	50.4	27.0
55–64 years	32.1	15.6

Source: Central Bureau of Statistics; Forecasting Information 1965:5. The women in the labor force 1. Table 22.

[1] An average of the data from the surveys in 1961–1965.

preschool age. Between 1961 and 1965 about 160,000 women, one-third of all the mothers of preschool children, were in paid employment. The special breakdowns given by labor force surveys on part-time work show that about 50 percent of the married women in paid employment worked less than half a day. The shortage of institutional facilities for child care is one of the factors which keeps mothers of small children out of the labor market.

The declining incidence of mature married women in paid employment is related to the difficulty of finding suitable jobs for many of them. A large proportion of these women, having been out of the labor market for a long time, lack training or possess skills which are no longer marketable. Not until the last few years have government labor officials come around to the view that special measures are needed to find better job opportunities for mature women. A significant sign of the new straws in the wind is female enrollment in elementary and advanced training courses and in retraining courses: the proportion, which was almost negligible at the end of the 1950's, rose to about 45 percent in 1965. In addition, tax-exempt training allowances are now much more available to married women— though not to the unmarried.

Implications of Full Employment for Women

The ever increasing proportion of gainfully employed women is closely related to the labor shortage that Sweden has had since the end of the 1940's. Both government and business have begun to realize that women are the only major resource we have left to alleviate the shortage. Among other things, this has meant that business employers have undertaken to revise their recruitment policies.

As for the official attitude, a good starting point for examination is the ILO report entitled "Women Workers in a Changing World". In addition to quoting employment statistics for women in different countries, the report describes the positions taken by governments. These are marked in most cases by strong reservations. The chief aim of government labor policy for women, we are told, should be to further the fulfillment of family obligations; paid employment for them is a secondary consideration.

Some of the countries, however, were decidedly more radical in their approach, and Sweden most of all. According to the Swedish Government, labor legislation should be identical for men and women, with separate provisions for pregnancy as the only allowable exceptions. Responsibility for child care and family maintenance is to be equally vested in both sexes; government should provide the same facilities for helping men and women enter the job world; part-time work ought to be arranged for both men and women who want it; and discrimination should be abolished generally.

The official Swedish position accords with the present-day views of organized management and trade unions. As yet, however, these are more in the nature of aspirations than actual achievements. Indeed, no more than lip service is often paid to the aspirations themselves, as witnessed by the absence of radical measures for change in most of the fields where the woman-at-work problem is relevant.

Thus we still have a system of taxation which postulates that man is the meal ticket and woman its beneficiary. The 1964 report of a government commission appointed to revise the system made not the slightest attempt to tackle this problem from a new angle. Further, the planning of community service agencies has proved unable to keep pace with the needs of breadwinners in general and families in particular. Although the drudgery has been taken out of housework, a great deal more could be done to lighten it. A particularly chronic problem, discussed below, is the provision of group arrangements for child care.

Inadequate Child Care

As of 1966 there was accommodation for 12,500 children in day nurseries and for 8,000 in private homes authorized by the local authorities to mind children. This makes a total of 20,500 places available to the 200,000 children under seven whose mothers and fathers are working—including those children who have only one parent. The majority of parents are therefore forced to make private arrangements for the care of their children, which is a difficult task at best. As in other countries the domestic service occupations have lost much of their appeal in Sweden because of better-paid jobs in other fields.

In spite of greatly increased national-government support of institutional facilities for child care, the local authorities are reluctant to expand them. For the most part they have preferred to invest their resources in family child-minding, which though cheaper tends to be instable: many of the mothers enrolled in this service tire of their duties, with the result that their charges often have to change environment. By comparison, the day nurseries are not only more stable, but they also provide the group comradeship which many children in isolated urban flats so sorely need. For this reason, current debate favors the nurseries, while the child-minding services are to cater primarily for those children to whom the nursery form is unsuited.

A recurring question in the debate on collective care concerns the risks it poses for the proper bringing-up of children. However, less interest has been shown in the risks of cutting off a child from other children and from adults other than its parents. Such risks follow from increasing urbanization, with its tendency to cluster people in dormitory suburbs where apartments are frequently small and outdoor play space is inadequate. The resulting isolation, of course, also affects mothers, with inevitable consequences for their mental health; but neither has this aspect received close attention.

In the view of child psychologists, it is fundamentally wrong to phrase the issue of collective upbringing in either-or terms. Nurseries, kindergartens and other common facilities should not be thought of as replacing parents but rather as supplementing them.

The effect on children of having both parents gainfully employed has been the subject of both Swedish and foreign studies, which show that the quality and not the quantity of parental contacts with children is crucial; the fact that the mother works outside the home is of less importance. Psychological research also reveals that children should have closer ties with the father.

One partial solution given for the problem of child care is to provide more part-time jobs for the parents, fathers included. Further, the disadvantages of having both parents work full time could be greatly lessened if many more service flats were built, or if housekeeping chores could otherwise be lightened to permit parents to spend more unhurried time with their children at the end of a workday. One bright star on the horizon is that the increased leisure which comes from shorter working hours will be devoted to those shared experiences that can make family life more secure and meaningful.

A Segregated Labor Market

Swedish long-range forecasts predict a sharp increase in the number of married women entering the labor market in the next decades. However, it cannot be assumed out of hand that greater equality of opportunity will result. As long as only the woman is supposed to play both a vocational and a family role, she will constantly lag behind the man in the job world. This produces a recoil effect: women will still be getting the worst-paid jobs, and hence their contribution to the family finances will be secondary to that of their husbands. Even women without direct family responsibilities will be disadvantaged, since employers tend to think in terms of "womanpower" as a universal category. Because men are looked upon as the chief providers, their work is considered more important and better geared to incentives for getting ahead. The women, as beneficiaries of the meal ticket, are second-rated on both counts.

The Occupational Pattern

It will already have emerged from the foregoing account that the fact of being male or female makes a big difference for the pursuit of a vocation. The labor market in Sweden, as in most other countries, splits into two parts, one which employs preponderantly men and the other women. Most of the gainfully employed women are engaged in occupations which they dominate totally or nearly so. The 1960 census showed that 71 percent of women in the labor force were working in some twenty occupations which employed only 12 percent of the men. In other words, the majority of occupations are more or less "masculine".

The occupations in which women comprise between 90 and 100 percent of the labor force bear familiar names: nurse, teacher, maid, charwoman, seamstress, physical therapist, prescriptionist, telephone operator and hairdresser. More than half the twenty "female trades" evoke associations with what women are traditionally supposed to do: nurse, sew, clean, cook or make themselves beautiful.

Different Levels

In fields of activity where men and women are more or less equally represented, they are put to completely unlike tasks with wide differences of status and pay levels. A look at the Swedish white-collar sector, which is very large numerically and where about half the employees are women, shows that 90 percent of them are doing clerical work as compared with only 33 percent of the men. More than half the men are in engineering or managerial positions, but only 8 percent of the women.

The majority of women occupy the lowest rungs of the white-collar ladder both in business and government, while men predominate at the middle and upper levels.

Underutilization of Womanpower

According to studies of the Swedish labor force, a considerable proportion of the women who would like to work cannot take jobs owing to obstacles of one kind or another. In the spring of 1965 it was estimated that 104,000 women were thus denied the opportunity to contribute their services. This figure forms the larger part of a total of 186,000 unemployed women at that time, making for an unemployment rate of 8 percent as compared with only 1 percent for the men.

Although no research has been made to identify the exact causes of this high unemployment rate for women, some illuminating statistics can be cited. For example, our population censuses show that the proportion of gainfully employed women varies sharply by geographic location. For married women the dispersion is as wide as 7 percent to 45 percent. The lowest proportions are found for sparsely settled areas, which is due to the paucity of job opportunities they offer. But the proportion is also low in localities of severe labor shortage; here there is a great wastage of womanpower because the local economy is dominated by industrial firms which employ men almost exclusively. In other words, the degree to which married women are employed depends largely on the economic pattern and on the traditions that have evolved in the hiring of womanpower. The unemployment rates are sent further soaring by the fact that many women have no vocational training; or if they do, their training is no longer marketable.

Women: a Qualitative and Quantitative Resource

As was noted above, women have begun to penetrate occupations in manufacturing industry that were formerly reserved for men. The metal fabrication industries are showing the way, but so far their female help is being put mostly on the assembly line. Very few women work as engineers, and here again hidebound tradition is keeping them back. At a time when engineering ability is a scarce commodity in our society, the failure to exploit woman's technical gifts becomes even more inexcusable. The anomaly is no less glaring in other industries, where the vast majority of women perform the least sophisticated tasks at the lowest levels.

Educational Discrimination

It follows from the foregoing that the vocational role of women is crucial not only for the achievement of greater sexual equality but also for the improved performance of the national economy. The machinery for change has been set in motion by a series of government reforms in education. An important objective of public policy in this field is to advance the educational aspirations of girls. Stronger emphasis is put on vocational orientation and guidance to stimulate girls (and boys, too) to apply more unconventional criteria to choice of careers. The current expansion of our educational system has affected girls in great measure: they now account for half the enrollment in pre-university schools and each year they comprise a larger proportion of the university entrants.

However, the curricula offered by upper secondary schools and universities still adhere to the labor market's cleavage of occupations into "male" and "female" sectors. Under the dead weight of tradition, moreover, girls continue to study for shorter periods than the boys do, which can only mean that they are preparing themselves for subordinate positions in the job world.

In the *gymnasium* or pre-university school, girls far outnumber the boys in the language curricula, while boys preponderate in science and technology. At the university level, girls tend to select courses which are not oriented to specific vocations. In 1960 they comprised 58 percent of first-year students in the humanities and about 25 percent in the social sciences. Corresponding proportions at institutes of technology, business colleges and schools of medicine were 5 percent, 14 percent and 21 percent, respectively. The professional study with the largest component of girls is dentistry, with 40 percent of the enrollment.

(Actually, a higher percentage of girls go in for pharmacy, but most of them stay only long enough to complete the course in prescription-filling, for which no graduate qualification is required.)

The male–female cleavage is especially pronounced in the trade schools, where most of the girls take courses leading to low-level positions in offices and the distributive trades, or to occupations in home economics and nursing. By far the greater number of boys go in for the technical arts and applied sciences.

Thus the traditional "allocation of roles" in the job world is intertwined with choice of education and career. Thanks to the lively public debate of the past few years, a growing number of government and business leaders have gone on record as favoring the selection of more unconventional careers for both boys and girls. At the level of practical affairs, however, there is decided caution. Parents, teachers, employers and politicians still seem unable to cut loose from the patterns they themselves grew up in. No real freedom of educational and vocational choice can be achieved until the true state of affairs is more energetically portrayed, beginning in the formative school years.

Formal Equality Is Not Enough

As events in Sweden and elsewhere have shown, the formal provision of equal rights for men and women is no more than a start. It is clear that traditional conceptions of sex roles are affected by economic trends, which in turn determine the degree of equality that a social system can tolerate. The process of social and economic development has also put the equality problem in another perspective. The reasons why woman still lags far behind the man in the labor market must be sought in the family role she is expected to fulfill. Most of the highly industrialized countries stress even more strongly her primary responsibility for the care and upbringing of children. In the old multi-generation family, women also used to contribute to its support, as did the men with their work within the family framework. The man's role as provider is now emphasized just as strongly.

As motivations, evaluations and incentives inside the home were hived off from those outside, a decisive impetus was given to segregation of the sexes. This trend has continued in spite of a closer identification between men and women in many aspects of their lives.

Values of Paid Employment and Family Life

Paid employment has become more attractive in prosperous countries. Opportunities for a good education and more interesting jobs are available to a much greater extent. Developments in Sweden have been marked by steadily rising wages and salaries, shorter working hours, greater security on the job, and improved amenities and democratic relationships at the workplace. These factors have combined to make paid employment more attractive for both men and women. And it is becoming increasingly accepted that women have just as much right to career aspirations as the men.

Other benefits accruing to women from paid employment are the financial independence it gives them, opportunities for contacts outside the family, and even prestige and power in certain cases. At the same time, it is emphasized in the public debate that the values related to participation in family life and work must not be forgotten. If women are enabled to enjoy a greater share of the values which come from the pursuit of vocations, then men should also be given greater opportunities to enjoy the values related to the family.

Memorable Dates for Swedish Women

1859 Enlarged liberty to pursue trades; more positions opened in elementary schools; women who seek to teach at elementary level are given their own normal school. (Teachers' training establishment.)

1863 Women admitted to positions in the telegraph service. Law makes women sui juris at age of 25 without resort to courts.

1870 Women entitled to take the Certificate of Secondary Education (studentexamen) qualifying for university entrance.

1873 Women entitled to take degrees in all branches of learning except theology and advanced law.

1884 Unmarried woman becomes sui juris at age of 21.

1909 Women entitled to run for elective office in local government. More teaching positions in State schools are opened to them.

1918 Women qualify for positions as senior masters and principals at secondary schools.

1919 Parliament amends Constitution to give women the suffrage and the right to stand in general elections.

1921 New Marriage Code abolishes the husband's guardianship status, prescribes mutual economic dependency, and alters the divorce laws.

1925 New law gives women the right to hold any position in national government service.

1929 Girls are admitted to the upper secondary schools.

1939 New law (amended and enlarged in 1946) bars employers from dismissing employees on grounds of marriage or pregnancy.

1958 Women are enabled to take Holy Orders in the established Church.

Britt Marie Svedberg

Born in 1919. Journalist, all-round reporter for magazines and
newspapers, employed since 1956 with Dagens Nyheter. Combines
know-how with a bantering style which has made her known and
respected. Has decided opinions and no apologies for them, either.

Welfare from the Cradle to the Grave

The alpha and omega of social security in Sweden are neatly summed up in a modern lullaby, written for a revue. Sung by a robust young mother, it tells of the riches that will descend on the house thanks to her child.

Actually, Svenson Junior was bringing money home before he was born. His mother could draw 300 kronor of the maternity grant 120 days before the youngster's expected coming. His father began to suspect that raising a family was good business, and nothing happened in the ensuing years to change his mind.

Young Svenson didn't cost a penny when he finally arrived. In Sweden every mother qualifies for free delivery and medical care, either in a maternity ward or at home. Nowadays, however, the obstetrician has largely replaced the midwife.

In the case of young Svenson, he spent the first week of his life in the maternity hospital, well looked after in a plastic box. There he enjoyed free care, free laundry, free diapers and free health checkups by a pediatrician.

After a few days on earth he was baptized, also for free. Swaddled in a red blanket, and with a pink rose and a name card lying on his tummy, he and 11 other babies were rolled on a cart into the hospital baptistry. Young Svenson was christened Carl Gustaf after the Swedish crown prince, reflecting the solid taste for royalty acquired by his mother from reading the glossy magazines.

When Carl Gustaf was born his mother picked up the rest of the maternity grant. All told this social benefit amounts to 1,080 kronor, and it goes a long way to explain the thriving state of the Swedish baby carriage industry. That's because the first thing a young mother buys for her offspring is a large baby carriage of the latest design, with the year's approved standard of mudguard shape and wheel diameter.

Carl Gustaf himself was earning money even before he learned how to turn over for diaper changes. Until the age of 16 every child is subsidized to the extent of 900 kronor a year. This benefit is a family allowance paid to the mother, a form of discrimination that offends many male Swedes. If a child is placed in a foster home for any reason (the housing shortage is the most common), the money is paid to the foster parent. Benefits are paid out every three months on the 21st, a date reinforced in the mind by the saturation advertising of firms which sell children's wear.

If Carl Gustaf had been born out of wedlock, his interests would already have been looked after in advance by a specially designated child welfare officer, usually a woman who has graduated from a school of social work. Her first job is to get the child's father to acknowledge paternity. If she is successful, he is made to pay a certain monthly amount toward its support. Sometimes the courts have to be brought in and there are recriminations all around. If the father refuses to pay, or simply disappears, the government advances a sum roughly equal to the minimum maintenance ordered in other cases.

A child pension of 1,375 kronor a year is payable if either the mother or father die, and of 1,925 kronor if both parents are dead.

The only need that isn't automatically catered to upon a child's entry into the world is a place to live. Although a married couple with a child move up a few notches in the housing queue, they must have more offspring to be eligible for priority placement on hardship grounds. The definition of hardship varies from one community to another.

Our Carl Gustaf, however, was lucky: his parents actually held the lease to their own apartment, and as such they belong to the only truly privileged class in present-day Sweden. Anybody with a lease enjoys secure tenancy as long as he pays his rent and behaves himself.

It was a nice apartment, too. The kitchen contained a combination refrigerator-freezer, an electric cooking range, and a stainless steel sink. The bedroom was big enough for baby's crib and other immediate necessities. Lastly, there was a living room, but since this had a parquette floor, teak furniture and the family TV set, it would be off limits to Carl Gustaf indefinitely.

When Carl Gustaf got to the toddling stage, the kitchen made room for his playpen. Mother found a storage place for the toys by cleaning out a bottom cabinet that had been built in for the express purpose of containing baking utensils.

The Swedish government's family allowance managed to keep pace with the consumer wants of Carl Gustaf. He was given a closet that befitted his growing station in life. Where once he lay nicely in his baby carriage, there to be regarded as a radiant extension of Mother's elegance, he now furiously pedalled his own kiddie sports car replete with tail fins and chrome finish. By this time, though, Carl Gustaf had spared Mother a considerable invisible expense (visible only in the sense of an abnormal protrusion of the derriere) : the countless number of paper diapers that Swedish mothers buy from the supermarkets in giant packages.

But we are getting ahead of our story. As soon as Carl Gustaf came from the maternity hospital, he qualified for free health care at an infant welfare center. There he was weighed, measured and inspected by a kindly doctor, and there too he underwent the required series of vaccinations. The center also had a kindly but firm-minded nurse, who would make regular home visits to impress on Mother the importance of breast feeding in the first few months.

Little Carl Gustaf, in short, received all the treatment in the book and more besides. It wasn't lost on him, either, for he developed into a model of good behavior. He never bit other children in the municipal sandlot, and he only beaned them with his wooden toy truck in self-defense. Of course he did have to defend himself from time to time, because a couple of the other children had the nasty habit of making off with his pail and shovel, or kicking his sand patties to bits. Then Carl Gustaf would run in tears to Mother, who sat on a nearby bench knitting with the other mothers. On at least one occasion Mother was distinctly heard saying, "You know, there are places in Sweden where they treat aggressive and maladjusted children."

What we were trying to say is that children with behavior problems also get looked after free of charge. In this sector, however, the waiting lists are long because there isn't enough staff to cope with the demand. After studying a problem child, psychiatrists and psychologists will recommend play therapy or some other treatment. In a difficult case, if the parents are considered unfit, the child may be placed in a foster home or a special home for children, where they can receive both therapy and a change of scene.

"It must be because his mother is a housewife that Carl Gustaf turned out so well", said his grandparents and all three aunts. According to one of the most tenacious bits of Swedish folklore, the constant presence of a mother at home guarantees the best environment for a child's upbringing. Hence the inadequate provision for day nurseries and other facilities for gainfully employed mothers. The local authorities can get government subsidies toward nurseries, but much of the money is never spent. Labor market officials have spoken eloquently of housewives as a huge reservoir of "manpower" that will save the Swedish economy, but their words have not penetrated at all the local levels.

If Carl Gustaf's mother had wanted to work outside the home, she would have had to apply for nursery accommodation before he was born. And even if she were the sole support of the family, she couldn't be sure of getting Carl Gustaf placed in a nursery.

Alternatively, it might have been possible to make some arrangement with a "family nursery", which is simply a place where a stay-at-home mother takes care of one or more children besides her own. The local authorities will guarantee her a certain income once they have inspected and approved her and the home. The parents pay a fee prorated to what they can afford to pay.

Many local officials prefer this form of care. There are strict regulations as to how a day nursery should be built and furnished. When to this is added the salaries payable to a professional staff working under union contracts, the cost of a day nursery runs into big money for the community. Since the parents pay in proportion to their incomes, the fees cover only a small part of the costs.

When Carl Gustaf reached the age of four, Mother began to

notice that it was difficult to keep him occupied at home. To be sure, the community had provided a nice playground, but the children there were too many and too big. Carl Gustaf seldom managed to elbow his way to the slide and seesaws.

"He ought to go to kindergarten", she thought. But when she called up about it she was not even offered the consolation of a waiting list. In most towns the kindergartens are so swamped by applications that only six-year-olds can be accepted.

"Isn't that strange?" said Mother, turning to Dad. "You'd think that with 120,000 babies born every year, they would figure out that 120,000 places in day nurseries and kindergartens will have to be ready several years later."

"There's enough public spending as it is", grumbled Dad, clutching at his wallet. "Anyway, it comes out of our taxes."

At long last Carl Gustaf reached the magic age for starting school: seven years. It was an adventure for the whole family. Carl Gustaf was going to enter a basic school, a combination of elementary and lower secondary grades—the product of a sweeping education reform that had been enacted and carried out during the 1960's. Many of its most ardent spokesmen had waxed eloquent on the subject of new and closer ties between the school and the home. But they could not completely dispel the mystery, because the new basic was a far cry from the old place of grind and swot that once served Mother and Dad.

Carl Gustaf's parents did not know much about the basic school and even less about what lay beyond: gymnasium, continuation school or vocational school. They carefully read through a pile of brochures, but the more they read the more they floundered in confusion among the curricula, levels, electives and the rest.

But Carl Gustaf took teacher's hand in his and stepped trustingly into the first grade.

He liked the fine, low-slung schoolhouse with its glass-surfaced exterior and mosaics in the hall. His classroom was a cheery place, with furniture ideal for children, potted plants and colored charts. And it gave him a thrill to receive new books with colored pictures inside, plus crayons, pencils, a blue-yellow eraser and lots of paper.

Everything was supplied gratis by the community. Going to

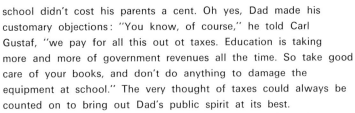

school didn't cost his parents a cent. Oh yes, Dad made his customary objections: "You know, of course," he told Carl Gustaf, "we pay for all this out ot taxes. Education is taking more and more of government revenues all the time. So take good care of your books, and don't do anything to damage the equipment at school." The very thought of taxes could always be counted on to bring out Dad's public spirit at its best.

As for Carl Gustaf's classmates, they couldn't care less about taxes as they carved the names of their pop idols on the new school benches.

The instruction and materials given to Carl Gustaf were not the only free things. He also received a free medical examination, and his teeth were fixed free of charge as part of the National Dental Service. Every day he ate a free breakfast at school, a privilege enjoyed by schoolchildren in the vast majority of Sweden's communities. However, the financing of school meals varies from place to place, and in some of them it takes no little ingenuity to provide a proper diet with the money available.

Carl Gustaf was happiest when pancakes or sausages were served for breakfast, though he could eat baked beans and fried bacon at 10 a.m. with equal relish. Nutritionists occasionally wrinkled their noses at the stodgy school food. There was once a rumor, which spread with the wings of panic, that pancakes would be removed from the menu. The pupils put a stop to it by signing their names to long petition lists.

In so doing, they achieved one of the major goals spelled out for the basic school: it had taught them to "think for themselves, exercise critical judgment, and develop the ability to cooperate". The sentence is quoted from an essay on educating young people for good citizenship in a democracy.

Some of Carl Gustaf's classmates had wage-earning mothers. When school let out for the day, they would go to an "afternoon nursery". This is an extension of the regular day nursery, where children can eat a snack, play games under supervision, or perhaps get help with their homework until mother comes to fetch them.

Came the summer, and the children didn't have to hang around waiting for their mothers to take a vacation. Some of them were sent off to a summer camp—an old institution dating from the times when there were really poor children in Sweden and private charity had to step in to make life more bearable for them. Others were taken into private homes in the countryside as summer boarders. This costs money, of course, but the fees are kept low by a local authority subsidy. Children are also enabled to take free holiday trips if the family income falls below a certain ceiling.

In rural Sweden, where home and school are often far apart, the children are picked up by buses. Gone are the days when children would have to trudge long miles to school and back.

Little Carl Gustaf was tested and found to possess a musical gift. So he started to go one afternoon every week to the municipal school of music, where he learned how to play a recorder. The lessons were free. So was any book that he might like to borrow from the school or city library. And if there were any time left over after music and reading, he could have become an amateur actor at the municipal children's theater.

The demands on Carl Gustaf's time kept increasing. Beginning with the fourth grade, his program of studies included English. Towards the end of the sixth grade he had to start thinking about the alternatives that would come in the seventh year, the first rung in the higher level of the basic school. His parents aged noticeably that spring as they dashed off to PTA meetings, read brochures, and tried to figure out whether Carl Gustaf ought to major in German and French, or in either German or French plus Swedish and mathematics, or in any of three other subject combinations. Should he spend two terms improving himself in Swedish and mathematics, or would one term be enough? The choices seemed infinite and equally perplexing.

Carl Gustaf sprawled prone in bed to the sound of recorded pop tunes and let his parents do the worrying. He had just become a teen-ager, a time of life when books should not be allowed to interfere with one's education.

During his eighth year in school, Carl Gustaf got his biggest kicks from practical vocational guidance. Over a total period of three weeks, divided into two segments, every pupil gets to tackle at least two occupations under the tutelage of willing employers. Less willing, perhaps, are the line foremen whose constant headache it is to find meaningful work for these hopeful 14-year-olds. In any case practical vocational guidance, though still applied on a small scale, seems destined to become a permanent part of the Swedish scene.

With the ninth and final year of basic school ahead, even more educational choices confronted Carl Gustaf's parents. Once again they diligently attended PTA meetings and read brochures. While thus preoccupied in the evenings, they had to neglect their son. Carl Gustaf, however, knew how to fend for himself: he would go to the nearby municipal youth recreation center, which had even better facilities for listening to pop music. There was no lack of other worthwhile things to do at the center, and its staff of specially trained youth leaders never tired of suggesting them. Everything free, of course—but so was the choice.

In school, the only limitation on Carl Gustaf's freedom of choice was that four others in his class pick the same combination of subjects (the National Board of Education said so). This complicated matters even more for his harassed parents. What should Carl Gustaf do after finishing basic school? First of all, there was the three-year gymnasium or pre-university school with its five curricula. Then there was the two-year continuation school (a follow-up on the basic), which offered three curricula and under them seven major courses of study in the first year, and fourteen different alternatives in the second year.

When the grade points had been ground through the central data processing mill, the result left Carl Gustaf somewhat crestfallen as he stood outside the gymnasium looking in. His point score just wasn't high enough. So rather than wait in too long a queue, he enrolled in a vocational school, which followed up on the prevocational courses he had taken in basic. In principle, the vocational school is on an even footing with the gymnasium and continuation school, and will eventually be merged with these in a single institution, roughly equivalent to the comprehensive high school in the United States. The merger is meant to overcome the obstinate prejudice against practical subjects as opposed to the academic, which have long held more "snob appeal".

The gymnasium is not what it used to be, either. Formerly, all seniors had to take a comprehensive set of final examinations to qualify for admission to a university. The new school does away with this requirement.

Upon reaching the age of sixteen, Carl Gustaf made his parents ineligible for the government family allowance. However, he had ceased to be a financial asset to Mother and Dad a long time ago. The cost of his clothes put an appreciable dent in the family budget. Carl Gustaf wanted pocket money, too, not to mention a tape recorder, a moped, and as many albums of pop records as his classmates. True, the government contributed 75 kronor a month toward the cost of his studies, but this benefit did not go very far.

Pupils from lower-income families could qualify for various other benefits subject to means or income tests: a travelling allowance, if the school was far away; a board-and-lodging supplement, if the pupil had to live in the school community; a study loan to finance secondary education, with no security required; and a string of others. In every case a mountain of forms had to be filled in.

At the age of 18, Carl Gustaf finished vocational school and promptly joined a regiment in central Sweden to perform his compulsory military service. For 304 days he was given food, clothing and shelter at the government's expense. Tears came to Mother's eyes when Carl Gustaf came home on leave in his natty gray-blue uniform. No longer was he her little Carl Gustaf; he was 19651208-32 Svenson. Even worse, he seemed to be enjoying his new role tremendously.

As a recruit his pay on a daily basis came to four kronor, just about enough for coffee at the post exchange and a moderate ration of cigarettes. If he were under obligation to support his family, he would also have qualified for a dependent's allowance and a housing allowance.

Next spring Carl Gustaf was back in civilian life. By then many of his old buddies had finished the gymnasium, and he saw without envy their attempts to enter the universities and professional schools. Once again the accommodation came nowhere near to meeting the demand. Not even the most brilliant grades could guarantee admission to, say, a medical school or an institute of technology.

The lucky ones who finally made it were not beset by serious financial woes. Today's undergraduate is entitled to study aid amounting to 7,000 kronor per year. Of this money, 1,750 kronor is an outright grant; the rest is a government loan repayable under lenient terms. Every student, moreover, receives the same assistance regardless of the financial status of his parents.

But Carl Gustaf already had a basic vocational education. He didn't have to wait in any queue. The free government employment service promptly got him a good job in the occupation for which he had been trained. Should he later decide to study some more, he knew he could always count on a further education grant plus study loan.

He put the thought of further education from his mind for the moment and decided to concentrate on his job. When payday came around, he discovered that he was pretty well-heeled for the first time in his life. He bought new clothes, a new tape recorder, and at length a small car. And after Mother had been nagging him for some time, he began to pay a small sum at home toward his room and board.

Carl Gustaf would have preferred to interpose some distance between himself and Mother's solicitude. He registered with the local housing authority (another free service) for a flat of his own but was told that many thousands were on the list ahead of him.

Always queues! You had to wait to get into a day nursery,

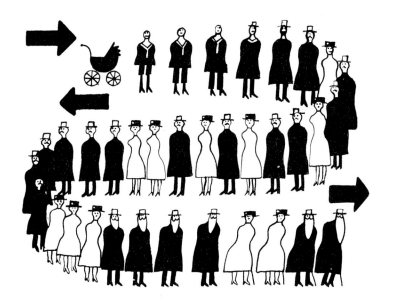

into a kindergarten, into a gymnasium, into a university. An undergraduate studying away from home had to wait to get living quarters in a student hostel, as many of Carl Gustaf's former classmates were now doing. Everything was well provided for in the statute books, but nobody seemed to have figured out how many preschoolers, schoolchildren and undergraduates eventually emerge from an annual baby crop of 120,000.

Carl Gustaf had reached the age of 21, with its attendant rights of buying what he liked at a liquor store and voting as he pleased at general elections, when he met Margareta at a restaurant on dancing night. Margareta was of the same age and had been named after a certain Mrs. Ambler, married in England but of Swedish royal blood. Margareta's mother also read the glossies.

An attractive blonde, Margareta liked to sew her own clothes and to bake cookies in her mother's thermostatically controlled electric oven. The vocational counsellors in school had failed to convince her that she ought to go in for electronics or civil engineering. When asked in questionnaires to state her choice of vocation, Margareta was one of those girls who always fill in the words, "Don't know". Anyway, the gyrations of the counselling mind were completely lost on Mother. As far as she was concerned, Margareta's excellent grasp of mathematics and physics would come in handy when she some day managed her own household budget and operated the thermostat iron and washing machine. And she certainly didn't have to become an engineer in order to marry and have children. Had Margareta's mother attended the new basic school, which she didn't, her own career might have taken a different turn: there they strongly uphold sexual equality and pour on more propaganda to get the girls into technical fields.

It was after finishing basic school that Margareta took a course in sewing. She changed her hair style twice a year and became quite expert in the art of applying mascara. With her good looks and good taste in clothes, she had ample potential for attracting the opposite sex, and she knew it. Carl Gustaf was not in the least sorry that she never undertook to study electronics. Quite the contrary: he took her in due course to the local housing authority, which in Sweden is the surest sign of a young man's honorable intentions.

Up to then the welfare state had done handsomely by both, but it failed them miserably this time. The authority had no flat to offer a young couple who wanted to get married. In five or six years perhaps, provided they had children by then.

Carl Gustaf and Margareta looked at one another. They knew of course that Sweden was short of housing; indeed, the shortage has existed as long as anyone could remember. But they had never lacked the good things of life before, and it seemed unthinkable that they would ever have to do without. They were well-fed, well-dressed, well-educated, well-adjusted. Carl Gustaf had a job with a future, and Margareta would have no trouble finding light work to tide her over until the duties of mother and housewife beckoned. And now there was no room for them amidst all the welfare.

What did they do? They got married, anyway. Margareta's parents vacated two upstairs rooms for them in their house. A closet was converted into a kitchenette, where Margareta could test her domestic talents on a hotplate. Mother would come up several times a day to make sure that everything was all right. She knew best how laundry should be folded and potted plants made to thrive. Past experience had also taught her how to save money on the food budget.

Margareta dried her tears on her apron. Carl Gustaf, frustrated because he could seldom spend a moment alone with his wife, found a way out by moonlighting. Sometimes the young Svensons would dine out with other couples who likewise had no place of their own. Another victim of the housing shortage was Carl Gustaf's small car: for lack of a garage, it spent all its life outdoors.

But young bliss cannot be denied for long, and Margareta provided it by giving birth to twins. In other circumstances the Svensons couldn't have asked for more, because their babies were both cute and lusty. However, they had extra reason to bless their good fortune because the twins propelled them very near to the head of the housing queue. So near, in fact, that the local authority soon called to offer them a three-room flat in a new suburban development. The rent was so high that 28 couples ahead in the queue declined to sign the lease, which moreover required a sizable down payment in cash.

Thanks to his night-time job, Carl Gustaf had saved quite a bit at the bank. Sale of the car netted some more cash. They acted fast and moved in before the twins were yet a month old.

Once again the welfare state had turned its kindliest face to two of its citizens.

The twins hadn't cost a cent. Margareta received free prenatal care, which included free iron and vitamin tablets. Her employer gave her the statutory pregnancy leave of six months, during which time she received extra cash sickness benefits under National Health Insurance. The regular maternity grant of 1,080 kronor was increased by 540 kronor, since she had given birth to two babies. Social security also covered three-fourths of the cost of having her teeth fixed during pregnancy.

Now that the Svensons had their own apartment they could also apply for a government loan to help set up housekeeping. This loan is available to any creditable couple upon publication of the banns and production of a lease. The National Bank of Sweden will advance up to 5,000 kronor toward the purchase of furniture and household goods. An unmarried mother or father also qualifies for the loan. Carl Gustaf and Margareta satisfied the bank as to their economic integrity by proving they had life insurance and no car. As soon as they picked up the money they bought a sofa in black imitation leather and a washing machine.

One evening they turned off the TV set, brewed some extra strong coffee, and sat down to read the rules on housing allowances for families with children. After the third cup they found that everything matched perfectly: they had at least two children, a taxable income of less than 12,000 kronor a year, and a modern flat of at least two rooms and kitchen. The government was willing to help defray their housing expenses by 330 to 390 kronor per year, plus 180 kronor for each child.

On the other hand, Margareta could not get a free vacation trip for housewives having at least two children under 14 years of age. Here the Svenson income exceeded the stipulated ceiling. But that was a minor setback. When the statutory four-week holiday came, Margareta and Carl Gustaf left the children with Grandmother (as so many young parents do) and set off for the Canary Islands, which over the years had become something of a Swedish recreational preserve.

By now the young Svensons were happily adjusted to the "People's Home", the name given by Swedes to their welfare state. Sure enough, the governing party put out an election campaign folder holding up the Svensons as shining examples of what the basic school could produce.

For this bit of testimonial advertising they were paid a modest fee, which went toward the purchase of a brand new car on the installment plan. When the next vacation rolled around, the Svensons, armed with a credit card from the local department store, bought a large tent with porch, a camping stove, sleeping bags and a collapsible dining table. Then they did a grand tour of the country side, stopping overnight at the camping grounds with their running water, candy stands and other conveniences that make many communities beam with pride. Unfortunately, it rained most of the time; this was probably to be expected, since the weather in Sweden has always been stubbornly unamenable to legislation.

In the following spring a third child was born to the Svensons, likewise at no expense. A homemaker took care of the twins while Margareta was in the hospital. A local government employee, the homemaker is paid according to a family's financial means.

That three-room apartment was obviously getting a little crowded. "Let's build a house," said Carl Gustaf. They applied for a government housing loan to cover 20 percent of the mortgage and borrowed the rest from a bank. The required cash payment came from the sale of their equity interest in the apartment and a loan from Carl Gustaf's parents.

The Svensons dearly loved their new house. If leisure had been a problem for them after the twins were born, it was certainly no problem now. They dug and planted and painted, mowed grass and shoveled snow. And the children were still small and innocent enough to like nothing better than to tag along everywhere and help out. It never occurred to Carl Gustaf and Margareta that the bank actually owned every inch of the house right up to the the roof ridges.

Life seemed rosy to them, though Carl Gustaf would sometimes mutter on the subject of taxes, just as his father had done before him.

Carl Gustaf was cocooned in security at his workplace, too. There was full employment in his line of business as in most others. He was employed under a collective agreement, enjoyed four weeks of vacation with pay under law, and worked a fixed number of hours in a five-day week. A new wage round was negotiated every second year, and each one concluded with a higher pay packet that just about covered the rising price level in the interim. But as far as Carl Gustaf was concerned, the main thing was that more money was being paid every year into his salary checking account.

He also belonged to an unemployment benefit society, which guaranteed him a maximum 40 kronor per day plus two kronor for each child if he should lose his job through no fault of his own. If it should ever be necessary to learn a new occupation, he would receive a training allowance. Moreover, if the new job compelled him to resettle in another community, the government would also pay him a moving allowance.

In spite of the precautions taken by the industrial safety officer,

Carl Gustaf happened one day to break his leg on the job. The costs of his hospitalization were covered by health insurance. He also received cash sickness benefits which, with supplements for the children, were high enough to keep his family in almost the same comfort as if he were still on the job. If the leg fracture had taken more than 90 days to heal, the costs of treatment would have been met by workmen's compensation. This is paid for by the employer, whereas health insurance comes as a special rate on the income tax.

When the children started school they contracted measles, whooping cough and roseola in rapid succession. Doctor Anderson came, looked down their throats, and consoled their mother. Health insurance paid three-fourths of the medical fee, or rather three-fourths of the fee set forth in an official schedule of rates. The doctor charged his own rates, and they were higher.

When the doctor prescribed medicine, the local pharmacy discounted 50 percent on every purchase above three kronor. For some diseases, such as diabetes, the medicine costs nothing.

One night Margareta felt sudden jabs of pain in her abdomen. Doctor Anderson diagnosed appendicitis and sent her to the hospital for an immediate operation. Health insurance took care of the hospital fee, but it paid her a sickness benefit of only six kronor per day, plus a modest supplement for each child. That money didn't go very far when Carl Gustaf had to take time off from work to look after the children. The Svensons had tried to engage a homemaker, but ran into the usual frustration: too big a demand chasing too small a supply.

Illness turned out to be an expensive business on this occasion. So after discharge from the hospital, Margareta signed up for supplementary health insurance which would give her higher cash sickness benefits. However, she had to pay the extra premiums herself.

If nothing else, the experience had taught her the value of her work in the home. The realization gave her a new self-assurance, perhaps too much so, because she started putting up fierce arguments over the dinner table. Or the marriage bond may have loosened from sheer inertia. No one knows. Anyway, one evening Carl Gustaf pounded his fist on the table and said he wanted a divorce.

The shock galvanized Margareta into new activity. As an incomeless housewife, she knew she was entitled to free judicial proceedings under the legal aid service. This is a right accruing to anyone of small financial means.

At the same time, however, she could also seek the free services of a family counselling bureau. Which is what Margareta in fact did. She unburdened her woes on a kind, motherly woman, who in due course also brought in Carl Gustaf for a talk. The confrontation made it clear, under the matron's skillful questioning, that the disharmony was not about fundamentals. Actually, the Svensons were too fond of one another to want a divorce.

But Margareta wondered if it wouldn't be for the family's best to work outside the home, so that she too could enlarge her interests and meet other people. Before long all her children would be in school, and she would have several spare hours every day.

She went to the employment office. Its staff was well equipped to cater to housewives who wanted to resume their former occupations or to undertake a brand new occupation. There were plenty of training courses for women in Margareta's situation: she could take up office work, pursue a career in nursing, clerk in a store, run a trolley, or work in a factory. Whichever course she chose, she would receive a training allowance. And the employment office could help to place her in the most suitable job.

Thus began a new phase in the Svenson Saga. While Carl Gustaf worked in his factory or addressed union meetings with a respect-inspiring voice (by now he had advanced to the position of shop committee chairman), Margareta drove a big transit bus through the city streets.

The children fended for themselves when they came home from school. Precooked dinners were kept in the freezer and needed only to be heated before the parents were due to come. The children went their separate ways at evening time; indeed, they could vanish as if by magic whenever Carl Gustaf wanted help with shoveling snow or mowing the lawn. He began to grumble about the lazy younger generation, just as his father had done when Carl Gustaf failed to qualify for the pre-university-school. With increasing frequency he caught himself thinking, "You know, the Old Man was right in a lot of things".

The "latchkey child" is one who returns to a parentless home after a day in school. Both his mother and father are gainfully employed.

The Old Man was in fact an old man now. He and Carl Gustaf's mother had been on government pension since the age of 67, amounting to about 3,500 kronor a year each. They had also moved into one of the new local-authority housing units for retired people. Though of dollhouse dimensions, their flat still had room for their most prized possessions. In addition to the national basic pension they received a rent allowance from the community. Carl Gustaf's mother quickly adapted to her new life as she fussed with the flowerpots and busied herself with all sorts of small domestic chores. The daily even round was occasionally livened up with bits of excitement, such as the church outings for pensioners.

Carl Gustaf's father was never much for the ecclesiastic way of life. A sprightly man for his years, he went in wholeheartedly for the calisthenics classes for old-timers (no charge, incidentally). Mrs. Svenson didn't attend. Decades of tramping in the former household had given her sore feet, and she was better served by the treatments of the visiting municipal chiropodist than by calisthenics.

The elder Mr. Svenson had also become an active member of the National Swedish Association of Pensioners, which would petition the government at regular intervals for increased benefits. As pensioners, the Svensons were also entitled to special fares from the Swedish State Railways; for ten kronor a year, they could buy a card with which they could travel round trip on a one-way ticket during the off season. In this way they got to see a good deal of Sweden in their sunset years.

Time had made Carl Gustaf's mother partially deaf. She was given a free hearing aid and attended a free course on how to use it. After that she put the aid in a drawer. "There's so much on the radio nowadays that isn't worth hearing," she said.

Election campaigns always gave the elder Svensons an extra lift. All the parties would outbid one another in promising new benefits and better pensions. Came election day and the party representatives would line up to offer them a free ride to the polling booth. Mr. Svenson would wink at Mrs. Svenson and pick the classiest-looking car. As he put it, "After all, we have the secret ballot in Sweden. We ride with whom we please and vote for whom we please."

If fate had been so unkind as to leave Mrs. Svenson a widow before she reached the age of 67, she would have received a widow's pension of 4,585 kronor a year, provided she had children under 16 living at home with her or was herself at least 50 and had been married at least five years.

Even the reduced chores of maintaining a small flat eventually became too much for Mrs. Svenson. "That does it!" shouted Mr. Svenson one day when she climbed unsteadily up the kitchen ladder to clean the windows. It didn't occur to him to try his hand at the windows, since he belonged to a generation of men who considered housekeeping beneath their dignity. He phoned the local social welfare office, which channeled him to a domestic aid committee. A "home samaritan" then came for two hours each day to clean the flat, buy the food and cook it.

"It's the kind of help we can accept with good conscience," said Carl Gustaf's father. "Social assistance is for people in distress because of old age or a temporary emergency. What we get from it is still no more than a fraction of what we've been paying in taxes over the years."

Even so, it frightened the elder Svensons to think of a possible future day when they could no longer take care of themselves without outside help. True, they could then be looked after in an old-age home. But this sector of Sweden's geriatric program is another of those which fall far short of need. With ever increasing life expectancy, the number of senior citizens grows larger and larger, and the old-age homes just cannot accommodate as many as they would like. The very last queue in Sweden's "People's Home" is lined up in front of the old-age homes.

Carl Gustaf and Margareta worried about their parents a great deal. They themselves belonged to ATP, the national supplementary pensions scheme, and thought that things were much better ordered for their old age than was true of their parents.

Actually, none of them had managed to make sense of the intricate rules for computing pensions, pension points and pensionable income. For sheer mysteriousness ATP was surpassed only by the system of reviewing farm prices, of which it was said that only three people in the country could fathom it.

Even so, the younger Svensons were not entirely in the dark. To begin with, if Carl Gustaf should be struck down in the prime of life, Margareta would receive an indemnity of 31,500 kronor under group life insurance, plus 7,000 kronor for each child. However, that wasn't a part of ATP but rather a benefit negotiated by Carl Gustaf's trade union with management.

If Margareta were widowed, ATP would pay her 35 percent of the pension to which Carl Gustaf was entitled, plus 15 percent for the first child and 10 percent for each additional child under 19 years of age. If Margareta had no children sharing her roof, she would get 40 percent of Carl Gustaf's pension, provided the marriage had lasted at least five years and was entered into not later than the 60th birthday of the deceased husband. Should Margareta remarry, the widow's pension would terminate; but if the new marriage were dissolved within five years, the pension could be reinstated.

It was pretty simple so far.

An orphan would get 40 percent of the father's or mother's pension, while three orphans would be entitled to 60 percent $(40+10+10)$ of whichever pension was the larger.

If Margareta, who now earned wages as a bus driver, were to die her children would be pensioned. But her husband wouldn't get anything, though his standard of living would be bound to decline with the removal of both her income and her work in the home.

But the real complications came in figuring out Carl Gustaf's pension. Assuming he lives to pensionable age, he must amass 30 pension points to qualify for the full pension. The pensionable income is divided by something called the "base amount" in order to accumulate the pension points. The base amount is subject to annual revision to preserve the value of the pension against inflation. Pensionable income in any one year is the figure remaining after the base amount is subtracted from actual income.

When the Svensons got this far in their mathematical endeavors, Margareta would rise silently from the sofa and leave for the kitchen to brew some really strong coffee. Then she'd return to the living room and say, "Well, after all, I know people who are getting their pensions. So the system must work somehow."

As an employee Carl Gustaf is not required to contribute towards his supplementary pension. His employer does that. But if Carl Gustaf were working for his own account, he would still get the pension, though he would then have to pay for it.

Anyone who is incapacitated for work because of illness or physical handicap qualifies for a disability pension. This scheme is only slightly more complicated than ATP.

When Carl Gustaf and Margareta sit on a Saturday evening to have another go at figuring out their benefits under ATP, they always succumb in powerless admiration for this crowning glory of Swedish social security. And they feel a strong solidarity with the People's Home.

And the evening usually ends with a mutual resolve to keep themselves able-bodied as long as possible, the better to put off that fateful day when they must really figure out what pension they have coming to them.

On Sunday mornings Margareta returns to more comprehensible tasks. While the youngsters are still asleep after the Saturday night school dance, she cleans up the kitchen and puts a plate of frozen Danish pastry into her new electronic oven.

As for Carl Gustaf, he's gone out to the front yard to raise the blue and yellow colors of the Swedish flag.

Gunnar Smedberg

Born in 1911. Clergyman in the Swedish Church with location in Uppsala. Has published a number of writings on the sociology of religion.

The Religious Organization

Pastors who preach for nonconformist sects make frequent home visits as part of their calling. In this picture, taken in 1963, a traveling evangelist of the Swedish Missionary Society is visiting new converts in a far northern village. Photo: Sune Jonsson.

If anything about the subject matter of this chapter can be assumed as widely known, it is that Sweden is supposed to be one of the most secularized countries in the world. The more initiated reader may also know that Sweden has long had an established or State Church. The parallel existence of "non-established" churches is more or less taken for granted.

Accordingly, the religious life of Sweden might be described by dividing it into two sectors: the Church of Sweden and the nonconformist or Free Churches. But before we go any further, it should be made clear that there are many connections between the two. A typical feature of the Swedish religious scene is "overlapping membership": in other words, the majority of Free Church adherents remain bound to the State Church, and hence pay double church tax. Understandably enough, this surprises foreign observers, and trying to explain it is not easy.

Free Church leaders have pointed out from time to time that adherence to two churches is wrong in principle, but their argument does not seep down to the lower echelons. The idea of being beholden to the State is only one of several areas of controversy, and probably a less important one at that. The essential confrontation is between two different types of piety. Generally speaking, the Free Churches are revivalist in their aims and seek to build up congregations of believers, whereas the State Church wants to provide a Christian education and build up a "national" church. The two types also have different roots: the Free Churches stem largely from British and American ancestors, while the State Church has adopted the Lutheranism which originated in Germany. However, such distinctions are too neat to be satisfactory. The origins of both "camps" are actually more diffuse than we have indicated, and indeed the two have continually interacted with and influenced one another.

It would also be incorrect to say that revivalist movements are a monopoly of the Free Church sector. There also exist intermediate forms, of which the best known is the National Evangelical Society. By the same token, the Free Churches are far from being a monolith. A Council of Free Churches does exist, but its membership does not include all denominations.

The outlines of our approach to the subject now begin to emerge. Religious life in Sweden does not present a united front, yet neither is it split down the middle into two opposing fronts. If similar dichotomies occasionally creep into the following paragraphs, the attempt to achieve greater clarity is their sole justification.

There is yet another way to characterize the different religious groups, and that is by use of the terms "left" and "right". The farther we move to the right, the greater the emphasis on the Church, the sacraments, and the ministry. Denominations of British or American origin may be said to cluster at the left end of the spectrum, to the right of them is the Lutheran Church, and at the far right we come to the Roman Catholic Church.

"The free denominations". First a few words about Swedenborgianism, which we have placed at the left end on liturgical grounds but is otherwise difficult to classify. Emanuel Swedenborg (1688–1772) was a Swedish scientist and religious mystic who is perhaps better known abroad than at home. His system of beliefs, embodied in the "New Church" or "New Jerusalem Church", is a kind of theosophy. Swedenborgianism has never won a wide following in our country, and its present-day adherents can be counted in the lower hundreds. The experience of other theosophies in Sweden, among them the anthroposophy of Rudolf Steiner (1861–1925), suggests that Swedes don't take readily to mystico-religious systems.

To continue our tour of the Swedish religious scene from left to right, the denominations we find at the far left share a common American ancestry. The oldest in Sweden is the Mormon Church, but since almost all the original converts emigrated to Utah, there was not much left on which to build a significant Swedish movement. Another denomination of long standing, the Seventh Day Adventists, likewise lacks a major following. That distinction goes to the Jehovah's Witnesses, who form a zealous, not to say fanatical group. However, these denominations have a common identity all over the world and as such are much too well-known to make further description necessary.

A little further to the right we come to the Pentecost Fellowship, whose 90,000 adherents make it one of the largest Free Church denominations in Sweden. The roots of pentecostalism are also American: it first came to prominence in Los Angeles in 1906, and soon went international on a big scale. Nowhere has it acquired as many adherents in proportion to population as in Sweden. The movement started out as a generator of great emotionalism, devoted to seeking the gift of tongues and the working of miracles, but the years have calmed it down considerably. In common with its foreign counterparts, the Swedish Pentecost Fellowship is strongly congregationalist—that is, it does not claim to be a church or even a denomination, but consists solely of independent self-governing units. Still, that hasn't prevented the Pentecostalists from forging a cohesive body in their relations with other interests; most of the credit for this feat goes to Pastor Lewi Pethrus, who has skillfully led the Stockholm congregation since 1911, and in this capacity also served as the movement's guiding genius. The Fellowship publishes its own newspaper and weekly, and also wields considerable political influence.

Of comparable size is the Swedish Missionary Society, with about 90,000 members. Most Swedes would probably regard it as the typical example of nonconformism. The Society has drawn upon both Anglo-American and German-Lutheran sources. It too upholds the independence of congregations in principle, but over the years has developed into an entity that is now even more closely knit than the Pentecost Fellowship. The Society champions no particular body of doctrine but welcomes all believers into its ranks. It doesn't even maintain a position of its own in the important matter of baptism. This sacrament is extended to both infants and adults. The Society's founder, P. P. Waldenström, was a warm advocate of infant baptism. Many members of the Swedish Parliament are among its adherents, indeed in far greater than proportionate numbers—indicating that the Society is very much in touch with public affairs.

The Baptists do not enjoy anywhere near as much preeminence as in, say, the United States. In Sweden they have suffered heavy losses to the Pentecost Fellowship and in consequence of later sectist offshoots. Together, the various Baptist denominations have about 50,000 adherents. Their creeds and forms of worship generally resemble those of Baptist groups in other countries.

The Salvation Army hardly needs any special presentation. It has never attained a wide following in Sweden, perhaps because it has always been an urban movement with only a very small rural admixture. Our country was still an agrarian society when the Salvation Army first arrived. After a flourishing period around the turn of the century, the Salvation Army did not make further headway and now numbers about 40,000 members. It is greatly esteemed and never has any trouble collecting funds for its activities.

The Swedish branch of the Methodist Church is not large, either. It is interesting to note that Methodism came to us from America in its episcopal form and not from Britain. As such, it represents a backwash of the heavy tide of emigration from Sweden to the United States in the 19th century.

Characteristically, nonconformism in Sweden has long been a movement towards the right. Where the congregationalist bodies have not taken on a more organized pattern they have at least tended to become more ecclesiastical in form. Many of them have introduced liturgies and handbooks for the conduct of worship services, adopted a large part of the church calendar, and embraced the system of texts developed by the State Church —all of which they had sharply rejected originally. Their pastors wear clerical garb and preach in quarters that today are called "churches". These buildings, once so bare and meager, are ornamented with flowers, lighted candles and even steeple bells. The same liturgical tendencies are manifest all over the world.

Many observers would no doubt also note that the Free Churches have come a long way from their revivalist beginnings. Their present emphasis is on Christian upbringing rather than religious awakening. Towards this end they have gone in for

The Pentecostal Movement, which has a decided congregationalist bent, runs two annual series of prayer meetings as a connecting link. One of these is located in a village of Lapland, where this picture was taken. It shows a woman who has been moved by the spirit. Photo: Sune Jonsson.

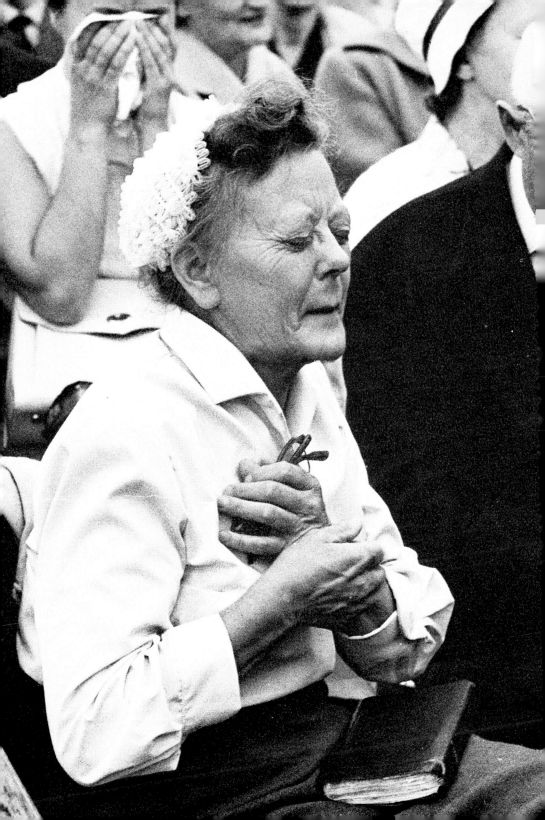

study circles and other educational programs, thereby adding another likeness to the established Church of Sweden. On the other hand, the Free Churches have largely retained their pietist way of life. Thus the true practice of Christianity is held to be incompatible with dancing, the consumption of alcohol and, usually, smoking. In these matters, however, the younger generation of worshippers may be expected to prefer eased restrictions.

If heads alone were counted, the Swedish Free Churches would appear to be anything but influential. Their combined membership comes to about 320,000, which equals only 4.2 percent of the population. Yet statistics like these are grossly misleading. They leave out large numbers of "sympathizers"—in short, ignore the fact that nonconformism reaches out to many sections of the community. And as we noted earlier, the nonconformists are strongly entrenched in the Swedish Parliament. Be that as it may, the majority of Free Churches are losing adherents at the present time.

The *Church of Sweden* lends itself to four descriptive terms: State, national, episcopal and Lutheran. Its first and most striking characteristic is its connection with the State. This tie is considerably less strong than it was in the 17th century, but it remains important. Thus the Riksdag (Parliament), acting jointly with the Church Assembly, enacts ecclesiastical law, authorizes the books to be used in church, and so on. The Cabinet appoints bishops and certain other high-ranking clergymen. Of extreme importance is the right to tax vested in every parish. Every person who has not withdrawn from the State Church is subject to this tax, which is levied as part of the regular national income tax. Since corporations and other legal entities cannot leave the State Church, they too must pay the church tax. Although very low by comparison with other levies, the church tax nets a good-sized revenue, which enables the Church of Sweden to function without major financial worries.

By virtue of its ties with the State, the Church of Sweden also performs an important demographic function. Every person living in the country, whether he belongs to the Church or not, must have his name and other vital particulars entered in a parish register, which also serves as a civil register; hence that familiar

Continuing secularization to the contrary, many new churches have been built in Sweden in recent years. They often depart from traditional architectural design. This church, built in 1966, is at Klippan in the south of Sweden. Architect: Sigurd Lewerentz. Photo: Ingvar Andersson.

institution of the Swedish scene known as the "pastorsexpeditionen" (parish office), where people go to obtain certificates of different kinds, report new addresses after they have moved, or officially make known their intention to wed.

Ministers of the Church of Sweden are classified as civil servants and rank fairly high on the government pay scale.

It is equally correct to use the word "national" to describe the Church of Sweden. If both parents or either of them are members, their children become so automatically. Membership may be resigned freely, requiring only a written application, but not many have availed themselves of the opportunity. About 97 percent of the Swedish people still belong to the Church. A large part of the remainder, moreover, consists of aliens. The figures for baptism and confirmation are also high, amounting to

87 percent of the population. Both these rites obviously exert a strong hold on the people, rooted as they are in long-standing family traditions.

Confirmation is preceded by a period of intensive study, usually accompanied by regular attendance at worship services (at the insistence of the clergy). The present tendency is to make these requirements more rigorous, but that doesn't discourage the boys and girls from taking their confirmation.

Brides and grooms may marry either in church or before a civil registrar. The right to perform marriages is vested in most Free Church pastors, and the same legal consequences ensue as if the marriage had taken place in the Church of Sweden. A civil service is not compulsory, and in fact about 94 percent of the couples prefer to marry in church.

The ceremonial status of burial is even more strongly impressed on the laity. All in all, therefore, the Church of Sweden still commands a very high degree of loyalty in birth, confirmation, marriage and death. The exact value of this loyalty in religious terms is of course difficult to assess. A glaring weakness, on the other hand, is the low attendance at worship services. On this count Sweden's reputation as a secularized country is justified. Strictly speaking, attendance is the general custom on only two occasions: the first Sunday of Advent, and "Julottan", the early-morning service on Christmas Day.

The Church of Sweden may also be called an episcopal church. It has 13 dioceses, each with its own bishop, whose primate is the Archbishop of Uppsala. The incumbent from 1914 to 1931, Nathan Söderblom, achieved international prominence for his work on behalf of the ecumenical movement. His successors, among them Gunnar Hultgren and the present Archbishop Ruben Josefson, have also been active in the cause of worldwide Christian unity.

Lay members are enabled to influence the management of Church affairs by participation in the synod at national level and the vestries at local level. However, there is a considerable body of thought which favors a more generous infusion of democratic procedures. Many observers feel that the Church of Sweden is an aristocratic institution in which the layman has too little to say.

A highly distinctive attribute of the Church is its decentralization of authority—a consequence of the episcopal form of government.

Women have been permitted to take Holy Orders in the established Lutheran Church since 1958. The first to carry out a regular morning service was Mrs. Barbro Nordholm-Ståhl. Her husband is a clergyman, too. The couple are shown here baptizing their daughter. Photo: Bo Schreiber.

In a very real sense every diocese is a self-contained unit. The Archbishop of Uppsala has no authority over the other bishops. Each diocese tends to be unlike the others in one or more respects, which makes it difficult to portray a composite picture of the Church. The experiences of any one diocese cannot be generalized for the country as a whole. Much of the Church's work is conducted within the dioceses, not least as regards programs for young people. A weekly paper, "Vår Kyrka" (Our Church) is published, but it lacks official status and is of limited circulation in some dioceses. On the other hand, the dioceses each put out their own papers, whose combined circulation far exceeds that of "Vår Kyrka".

We now come to our last descriptive term for the State Church: Lutheran. Among the various articles of the Lutheran faith recognized in Sweden, the most important are those contained in the Augsburg Confession. Incidentally, the church founded in the United States by Swedish emigrants, and which until 1948 was called the Augustana Evangelical Lutheran Synod, stems from this basic document. In recent years the Lutheran articles of faith have figured prominently in Swedish public debate, though not to the same extent in practice. Even so, the Church of Sweden has largely retained its Lutheran character throughout the years. During the 19th century, it too came under the influence of revivalist movements, originating chiefly in Britain and America. Adoption by the Church of Sweden of the Sunday School, foreign missions, youth programs and other new types of activity date from this period. Since then winds from the right have blown in both the established and non-established sectors. The conduct of worship services has changed a great deal in the last 30 years alone. Altar-services robes are in general use and Holy Communion is administered much more often than in the past— to name only two of the more remarkable developments. It is relevant here to mention the influence of High Church beliefs in the Church of England, which began to enter the Swedish clerical ranks around 1910, though its more outward manifestations did not come until the 1930's. The gulf caused by this and other factors came into sharp focus in 1958, when women were allowed to take Holy Orders. As of 1967 there were 20 women priests in Sweden. Clergy and lay members opposed to this innovation have hived off into a group known as the "Ecclesiastical Assembly".

A few words on how the Church of Sweden works are in order. It is taken for granted that the Free Churches carry on missionary activities in non-Christian countries. But so does the Church of Sweden, which might come as a surprise in view of its established status. It may come as an even greater surprise to the reader to learn that the rules governing the Church's missions are laid down by the Crown. However, that is as far as State control goes: the missions themselves are financed entirely from donations. At present about SKr 12 million a year is being collected for missions in Africa and Asia. However, the Church of Sweden still falls far short of what the Free Churches are doing in this field.

The welfare programs run by the established Church on behalf of Swedish seamen also come under Crown regulations. They operate at 34 stations throughout the world and 90 percent of their expenses are covered by donations. In this field the Free Churches play no more than a modest role.

Visitors from abroad sometimes ask where the Church of Sweden has its headquarters. Surely there must be a central place where one can obtain information and the like. Yes, there is such a a place: the Central Council of the Church of Sweden (*Svenska kyrkans centralråd*). However, it is vested only with powers to advise, not to make decisions. As was observed earlier of the Church missions and seamen's welfare programs, the Central Council occupies a peculiar intermediate position between the official and the autonomous.

The Church of Sweden runs five schools for the training of deacons and deaconesses, who are the Church's welfare workers. These schools are independent of State control, as is the Swedish section of the Lutheran World Federation. Within only a short time, the section's "Luther Aid" program has developed into one of Sweden's most important instruments for assistance to the developing countries. Its collection drives now net about SKr 18 million, a good performance for a church community which is not otherwise noted for its willingness to make sacrifices. A quite different attitude prevails among the Free Church adherents, who often pay the full Biblical tithe to their denominations.

The Archbishop lives in Uppsala and the Central Council of the

Church of Sweden is located in Stockholm. But if one wants to form an idea of how the Church works today, perhaps the best place to visit is Sigtuna, an ancient town of narrow crooked streets which occupies a very beautiful site on the shores of Lake Mälaren. Besides being noted for its educational institutions of ecclesiastical origin, among them the Swedish Church School, Sigtuna is the home of several old churches and religious foundations.

What does the future look like for the Church of Sweden? A great deal will depend on the coming nature of its link with the State. Many insist on a complete "divorce" between the two, arguing that the present system of conferring privileges on one religious body militates against full freedom of worship. Others want disestablishment in order to give the Church more freedom, since they feel that the State is slowly but steadily enlarging its control in the religious sphere. A government commission of inquiry has been at work for several years trying to clarify the issue. Its task is not an easy one; after all, Church and State have been intimately bound up with one another in our country ever since the 11th century. There is general agreement on one point, however: the Church would be faced with great difficulties if it were to be completely disestablished. Not only would this entail financial difficulties, but a schism within the Church might very well ensue. Without the State as a unifying factor, we might have two Churches instead of one. The cleavages are already evident, and the dispute over the right of women to take Holy Orders is only one of them.

Another factor that will inevitably mold the Church's future is the large-scale migration of people from the countryside to cities and towns. A government commission of inquiry recently recommended the closure of small, marginal farms. If the recommendation is carried out, our rural areas will be even more depopulated, especially in the far north. The Church of Sweden has long had its strongest roots in the rural parishes. Will the Church be able to adapt itself to Sweden's increasingly urban way of life? On present performance, the outlook is not very promising: the Church has not readily responded to change, and the present "cultural lag" is widening. The same observation can be applied with equal force to the Free Churches. If anything, future difficulties will grow rather than diminish.

After this fairly exhaustive account of the established Church, we still have to come to the far right end of the Swedish religious spectrum: the Catholic Church. By tradition, Swedes have taken a deeply suspicious view of Catholics. Up to World War II there were only about 5000 of them in Sweden, but their ranks have since swelled owing chiefly to immigration from Catholic countries. As yet, however, Catholics are not sufficiently large in numbers to make mixed marriages an appreciable problem in our country.

There are in Sweden around 14,000 adherents of the Jewish faith (1966).

A very large influx of immigrants has entered Sweden during the postwar period. The 1960 Census counted 190,000 aliens. The number has not changed very much since. About half the immigrants are Scandinavians (and as such mostly Lutherans, of course). Of the remainder, an estimated 25,000 are Roman Catholics; this has to be an informed guess, since no separate religious statistics are kept. There are probably at least 15,000 members of the Greek Orthodox Church. Other confessions are represented by only very small groups; the number of Islamites, for example, reportedly does not exceed 300.

Sten Lindroth

Born in 1914. Professor of the history of ideas and science at Uppsala University. Specializes in the history of Swedish biology, medicine and mining. His latest work is a history of the Royal Swedish Academy of Sciences during the 18th century.

Bo Oscarsson

Born in 1938, Master of Science. Attached to the Secretariat of the Government's Science Advisory Council.

Science and Technology

Carolus Linnaeus, or Carl von Linné (1707–1778), is the most renowned of Sweden's scientists. His most notable work was in botany, and his "Systema Naturae" became the bible of natural history.

Sten Lindroth

The Scientific Heritage

Scientific research in the more modern sense of the term is not of very long standing in Sweden. As late as the middle of the 17th century, higher education in our country was still on the old-fashioned, somewhat ponderous side. Orthodox Lutheran theology and scholastic philosophy were the chief offerings at the universities. In the rest of Europe the trail-blazers of a new scientific order had risen up in arms against the existing scheme of things. However, their revolutionary ideas of a new world picture made sluggish headway against the general inertia of Swedish culture.

There was admittedly one man who stood head and shoulders above the rest: Olof Rudbeck (1630–1702). Already as a young student at Uppsala, in the early 1650's, he made a remarkable contribution to the history of medicine: his discovery of the lymphatic system, which he described with superb clarity. Yet Rudbeck somehow remains an isolated figure in the cavalcade of scientific research. In Sweden as elsewhere a new intellectual climate was needed to give impetus to modern science and help make it into a reshaping force. The change, or the beginnings of change, came when the philosophy propounded by Descartes attained respectability. The Cartesian philosophers at Uppsala, Lund and Åbo (Turku) looked upon the universe as one huge problem in mechanics; they obtained air pumps and barometers and began to make experiments. It was this new educational environment that nourished the men who laid the basis for a firm scientific tradition in Sweden around the turn of the 18th century. Among the memorable names we now encounter are Urban Hiärne (1641–1724), the physician and chemist; Christopher Polhem (1661–1751), an engineer of brilliant gifts; and his admiring disciple, Emanuel Swedenborg (1688–1772), who fervently tackled the most formidable problems of science and technology. Swedenborg's major scientific opus, "Principia rerum naturalium" (1734) is an ambitious attempt to embrace the whole of creation and explain it in terms of mechanics. This was about

Christopher Polhem (1661–1751) belongs to the legendary figures of Swedish technology. He is best known for his development of mining techniques, especially at the Falun copper mine, and his canal-building projects.

ten years before he definitely turned to the religious mysticism for which posterity chiefly remembers him.

With the 1740's, Swedish science burgeoned with a richness of bloom it had never attained before. The miracle, for such it was, is chiefly identified with Carolus Linnaeus (1707–1778), but he was only the first among equals. Men of science and medicine by the score gave Sweden an international reputation. As Linnaeus said with delight: "The Swedes will have to teach the foreigners to count the eggs in the polyps!" That matters should have reached this stage had its reasons, of course. The discoveries of science had come into fashion because the economic and political doctrines of the age were favorable to them. Utilitarian views of the economy were emphasized time and again. Industries and agriculture were to be encouraged at all costs— but they had to rest on the solid foundation of science. Since research took a practical and outward-oriented turn, it served the public interest and thereby gained in esteem. These aspirations were given material embodiment in 1739, when the Swedish Academy of Sciences was founded in Stockholm. Largely patterned after the Royal Society in London, the Swedish Academy soon became one of the foremost in Europe. Its "Proceedings", a motley mixture of household discoveries and laboratory reports, were translated into several languages, including German, French and Latin.

Under these conditions natural history enjoyed a special prestige, which came from its having tracked down neglected natural resources and raw materials. But the distinction it was long to enjoy as a kind of Swedish science par preference was due to Linnaeus. He founded his world reputation in the 1730's with a long series of books written during years of feverish youthful activity in Holland. Later, as professor at Uppsala, he formulated laws for all the world's botanists; his "Systema Naturae" (1735) became the bible of natural history. Linnaeus had an innate gift for bringing order out of chaos, and under his scrutinizing eyes the world's fauna and flora were arrayed in neatly ordered rows like so many platoon soldiers in a barracks square. The Linnaean zeal was imparted to his pupils, who were despatched far and wide to collect the missing links in his system of classification. Hasselquist travelled to Palestine and Forsskål to Arabia, Löfling to Venezuela and Thunberg to Japan. Several of them died a long way from home, others returned with a rich harvest—among them Pehr Kalm (1716–1779), who had journeyed to North America.

It is tempting to regard the quest for clarity and organization which Linnaeus incarnated as typical of Swedish science during and even after the 18th century. Originality of thought and boldness of intuition were rarer plants; the Swedes preferred to collect, describe and systemize. Still, this approach was not to be despised, and some of the luster also rubbed off on our mineralogists and mining experts, who had established a European reputation by the middle of the 18th century. Johan Gottschalk Wallerius (1709–1785), professor of chemistry at Uppsala, set up a system of classification for the inanimate kingdom with his "Mineralogia" (1747). Several years later Axel Fredrik Cronstedt (1722–1765) published his pioneering "Essay towards a system of mineralogy", in which he devised a chemical classification of minerals which long was widely used. Empirical, and at the same time of a collecting bent, were the two outstanding astronomers of the age: Anders Celsius (1701–1744) of Uppsala, best known for his centigrade thermometer, and his pupil Pehr Wilhelm Wargentin (1717–1783), who served the Swedish Academy of Sciences as its indispensable secretary and became the leading contemporary expert on the moons of Jupiter. To be sure, the age also had its theoretical scientists, men who cannot be fitted into the above pattern. In the 1750's Samuel Klingenstierna (1698–1765), an eminent mathematician, corrected Newton's theory on refraction of light in optical systems. And Johan Carl Wilcke (1732–1796) won later international fame as an experimental physicist, in particular for his research into latent heat.

The heyday of Swedish science was to last several more decades. During the Gustavian era of the 1770's and 1780's, two men were individually and jointly dedicated to enhancing Sweden's status in the field of chemistry. They were Torbern Bergman (1735–1784), a professor at Uppsala, and Carl Wilhelm Scheele (1742–1786), a self-taught pharmacist. Their laboratories spawned a sequence of chemical discoveries, the essentials of which formed the basis of the modern chemistry founded by

Lavoisier. Scheele was the brilliant experimentalist, Bergman more the man of theory and system, who inspired a number of disciples from various countries.

Before long, however, the Swedish flame faded, and science was in a rather sorry state by the beginning of the 19th century. This was a period of decline for Swedish intellectual life in general, exacerbated by despotic rule at the top. Science continued to live under a cloud even after political conditions changed for the better. The general spirit of the times was largely to blame. As the century proceeded, German romantic philosophy gained an increasing foothold; students at the universities of Uppsala and Lund ardently embraced the new esthetic gospel and gave themselves to dark metaphysical musings. Characteristically, the most influential teacher at Uppsala in the mid-19th century was Israel Hwasser (1790–1860), who was so completely immersed in mysticism as to lose all contact both with the sickbed and the

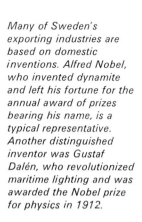

Many of Sweden's exporting industries are based on domestic inventions. Alfred Nobel, who invented dynamite and left his fortune for the annual award of prizes bearing his name, is a typical representative. Another distinguished inventor was Gustaf Dalén, who revolutionized maritime lighting and was awarded the Nobel prize for physics in 1912.

material world. Idealism and esthetic affectations were the order of the day, at least at our small provincial universities. Hence philosophy and letters, and to some extent the classical disciplines as well, represented the finest fruits of an academic education. To busy oneself with raw empirical reality was just not considered comme il faut. The natural sciences did not conform to good social usage, and were far from holding the center of the stage they enjoyed one hundred years earlier.

However, lack of social acceptance did not deter dedicated men from pursuing their researches at the universities, the Swedish Academy of Sciences, and elsewhere. The amiable Linnaean tradition could establish ready rapport with the romantic spirit, and botany therefore continued to flourish. It was still a one-sided discipline, with new species being described and classification systems constructed in epigonous style. Our internationally best known botanists in the first half of the 19th century were Carl Adolph Agardh (1785–1859) of Lund and Elias Fries (1794–1878) of Uppsala; both devoted themselves to the previously neglected cryptogams: ferns, mosses, algae and fungi. Zoology boasted such eminent names as Anders Retzius (1796–1860) and Sven Lovén (1809–1895). And a Swedish physicist of stature came in the person of Anders Johan Ångström (1814–1874), who is particularly noted for his work on spectroscopy.

However, there was no one to compare with Jöns Jacob Berzelius (1779–1848), who was the towering figure of Swedish science until his death. His chemical discoveries built on the tradition that had been interrupted since the days of Bergman and Scheele, and his simple laboratory became a Mecca for students from near and far. By virtue of his major analytical works Berzelius did more than any of his contemporaries to impart system and theoretical coherence to modern chemistry; if one so chooses, he could be called a brilliant representative of the fruitful Swedish sense of order. His career was beset by a running battle with romanticism, whose ethereal philosophy conflicted head-on with his materialistic convictions as a scientist. Berzelius eventually gained adherents, and in alliance with liberalism and other new ferments in Swedish society, the anti-romantic school erupted in violent opposition in the middle of the 19th century. Uppsala University was criticized from Stockholm as being a stagnant backwater unfit to bear the scientific mantle; if science were to thrive at all, it could only do so in intimate relationship with the productive society.

Even so, many years were to pass before academic conservatism lost its power in Sweden. The 1880's, it is true, signified a breakthrough for radical European ideas. Increasing industrialization set the stage for economic progress and instilled in the community a more mundane, pro-reform turn of mind. Several distinguished men of science came to the fore in this period, among them Svante Arrhenius (1859–1927) with his theory of electrolytic dissociation. And new universities were founded in Stockholm and Göteborg. The capital, where the Swedish Academy of Sciences also showed renewed vitality, began to play an increasingly important scientific role. But even as late as 1900 Sweden lagged behind as a nation of research, and a rather long time could sometimes elapse before fruitful new currents reached our professors from the Continent. When the change did come, it could only be for the better. The Swedish sciences were given improved resources and facilities, and young men of genius were enticed to the laboratories and out into the field. That brings us to the threshold of our own time, when the sciences once again enjoy the pride of place that was theirs during the glorious days of Linnaeus.

Bo Oscarsson

The Present Era

In the vast expansion of scientific pursuit during the postwar period, almost every country has aspired towards excellence in *all* branches of science, limited only by the extent of its resources. Now as the research and development entail more and more tremendous expense, the small countries in particular have found it necessary to open a discussion on how to order priorities, whereby certain branches are given precedence over others. In space research, to mention just one example, the resources required are already of such a scale that a small country cannot possibly hope to compete with the great powers. If it wishes to challenge their leadership, its only recourse is to pool facilities with other small countries. In Europe they have banded together to form ESRO, the European Space Research Organization. CERN, the European Organization for Nuclear Research, is another expression of the same development.

Even so, it is still possible for small countries to achieve international eminence by their own resources in selected fields of scientific and biomedical endeavor, which have not yet become Big Science to that extent, as for example space research or high energy physics. Here again, however, it will certainly be increasingly necessary for these countries to specialize just as the beginnings of specialization are apparent at the national level between universities and research institutions. A small country, probably, is well advised to concentrate on such fields in which it already occupies a leading position. In other fields chief reliance will have to be put on international cooperation. And if fragmentation of resources is to be avoided, it may be the better course to discontinue certain programs and instead acquire know-how from the outside by licenses or other means.

By international yardsticks, Sweden has so far managed to uphold a remarkably high standard in most of the fields of scientific and technological research. It is true that certain circumstances, related to a long scientific tradition, glowing examples of individual accomplishment, and geographic situation, have imparted a special character to science in our country. None the less, it is striking how complex and diverse Swedish research is. This makes it difficult to give, within the compass of a brief review, even an approximate picture of what is being done. The situation is further complicated by the increasing emergence of interdisciplinary research which brings existing disciplines into intricate interrelationships and makes traditional boundary lines between them out of date.

Although many names could be cited as examples of illustrious pioneering achievement in our time, we think it would be fairer to give a more general picture of current developments in the three major sectors: medicine, natural science, and technology. There is further justification for this approach in the growing trend towards conducting research in teams, which makes it difficult to single out any one individual for special mention.

Medicine

By common consensus, Sweden enjoys international eminence in the life sciences. Referring to what we said earlier of the increasing need to specialize, we can feel certain that medicine will continue to rank very high on the list of priorities in Sweden. The emphasis put on medical research is most tellingly illustrated by the near-threefold increase in government grants to the Medical Research Council in the past five fiscal years (figures are in million Swedish kronor):

1961/62	1962/63	1963/64	1964/65	1965/66
6.1	6.9	9.5	13.2	17.1

One field of rapid expansion is molecular medicine, which has evolved from morphology and biochemistry on the basis of modern methods derived from a number of basic research fields. A decisive impetus was given here by X-ray crystallography, making it possible to determine the structure of large molecules like proteins and nucleic acids. Research teams in biochemistry and X-ray crystallography are busy in several places, among them Göteborg, where a team has done outstanding work in structural analyses of the purely crystalline prostaglandins. In Uppsala and Stockholm, other highly qualified teams are working on problems of protein structure, with particular reference to enzymes.

High-quality research is also being done in genetics, a field where Sweden would appear to be especially well endowed, thanks in some measure to the church parish records that have been providing official demographic data since 1749. Research in medical genetics is carried on by an institution at the University of Uppsala as well as by scientists working individually. The cross-fertilization of genetics with cytology, known as cytogenetics, has assumed prominence. Progress in genetic research generally, however, is hampered to some extent for lack of trained personnel.

Traditions maintained since the days of the famed Berzelius have given biochemistry a strong position in our schools of medicine. Swedish scientists have done ground-breaking research on nucleic acids, carbohydrates and proteins. The several teams currently working in these fields have also contributed significantly to the development of biochemical methods now in active clinical use.

An example of how basic medical research has led to clinical applications is the work of the Royal Caroline Institute on blood coagulation. The translation of basic research findings into industrial production also has its examples, among them insulin and heparin. Another consequence of biochemistry's salience has been to elevate Swedish clinical chemistry to a top-ranking international position, as witnessed for instance by the discovery of Dextran.

A field of particularly vigorous expansion at the present time is neurophysiology, thanks in large part to the use of modern electronic techniques.

Medical bacteriology is fairly well established. Especially worthy of note are the projects in molecular biology designed to shed greater light on the viruses. Sweden would appear to be well equipped to make important contributions in immunology, to which some outstanding young scientists are devoting their energies. Immunology also has strong ties with clinical research.

Currently, the international limelight is monopolized by cancer research, understandably so in view of its more direct relevance for the layman. In Sweden a powerful stimulus to progress comes from the support given by the Swedish Cancer Society. Among the more noteworthy projects now under way are those of the Caroline Institute, which is concentrating on the properties of cancer cells with special reference to genetics.

The major part of research on drugs is conducted by the pharmaceutical industry. Here cooperation between physiologists and pharmacologists on the one hand and chemists on the other has resulted in a number of Swedish "firsts", among them Xylocaine, an anesthetic widely used in dentistry.

A great deal of clinical research is going into surgery. The enlargement of facilities for transplantation research is currently under way. Improved means of diagnosing tumors at an early stage have added to the importance of cancer surgery, at the same time that collaboration with experts on radiation therapy and endocrinology has increased. Another central field is cardiovascular surgery, where Swedish researchers have brought international attention to their endeavors. Great interest is also being shown in the development of surgery as a science in the cause of preventive medicine. In this connection there has been a demand for cooperation between medicine and the engineering sciences. Medical engineering, concerned with the development of technical apparatus for therapy, is an example of inter-disciplinary work that is already established.

Natural Science

Cooperation so fruitful that one can speak of a virtual coalescence has developed in recent years between medicine and certain branches of natural science. This is especially true of research in genetics, microbiology, cytology and related life sciences, which is pursued at both medical and scientific institutions. The Caroline Institute, which is a school of medicine, also does internationally noted research in natural science at its departments of bacteriology, virology and other departments concerned with basic work in biology. The greater part of biological research, however, is carried on at the universities. Together with physics, the life sciences are the most vigorously expanding sectors in Sweden today.

As a result of these emphases, the systematic sciences of botany and zoology have lost some of their former dominance. It should be pointed out, however, that Swedish scientists have long held international eminence in botany, in accordance with traditions that date back to Linnaeus (see "The scientific heritage"). An important center of the zoological sciences in Sweden has long been the Museum of Natural History.

As to physical science, to begin with, Sweden's limited economic resources have prevented her from developing high-energy physics on any appreciable scale. In other branches of physics, however, her achievements stand up pretty well to international comparisons. Theoretical physicists are tackling most of the core problems in this science, and in addition have set up machinery for cooperation with scientists in the other Scandinavian countries; this is NORDITA, the Nordic Institute for Theoretical Nuclear Physics.

Much important work has been done in experimental physics. The departments of physics at Uppsala and Lund Universities, and the Institute of Atomic Physics at Frescati, have increasingly concentrated their efforts on nuclear research. Large resources have been invested in experimental facilities. The biggest accelerator plant, located in Lund, includes a synchrotron with a capacity of 1.2 GeV.

The spectroscopic study of molecules, atoms and nuclei is another branch of experimental physics that Sweden is backing heavily. Plasma physics, which is a modern application of spectroscopy, is being particularly stressed at the Royal Institute of Technology in Stockholm.

In chemistry, Sweden can again point to outstanding work, especially in the branches of physical chemistry and biochemistry, which has netted a couple of Nobel prizes. Current interest in the inorganic sector is attached to physical chemistry, where structural determinations by means of X-rays have long been carried out. Electronic computers have now made it possible to analyze highly complex structures.

Research in organic chemistry commands much smaller resources, which is probably the main reason why Swedish industrial production of plastics, synthetic fibers and the like still ranks rather low by international standards. Here again the lack of trained personnel is probably one of the hampering factors. In this sector, too, research projects cannot always be counted on to produce successful results, and manufacturers have accordingly hesitated to risk the capital for the long-range investments which are often necessary.

Under the head of natural science, mention must also be made of astronomy, where a great deal of work is now going into projects concerned with explaining the structure and rotation of the Milky Way and other galaxies.

A field of research with a broad purview is geophysics, which is the subject of study at a large number of institutions. It is currently undergoing rapid expansion, not least because of its significance for space research.

A border area between natural science and technology is occupied by environmental research. Although it has not yet attained large-scale proportions in Sweden, we may expect considerable expansion in the near future.

Professor Hannes Alfvén, who teaches plasma physics at the Stockholm Institute of Technology, is one of the best-known Swedish scientists abroad. He is also active in public life as a spokesman for the scientific community. Photo : Sven Åsberg.

Technology

A high standard of technology is essential to industrial progress. It is therefore natural for private enterprise to underwrite the major portion of research and development in this field. According to the most recent surveys, Swedish firms are now spending more than SKr 800 million a year on R & D work. As in many other industrialized countries, R & D outlays are highest both in amount and in relation to production value for the electrical engineering, metal fabrication and foundry industries. Tougher international competition has compelled the shipbuilding industry to increase its R & D budgets. The forest product industries have also enlarged their R & D programs in order to cope with the falling price tendencies for wood products during the past ten years.

The largest companies in any industry are of course better equipped to finance expensive R & D programs. Smaller companies usually have to set their sights lower. Inasmuch as small and medium-sized establishments predominate in the Swedish business structure, only a few industries can afford research and development in which an immediate payoff is not expected. Other industries just don't have enough venture capital to justify the risks involved in such research. As a result 90 percent of the private R & D programs concentrate on development projects which are directly related to the industrial production process.

Because scientific and technological research and development of a general nature receive relatively little support from the private sector, the government has to shoulder much of the responsibility, and actually most of the government R & D expenditure is now going to research in applied sciences and engineering. Facilities for higher education and research are offered primarily by the institutes of technology and secondarily by the universities.

The radio astronomy observatory at Råö, built in 1950, forms part of the Chalmers Institute of Technology in Göteborg. Its largest instrument is a radio telescope with an aperture of 25.6 meters. Photo: Göran Algård.

To stimulate research and development in industry, and particularly in small-scale enterprises, the national government also grants money to several special bodies of an official or semi-official nature. One of these is the Technical Research Council with an annual budget of about SKr 17 million (1965/66). Another is INFOR, which received a starting grant of SKr 20 million in 1964 to finance projects for turning research to practical account

in industry. A similar purpose is served by EFOR, the Foundation for Exploitation of Research Results.

Parts of the profits returned by the government-owned mines in Kiruna are earmarked for two R & D funds, known as the Norrland Foundation and the Swedish Ore Foundation for Scientific Research and Development. The former is especially concerned with the development of resources in northern Sweden as a means of stimulating economic growth in that part of the country. Together, these two funds receive annual grants of SKr 25 million.

Further support of the research efforts of private enterprise comes from the branch research institutes. There are now 30 such institutes in Sweden, which enable groups of firms with similar interests to pursue research in common. Some ten of them receive half their funds from the national government; the largest are the Forest Products Research Laboratory, the Institute for Production Engineering Research, and the Institute for Food Preservation Research. Several branch research institutes collaborate closely with the institutes of technology and in this way serve as liaison between government and business endeavors. Some of the institutes also have international ties. Their most important function is to provide facilities that would be too expensive for the member firms to finance individually. They also perform valuable services as documentation centers and as headquarters of material-testing and standardization programs.

Considering the extreme diversity of technological research, it is almost impossible to summarize the present situation in a few words. One field that is conspicuously expanding at the moment is electronics, with both government and business investing large sums. A great deal of research effort is also going into transportation, which involves such questions as highway engineering, user costs and relative economies between rail, road and water transport.

Mention should also be made under this head of nuclear energy, where government is the main driving force through its own company, AB Atomenergi, whose largest research station is at Studsvik. Swedish industry has recently undertaken the development of reactors on a commercial basis.

Other fields that rate high current priority include automatic controls for the process industries, petrochemistry, and technical microbiology. Great interest is also being shown in corrosion and materials science.

As science and technology continue their headlong pace, there is increasing need for updated information services to make the findings of basic research available to industry with minimum delay. Although several sciences are now collaborating in this field, it is realized that the provision of adequate information services will require a new kind of training and technology.

Göte Rudvall   Born in 1925. Lecturer in methodology at the school of Education in Malmö. Played a prominent role in the pilot program which preceded the introduction of nine years of compulsory schooling in 1962.

Ulla Åhgren-Lange   Born in 1934, Master of Arts. Department head at the Office of the Chancellor of the Swedish Universities, the administrative link between government and higher education. Her views on a non-religious ethic are portrayed in a polemical essay, *Morals for Doubters* (*Moral för tvivlare*).

Swedish Education in New Molds

Göte Rudvall

Much of the old formality has gone out of the Swedish school system. Early efforts are also made to individualize instruction. Two small girls are seen forming a make-believe picture of the world far beyond the borders of Sweden. Photo : Bertil Stilling.

Basic and Secondary Education

The Swedish educational system was strongly conservative up to the beginning of the postwar period. Although continuing democratization had long been permeating other sectors of society, little if any of it had rubbed off on the school. Until quite recently there remained a formidable barrier between the higher grades of the elementary school and the academic forms of secondary education. On both sides of the barrier, moreover, arbitrary power had been vested in the teacher, whose methods of instruction tended to make subject matter dull and the pupils even duller.

During the postwar years, however, Sweden has embarked upon a momentous program of reforms in the content and methods of education. Compulsory basic schooling now runs for nine years and is given in the comprehensive school. For the first eight years pupils are kept together in unsegregated classes, after which they are sorted out by their own indications into several streams or scholastic divisions according to their fields of interest.

All education beyond the ninth year is voluntary. From the tenth through the twelfth years it is given in the gymnasia, continuation schools and vocational schools. Here, too, however, the aim is to achieve a more unified organization, and a first step in this direction took effect as from the 1966/67 academic year, when the three types of gymnasium—general, commercial and polytechnic—were merged into one. At the same time, instruction is being increasingly focused on individual needs.

At bottom, the reforms in education and training of teachers are

211

one expression of the general quest for a better society. They aim to remove to the utmost degree those economic, geographic, social and psychological handicaps which have so far kept young people from selecting and assimilating the education that best fulfills their interests and abilities. The reforms, moreover, are meant to raise the level of education as well as overall cultural standards, to narrow the social and cultural gaps between different sections of the community, and to instill a sense of the equal worth and dignity of different trades and occupations.

In the past, when different types of school were catering for equivalent levels of education at the same time, pupils from the countryside and from the lowest income group (socioeconomic group 3) were largely overlooked. They were poorly represented in the secondary schools in proportion to their numbers. Moreover, a very strong traditional resistance had to be overcome, compounded by long distances between home and school and other practical difficulties.

With the arrival of the comprehensive school, which replaces the former separate provision for elementary and lower-secondary education, the same study opportunities are available for all nine years regardless of geographic location. Pupils need no longer board in another community to get their first taste of academic learning. The fact that streaming is not introduced until the ninth year meets another criterion of fairness: the experience of many countries suggests that the class grouping of pupils by ability entails a large measure of social discrimination. Pupils in socioeconomic groups 1 and 2 usually come from homes which give them more active encouragement in their studies as compared with pupils from group-3 homes. Deferred specialization acts to keep young people of disadvantaged background from getting bogged down in inferior school environments which offer them little intellectual stimulation. Apathy among them is all too likely to be the result after the most gifted pupils have been hived off into so-called progressive classes. It is considered much more desirable to have all categories of pupils learn to live and work together. Further, every effort is made to encourage the pursuit of theoretical studies on the part of gifted pupils whose development has been inhibited by disapproval or indifference in the home.

The Swedish school system attaches increasing importance to sexual education. Here is a demonstration of contraceptives in the ninth grade of the comprehensive school. Photo: Bror Karlsson.

The principle of free selection is strictly applied in the comprehensive school to the courses and subjects in grades 7 and 8, and also to the nine different sides in grade 9. No enrollment barriers are set up except for the least able pupils, who are given special instruction. The self-selection system has a special value in that it makes pupils assume more of the responsibility for their education. Besides, it is felt that schools run too great a risk of misjudging scholastic ability in the individual case to entrust them with the responsibility of assigning pupils to different fields of study. One consequence of the system has been to generate a heavy flow of enrollments into theoretical as opposed to practical courses.

For the present, free selection is restricted in secondary schools by the official policy of gearing accommodation to estimated labor-market needs of trained manpower in different occupations. As a rule, therefore, admissions are screened with reference to the marks received in the comprehensive school.

There is rather wide differentiation of facilities at the secondary level, inasmuch as many of the courses prepare for direct entry into the job world. This explains why gymnasia can only be established in the cities and towns. The impelling motivation here is to have all courses available at the same locality so as not to distort the vocational choices of young people. The geographical accident of birth should not be allowed to curtail opportunity; rather than have a pupil study for a vocation for which he may be poorly fitted just because the preparatory course happens to be nearest at hand, it is better to furnish him with travel allowances and stipends so that he can attend the school which is best fitted to serve him.

All types of school attach great importance to the pursuit of independent work. Individualized instruction, which permits different pupils to work at their own pace, is fostered in every way possible, and current educational research is intensively exploring new methods for this purpose. To a great extent, capability for independent study is developed by having pupils work together in groups. The emphasis is on cooperation rather than competition. Indeed, it is felt that the competitive element in education has been allowed to dominate too much in the past, and there is now a tendency to play down the significance of marks. The abolition of final examinations serves the same end.

Independent and group motivation are both stimulated by the important role which organizations of pupils and students have come to play in Swedish education. As from the seventh grade, most schools have similar bodies whose members are democratically elected and empowered to advise teachers and school authorities in educational matters. Most of them are affiliated with SECO, the Swedish Union of Secondary-School Students, which also has a well-developed regional organization. Each year SECO convenes its members in a "student parliament", where many proposals for educational reform are put forth and thoroughly discussed. SECO, which receives a government subsidy for its activities, also organizes large-scale programs for the training of officers who serve on the "student councils". SECO

A 15-year-old girl is gaining experience in a workshop, which will help her qualify for admission to a technical high school. The conventional demarcation of sex roles is severely criticized in present-day Sweden, but steps to demolish it are not making much progress. Photo: Lars-Olov Davidsson.

and its affiliates leaped into prominence in late 1966, when most of the country's organized teachers struck for higher pay. For lack of classroom guidance, the students had to be their own teachers, and it was their councils which largely filled the breach by assigning lessons and homework for the three weeks of the strike.

Beginning in the 1966/67 academic year, students in upper secondary schools are mandatorily represented in class and subject

conferences, as well as on joint committees, which concern
themselves with matters relating to deportment, motivation and
discipline in the schools.

Whatever the type of school or the courses it offers, great care
is taken to avoid "blind alleys". Government-financed tutorial
plans and other facilities have been devised to enable pupils to
switch from one line of study to another if they so desire. This
forms part of the general efforts to confer the same dignity and
prestige on all branches of learning. Thus a pupil who has already
gone in for a "practical" alternative does not thereby debar
himself from theoretical pursuits should he want to make the
switch in later life; the right to change one's mind applies the
other way around, too, of course.

Although the educational reforms were considered radical when
first enacted, society is changing so rapidly that clamor has arisen
for more reforms on the same sweeping scale. A committee of
the National Board of Education is already engaged in working
out a new program for the comprehensive school; one of its
objectives is to create a better balance between theoretical and
practical assignments in classroom work. Plans are in hand to
abolish the system of scholastic divisions in grade 9 in favor of
a system of subject electives similar to that of grades 7 and 8.
An important reason is that the prevocational courses have proved
to exert little appeal for the pupils.

In the meantime, the flow of admissions to secondary schools
has become so torrential that it may soon be necessary to add
two or three years to the comprehensive school. If compulsory
schooling is thus prolonged, the integration of courses and
curricula will probably have to be carried even farther. Here again
the inculcation of specific vocational skills may be expected to
give way to more direct concern with character development and
a broader content of general education.

Ulla Åhgren-Lange

Higher Education

Sweden, in common with many other countries, has experienced
an enormous growth in the number of people who pursue their
education beyond the secondary level. The undergraduate

population of our universities and colleges, at 15,000 in the 1940's, rose to nearly 60,000 in 1964. According to parliamentary decision, higher educational facilities are to be enlarged so as to accommodate 87,000 undergraduates by 1970.

This expansion is related to the reforms in basic and secondary education which began to be implemented in the 1960's. Whereas only six percent of an age group qualified for university entrance in 1945, the proportion rose to 14 percent in 1963. The new gymnasium or secondary school that took over as from the 1966/67 academic year is meant in due course to accommodate 30 percent of each age group, while 20 percent are earmarked for the newly established continuation school (where courses are for two years as compared with the gymnasium's three).

A far-reaching change in the scholastic qualifications of the labor force is expected to ensue from the current educational revolution. The National Labor Market Board predicts the following advances in educational levels from 1960 to 2000:

Educational Levels Attained by Persons Aged 15 to 65 Years (in percent)

	1960	1970	1980	1990	2000
University degree	2	3	5	7	10
Completion of secondary school	4	6	10	15	20
Nine years of schooling	10	20	32	43	48
Seven or fewer years of schooling	84	71	53	35	22

Recognition of the need to continue enlarging the democratic base of our society has served as the primary spur to overhaul of the educational system. At the same time, however, considerations of labor market policy have been very much to the fore, not least in the program calling for expanded secondary education. Thus there is deliberately greater provision for technical and business studies, which prepare for direct entrance into the job world, as well as for the science-oriented subjects which ultimately lead to the professions.

The expansion of higher education has been matched by increased demand for virtually all kinds of university-trained manpower. Since the headlong surge of technological advance makes it difficult to assess just how many graduates will be needed in different fields, the recent tendency in college-and-university facility planning has been to adapt total capacity to expected enrollments, after which a balance is struck between the different disciplines so as to gear capacity to expected trends on the labor market.

There is general agreement that the further expansion of higher education must waste no time. To prevent the expansion from becoming lopsided, existing resources must be deployed more efficiently. Except for the medical departments of universities and the professional schools, admissions to the universities have always been unrestricted. New ways must now be sought to reduce length of studies and to accelerate the throughput rate. In order to cater for the rapidly growing undergraduate population in the departments of humanities, social sciences and mathematics-natural sciences, the authorities since 1958 have applied a flexible system of grants, whereby added funds are automatically provided for extra teacher staffing in proportion to increases in enrollment. In addition, fixed curricula are now being introduced, which require undergraduates to pursue their studies in a given sequence of subject matter and to complete courses within specified times.

In due course admission to these departments will be made contingent on strict observance of the new curricula requirements. The aim here is twofold: first, greater efficiency will result when instruction in different subjects is coordinated; and second, it will be easier to keep track of the individual student and to take appropriate action if he doesn't maintain the prescribed pace. As a last resort a student who falls short of the mark can be debarred from pursuing a university education. The tightened rules will also apply to the departments of law and theology.

Affiliated universities for lower academic degrees in the humanistic, natural-science and social-science disciplines are being established, with the parent universities to function as overseers so as to ensure satisfactory scholastic standards. This decentralization will ease undergraduate loads on the home campus, and at the same time avoid the fragmentation of research resources which the founding of an independent university would entail.

In the following table, the number of undergraduates enrolled in 1963 are compared with the forecast for 1972. The breakdown figures shown for the humanities and natural sciences are approximate, since no official decision has been made as to the exact distribution between the two.

Discipline	1963 enrollments	1972 enrollments
Theology	913	1,500
Law	2,369	6,000
Medicine	3,959	7,100
Humanities	21,433	15,580
Social sciences (excl. economics)		13,220
Mathematics-natural sciences	7,989	21,630
Technology	6,632	13,740
Dentistry	1,197	1,650
Economics	2,275	4,400
Miscellaneous	1,460	1,900
Totals	*48,227*	*87,000*

The Arts in Sweden

The Swedish cultural scene bears a strong international flavor nowadays. Sweden—and Stockholm in particular—has become a meeting place for art and artists from all over the world. A not unimportant mediating service which Stockholm performs is to bring new American art into initial contact with European audiences.

That is probably the aptest summary of what this chapter has to say about current endeavors in Swedish cinema, music, ballet, drama, literature and the fine arts. Since 1945 the national, as understood in the narrower sense, has been giving up terrain bit by bit. Swedish artists have deliberately elected to expose themselves to the dictates of international competition, and in so doing have renounced whatever "security" provincial yardsticks of appraisal have been able to confer. A long period of cultural isolation was bound to follow from Sweden's non-involvement in both world wars. It is this isolation which has finally crumbled, and in its place there is growing commitment to events in the world of art as they unfold beyond our country's frontiers.

Ingrid Arvidsson

Born in 1919. Poet and literary critic. Cultural attaché at the Swedish Embassy in Washington since 1966.

Swedish Cultural Policy

Expansion has been the keynote of Swedish cultural policy in the past decade. Virtually all the arts have come in for greatly increased government support, a development made possible by growing prosperity. Once the community-at-large was satisfied that the country's material needs had been largely secured, it felt a similar obligation to impart a richer spiritual content to the life of the people. That this responsibility should be undertaken by the public sector has its reasons: with more discretionary purchasing power at his disposal, the average citizen has opted to spend the larger share on cars, summer houses and other creature comforts; his consumption of culture, on the other hand, tends to increase very slowly.

In a country as small as Sweden, very few authors and artists can make an adequate living from their works. The peace of mind they need in order to create art requires freedom from want and ample scope for their talents. Accordingly, State patronage of the arts embraces not only budgeted grants to schools and cultural institutions, but also an extensive system of bursaries payable to artists, writers, actors, dancers, craftsmen and designers. These bursaries are meant to foster the arts, and not to render public charity to practitioners who happen to be down on their luck. Artists are to be helped in every way as scientists because society needs their products.

Moreover, no strings are attached to public support. There is no regimentation from the top. Certain criteria of quality must be met, but the assessment of quality is largely left to professional experts. Were a politician to pontificate on art matters, he would get short shrift in Sweden, where freedom of speech and expression is of long standing. The only exception is film censorship, and even this is exposed to running fire as part of the tradition of public debate. Experience has scotched earlier fears that artists beholden to the State for their incomes would feel hemmed in, unfree to criticize the prevailing order or to create art that wasn't readily accessible to the layman. Quite the contrary: a Swedish artist who receives a bursary is as little bound to renounce his right of social protest as when he is paid a sickness benefit or family allowance.

Whether the field be art or science, there is always the risk that sensitive toes are going to be stepped on when grants and bursaries are awarded. The authorities have sought to guarantee impartiality by empowering professional organizations to make the awards, rotating the membership of grants committees, and by bringing in experts. The bursaries are thrown open to application, and a widely ramified network of national, local and private bursaries guards against gross negligence of deserving candidates.

Swedish writers were given the legal right to compensation for loans of their works from public libraries in 1955. It was considered preferable to pay writers out of tax revenues rather than charge fees to borrowers. The compensation, currently at the rate of six öre (about one cent) per loan, is paid into a special fund, from which grants are distributed. Administration of the fund is in the hands of trustees representing the government and different societies of authors. Total proceeds run at more than Swedish kronor 2,500,000 a year. Some of the money is directly paid to authors in proportion to the number of library loans. Another portion is payable as bursaries, assistance, travel allowances and pensions to authors of every category. The authors themselves have recommended this system, under which the more popular amongst them distribute the benefits more equitably to those with a smaller readership.

Public support of the arts is forthcoming in many other ways. Under this head we can mention the libraries and museums, professional schools of art, music and cinematography, adult education programs, the Royal Dramatic Theater and the Royal Opera. In recent years, moreover, special grants have been voted for touring concert and theatrical companies, travelling exhibitions of art, the activities of private theaters, the purchase of art for the ornamentation of public buildings, and the publication of literary periodicals. There is also the Nordic Cultural Fund, which finances interchange of programs between Norway, Denmark, Finland and Sweden.

It should not be concluded from the foregoing that Swedish artists live in an economic paradise, even if they are better off than their counterparts in most other countries. The highest bursaries, amounting to SKr 12,000–15,000 a year, fall far short of the income earned by an untrained clerk or salesperson. They are payable to a limited number of artists and run for only a few years. After that a beneficiary has to look to other and usually less lucrative sources. The most coveted awards, amounting to SKr 27,500 per year and payable for life, are reserved for highly deserving artists. They are reducible in proportion to an artist's own earnings, and their chief value comes from their being a sort of guaranteed pension. There are now about one hundred of these lifetime awards, which were established only recently.

Government grants to art, literature, etc. in millions of kronor.

	Fiscal year 1961–62	Fiscal year 1967–68
Stipends to artists (in literature, art, music, theater, film, dance)	0.6	2.9
Awards to artists		0.6
Ornamentation of public buildings	0.4	1.8
Remuneration to writers et al for library loans of their works	1.2	2.8
Grants to theaters (Royal Opera, Dramatic Theater, civic theaters, touring companies)	22.0	55.2
Grant to Special Cultural Purposes	—	17.5
whereof for theater	1.7	
whereof for music and dance	11.7	
whereof for art and exhibitions	3.2	
whereof for magazines	0.2	
Miscellaneous	7.0	0.7
Totals	31.2	81.5

Note: The decline in real value between 1961–62 and 1967–68 is estimated at 23 %.

Carl Henrik Svenstedt

Born in 1937. Author and critic of films and literature for Svenska Dagbladet. Has also represented the Swedish Institute for Cultural Relations with Foreign Countries in Paris, etc.

Cinema

Sweden also has a "new wave" of cinematic art, and its posture can be summed up in a single scene occurring in the film that established *Bo Widerberg* as a director. As "Raven's End" draws to a close, the revolutionary young hero is half-running with bag in hand to the train that will take him from Malmö's slums and resignation to Stockholm, symbol of freedom, where he and others of his generation will, in the shadow of World War II, shape a new Sweden closer to their hearts' desire. As he casts a last look at his back yard, he sees a young girl skipping rope. Her hair is flying and her feet strike a rhythm as if she, too, could fly. In the middle of one of her leaps, Widerberg suddenly "freezes" the picture: the image of a child is fixed on the retina, and with it a childhood of infinite opportunity.

The scene is a tribute to François Truffaut and "The 400 Blows", the film which tore cinematography loose from the studio straitjacket. At the same time it signifies a revolt against Swedish film-making of the 'forties and 'fifties—against *Ingmar Bergman* and *Alf Sjöberg*, against chamber dramas, tragedies and myths.

For years on end, one name alone has stood abroad for the Swedish motion picture: Ingmar Bergman, creator of "The Seventh Seal", "Wild Strawberries" and "The Virgin Spring", to name just a few. And quite right, too, for Bergman is still the only Swedish director who can hold his own with the international greats. Which also explains why the newcomers cannot ignore his work. Besides, why should they? It would be as if a Frenchman were to disavow Jean Renoir!

Yet we have that little rope-skipping girl to remind us that things can never be the same. There she is caught in mid-air, and no one yet knows which way she is going to bounce. New signals have been hoisted but it is still too early to interpret them.

Of the younger directors, Widerberg, a former writer, has flouted the Bergmanesque tradition most openly. Inspired by the "new wave" in France, he exchanged his typewriter for the film camera with its possibilities of capturing the here and now: *prendre la vie sur le vif.* With his debut work, "The Baby Carriage" (1963) he abandoned the studios for today's urban scene; in "Raven's End" he renounced philosophical broodings on good and evil for unvarnished social portrayal; and in "Love 65" (1965) he spurned contrived drawing-room dialogue for improvisation and spontaneity in the spirit of Fellini's "$8\frac{1}{2}$". Widerberg achieved his greatest international success with the bitter-sweet romance, "Elvira Madigan", done in color, which received a major prize at the 1967 Cannes Festival. Audiences and critics were perhaps more captivated by the melancholy love story as such between a deserting officer and a tightrope dancer, than by the "Mayerling theme" which Widerberg thought essential: to attack a social morality which forces an "impossible" love affair to end in murder and suicide.

Vilgot Sjöman is also committed to the revolution, but he is making haste slowly and methodically. No piling up of corpses at the barricades for him, which is the way Sweden prefers to carry out her revolutions. His first production, "The Mistress" (1962), describing a *ménage à trois*, was deeply marked by Bergman's style and visual technique. (Sjöman also happens to be a pupil of Bergman from his university theater days.) But in "491", dealing with teenagers on the twilight fringes of the welfare state, he joined forces with the fiercely rebellious author, Lars Görling. Their alliance produced a no-holds-barred film that remains unique in Swedish cinematic history. A reversion to Bergmanesque strains came with "The Dress" (1964), a chamber drama about two women, the one emerging from puberty and the other in her years of menopause. But Sjöman's most recent film, "My Sister, My Love" (1965), left not the slightest doubt that he has at last found his own way. It has nothing to do with Widerberg's "new wave", but takes off at a tangent from a road that has been well trodden in the Swedish cinema. In scenes of beautifully balanced cruelty and tenderness, he portrays the timeless drama of incest in a classical 18th century French setting.

Both Widerberg and Sjöman are on the sunny side of forty,

Jan Troell, teacher and successful maker of short films, scored a notable debut as director in 1966 with "Here Is Your Life", after Eyvind Johnson's series of novels bearing the same name. The plot, set in the far north of Sweden, is a penetrating portrayal of life in the days of World War I.

and so is the third director in this chronicle: *Jörn Donner* (who came over here from his home country, Finland). His cinematic style is "Continental" in the best sense: taut and sensitive, yet turning at times inward and elusive. Donner, once a militant Marxist, used to be fond of lambasting the film-makers for their shallowness, and his incisive writing did much to raise the standards of Swedish film criticism. When he left the newspaper world to become his own producer, it was widely expected that he would swoop down like young Galahad on the social evils of our time. But he has done nothing of the kind. Instead, he has dwelt in one film after the other on the problems of a man and woman living together, in "A Sunday in September" (1963), "To Love" (1964) and "Adventure Starts

Here" (1965). The last of these, however, suggests that Donner is beginning to look on the bedroom as too confined; his two principal characters act out their roles in a larger social context, and the milieus portrayed sometimes take on the universality of meaning imparted by Antonioni.

Having dwelt at such length on the doings of our younger generation, we do not wish to imply that the "old-timers" have shot their wad. Far from it: Sjöberg is still making films and Bergman seems to have suffered no loss of his powers. Also very much active is a third internationally known member of the old school, *Arne Sucksdorff*.

Indeed, such is the ferment in Swedish cinema today that even Widerberg, Sjöman and Donner cannot afford to rest on their laurels too long, for right behind them is a crop of even younger hopefuls. Among them are *Mai Zetterling* (admittedly a veteran as actress, but decidedly a youngster as film-maker), *Jan Halldoff*, *Peter Kylberg*, *Jonas Cornell* and *Jan Troell* (who presumably will be the one who tells us where Widerberg's girl bounces, to judge from his broad poetic description of poverty in Northern Sweden in the early 1900's, "Here Is Your Life" (1966), the most significant debut film in many years). This array of talent has started off with an advantage that was non-existent before 1963, when the Swedish authorities decided to establish a new agency, the Swedish Film Institute; financed from the receipts of cinema entertainment tax, the Institute works as a center of information, runs training programs, and awards prizes to quality films on the recommendations of an independent jury.

Ulf Linde

Born in 1929, Master of Arts. Art critic and essayist. Has contributed
prominently to the introduction of the latest currents in art and as
a fountainhead of ideas in the art debate. Among his writings,
Hommage à Marcel Duchamp has also been published in English.

Painting and Sculpture

It is scarcely possible to describe the present state of the plastic
arts in Sweden without at least one backward look into the past.
The decisive event took place as early as 1947, the year in
which a new generation of artists made their debut. During the
war years they had methodically assimilated the legacy left by
cubism and abstract art. They had not been in direct contact
with the originals; the inspiration was supplied by isolated issues
of such magazines as *Verve* and *Cahiers d'Art*, dating back to
the interwar years.

Works by these artists—Lennart Rodhe, Olle Bonniér, Lage Lindell,
Karl Axel Pehrson, Arne Jones and others—compelled a largely
unprepared general public to revise its provincial outlook. Their
debut foreshadowed the orientation towards international
modernism that has remained dominant in Swedish art up to the
present time.

Lennart Rodhe has emerged as the towering figure among these
concretists, as they are called. His art combines unflinching
austerity with unusual rhythmic power. Rodhe's particular forte is
the mural painting, and his works in this genre are among the
most noteworthy that now grace the Swedish public scene. (It
should be noted here that Swedish artists are often called upon
to work on the monumental scale. The integration of art with
architecture, so often discussed on the Continent as a utopian
vision, has here been implemented in actual projects. However,
it would be too much to say that this has instilled greater
appreciation of art among the "masses".)

Non-figurative art had other practitioners, too, and its position was
further strengthened in the early 'fifties by Olle Baertling in
a twofold capacity: as painter and as enthusiastic missionary on
behalf of Auguste Herbin. Before long, however, a reaction set

in. In 1952 a young painter, Torsten Renqvist, appeared with ostentatiously figurative canvases, executed in harsh, aggressive brushwork. Other artists followed suit, and before long the critics were talking about a wave of *neo-expressionism*. It soon proved to be a very roomy classification: two well-established older artists such as Siri Derkert and Evert Lundquist found themselves grouped with the "neo-expressionists", for reasons neither they nor most others could quite grasp. Both Derkert and Lundquist have survived the label (and Renqvist, too, for that matter), of which little is heard nowadays.

Towards the end of the 'fifties the Swedish art scene, as in most other Western European countries, was dominated by the "informal" style. The era may be said to have been launched by Georges Mathieu during a visit to Stockholm in the summer of 1958; while an invited audience looked on, he painted a huge battle scene in the garden of a famous old patrician town house. In the ensuing years the word informal seems to have been interpreted a little too loosely; this was certainly very much in evidence at the regularly recurring "salons" in the Liljevalchs Gallery.

In any case, little of Swedish informal painting is truly original. The notable exceptions belong to Rune Jansson and Eddie Figge, but both already did their softly lyrical abstractions a decade before Mathieu arrived. (As usual, pioneers wear best in the long run!)

By the middle of the 'sixties, communications were working so fast that Swedish and foreign art became, to all intents and purposes, fully synchronized. Ideas are rapidly spread by magazines, the young artists leave early for foreign pastures, and so on. However, a very important factor in the synchronizing process has been the activities of the Museum of Modern Art in Stockholm. Artists like Jasper Johns, Rauschenberg and Tinguely —to name just a few of the more significant—have been most typically represented at the Museum. Even more important, their works have been shown early! The Museum was the first in Europe to present a major exhibition of American pop art. Stockholm has certainly become one of Europe's most eventful art capitals thanks in large part to the Museum. Much of the credit also goes to the art trade: there are some 40 private galleries in Stockholm, a remarkably high figure when related to the city's population.

All this has enhanced the critical awareness of today's Swedish artists. Epigones who try to pass off imported ideas as their own are more readily exposed as shams. That may explain why it is more difficult today to connect the more interesting young artists with foreign prototypes, though neo-provincialism need not be imputed to them for this reason. Names such as Per Olof Ultvedt, Öyvind Fahlström, Elis Eriksson and Carl Fredrik Reuterswärd have also turned up internationally—and *without* the benefit of trumpeting by public relations men. The originality of their work has sufficed to speak for itself.

Summing up, Swedish art of the 'sixties is highly vital. Above all, it is rich in alternatives. This should be viewed as a good thing, even if we allow that the classifiers—who are always with us—may have a hard time trying to sort out a distinctive "Swedish school", the easier to attract international attention (as the Danes once did with their COBRA group, for instance).

Runar Mangs

Born in 1928. Music teacher and critic. Has also produced programs
for the Swedish Broadcasting Corporation.

Music

Until around 1950 Sweden was largely a blank spot on the
international music map. There were good composers before then,
to be sure, but for various reasons they have more or less been
overlooked abroad, and sometimes at home as well. As compared
with the other Nordic countries, Sweden has not had a composer
who could hold his own in such distinguished company as
Finland's Sibelius, Norway's Grieg and Denmark's Nielsen.

Credit for putting Sweden on the map goes to Karl-Birger
Blomdahl, Sven-Erik Bäck and Ingvar Lidholm, radicals all three,
whose works received critical acclaim at a succession of ISCM
festivals during the 1950's. Blomdahl's production from this period
is exemplified by his symphony, "Facets", the cantata, "In the
Hall of Mirrors", and the opera, "Aniara"; Lidholm's by
"Ritornelle" and "Motus-colores", both for orchestra; and Bäck's
by the "Chamber Symphony".

This breakthrough decisively altered the status of radical music
in Sweden, both in artistic and political terms. The former rebels
now hold leading musical posts: Lidholm is professor of
composition at the Royal College of Music in Stockholm, and both
Bäck and Blomdahl are with the Swedish Broadcasting
Corporation, the former as director of its School of Music and
the latter as head of its Music Department. The Corporation,
incidentally, is far and away the most important factor in
Sweden's musical life, having spurred developments in
a progressive direction before Blomdahl put his name on the door.

In addition to the foregoing trio, whose initial efforts go back
to the immediate postwar period, the composers who dominate
the current Swedish musical scene are those who have emerged
during the last ten years. An initial source of inspiration was the
pointillism of the Darmstadt School dating from the early 'fifties.
This was followed by further development of the musical colorism
stemming from György Ligeti and other foreign composers,

electronic experiments, "chance music", musical theater and other contemporary tendencies. A broad spectrum of talent is represented here: Bo Nilsson, the enfant terrible of young Swedish music, who maintains a precarious balance in his work between extremities of softness and brutality; Bengt Hambraeus, who writes music of tropically lush tonal color and strangely floating form: he is the father of "families", that is, of compositions which can be played either together or separately; Karl-Erik Welin, an extraordinary interpreter of modern organ and piano music and a flamboyant practitioner of musical theater; Johan Werle, whose opera, "The Vision of Thérèse", was a transplantation to music of arena theater, where the performers act out their roles in the center of a circular auditorium with the audience seated on all sides of the stage, while the orchestra is spread out along the outer wall; the fanatical young purist, Jan W. Morthensen, whose tonal blocks with their endlessly slow rotation reject everything that even resembles a human gesture; and the ferocious, exuberant and destructive duo, Jan Bark and Folke Rabe.

Is it valid to speak of specifically "Swedish" music? Are there any contemporary chords of which it can be said that the likes of them cannot be heard in any other country? Perhaps the best answer would be this: the general tendencies in radical music are the same here as elsewhere; the differences come from the way they are regarded and treated. In countries with strong, buoyant traditions, the radical attitude readily tends toward aggressive rebellion. Swedish music is unusual in not having been overly weighed down by such traditions; besides, the last vestiges of conservatism were pretty well trampled under foot by the victorious 'forties.

Whatever else one may call our new generation of composers, rebels they certainly are not. Now and then someone makes a show of storming the barricades, but such antics meet with shrugs. Where is the oppression to rise up against, when oppression itself has come under those trampling feet?

Contemporary Swedish music has opted for fun rather than cantankerousness. Yet it is the sort of fun that may well open more creative vistas than commonplace revolts, negatively tied to the conventions as they are.

Ludvig Rasmusson

Born in 1936. Journalist, specializes in art and jazz.

Jazz and Pop

Swedish jazz first made an international name for itself at the
1949 Paris Festival and was long regarded by American critics
as the foremost in Europe. Young musicians like Bengt Hallberg,
Lars Gullin and Rolf Eriksson stunned the other side of the
Atlantic with their skill in a métier that Americans had thought
was exclusively theirs. Most of what they heard, however, was
brilliantly imitative rather than original.

It was with Lars Gullin, the baritone saxophonist, that Swedish
jazz acquired its own distinctive style. Gullin blended native folk
music with jazz, and in so doing set off a school of playing
that is still thriving. Incidentally, our folk music has gained
converts abroad and has been recorded in this modern guise by
(among others) two Americans, Stan Getz and Art Farmer.

Towards the end of the 'fifties a new crop of musicians, inspired
by American hard bop, broke off with the prevailing trend. The
lead was taken by Bernt Rosengren, tenor sax, and Eje Thelin,
trombone, who have since considerably developed and modernized
their style. They have toured the whole of Europe, being
particularly well known in the Eastern countries. But they haven't
made the slightest dent in the U.S., where Swedish jazz no longer
enjoys the same excellent reputation but is bracketed together
with the French and British.

None the less, Stockholm remains one of the jazz centers of
Europe. Most American and European musicians of consequence
visit Stockholm several times over, and not a few of them stay
on quite a while after their concert appearances. One of them is
the pianist, George Russel, who teaches jazz theory in the capital
and directs his own international sextet (whose members include
Rosengren and the drummer, Al Heath).

For all the many concerts in Stockholm and its magnetic
attractions for musicians from the rest of Sweden, as well as
from continental Europe and the U.S., public interest in jazz is
surprisingly small. Audiences have dwindled alarmingly in recent

years, and to keep things going the national government and the city fathers have begun to award bursaries and subsidize concerts. Nowadays modern jazz is generally accepted as a serious art form.

Swedish jazz was long dominated by Gullin's internationally celebrated generation and the young innovators typified by Rosengren. Experimental jazz along the lines of Dolphy and Coleman lived in an eclipse. Now that the experiments have finally gotten under way, the Dolphy–Coleman school has been leapfrogged and a direct plunge taken into even more extreme forms. By the middle of the 1960's the experimenters outnumbered the moderates, and all of them had gone way out. Although the Swedish jazz scene was completely under their thumb, they hadn't yet made much of a name internationally.

Jazz happenings were launched in Sweden by the pianist, Lars Werner, first in partnership with the American, Don Ellis, and later with his own combo. As often as not, Werner and his boys are lining it out in an avant-garde theater. This group and the quartet of Nils Sandström, tenor sax, are influenced by contemporary American serious music, especially the works of John Cage. Sandström's combo is the most extreme in Sweden and plays an "open jazz", where the freedom of improvisation has been carried to great lengths. The young trumpeter, Bengt Ernryd, started out with Oriental scales but now makes free use of them in a style that sounds increasingly like Western art music.

Werner, Sandström and Ernryd all draw liberally on pop sources. Indeed, avant-garde jazz circles have been much concerned with pop, and pop has been a dominant subject of the jazz debate in the past few years. Many who play experimental jazz are also capable pop musicians.

After starting out as purely commercial or amateurish, Swedish pop music has gradually built up a high standard. It has broken off from the British prototypes and acquired its own image. Around the mid-1960's several of the pop bands, among them Ola and the Janglers, Lee Kings and Science Poption, are fully comparable with the jazz bands.

Madeleine Kats

Born in 1932. All-round journalist and ballet critic.

Ballet

Ballet may be said to have begun in Sweden after the war, even though the Royal Opera has been performing ballet programs since the 18th century. Then, too, there was a time at the beginning of this century when Jean Börlin and "Svenska Baletten" amazed the world, or at least Paris. But in 1945 the dancers rubbed their eyes and found a world beyond Sleepy Hollow: a world of dance with its own criteria and ruling passions. They found it in Paris and London, made regular summer pilgrimages there, and took training from the old Russian pedagogues. The next stage, logically enough, was the discovery of Russia itself.

Since the beginning of the 'sixties, all the impulses of any consequence have been coming from the United States. Which means that Sweden—at long last—is building up a modern dance art. The free idiom which had come here by way of Germany, only to die again, left remnants in the persons of three choreographers: Birgit Cullberg, Birgit Åkesson and Iwo Cramér. Birgit Cullberg gradually went over to the classical technique; she worked more and more with the opera ballet and in the process developed some promising young talent. Birgit Åkesson embarked on a path that is peculiarly her own. Iwo Cramér turned to the direction of operettas and later musicals.

The turning point came when a young American, Walter Nicks, was invited by the Ballet Academy in Stockholm to conduct a summer course in jazz dancing. This form of the art caught on like wildfire, first among the dancers themselves, then among actors and amateurs. Audiences who had been scared off by fairy tales and point shoes came back in droves to see and hear the blues. And they were piloted by way of Katherine Dunham to Martha Graham and so on.

All of a sudden the Swedish dancing scene was galvanized. American dancers, choreographers and teachers landed on our shores, and Swedish dancers descended on America. In due course a musical like "West Side Story" could be given with an all-Swedish cast—an event that would have been unthinkable only five years ago. Young choreographers began to stage their performances in parks, museums and in playhouses on off nights. Small ensembles were formed and dissolved again depending on how the money flowed in or didn't. Dancers who had learned to spell the name of Anna Pavlova found they could also spell Martha Graham's.

Eventually, Swedish TV got around to discovering that ballet was not only photogenic but also entertaining. Birgit Cullberg reciprocated the interest and before long her creations made European viewers sit up and take notice. Here she has had great help from a producer, Arne Arnbom, who readily conceded a vital point she insisted on: namely, the use of a single stationary camera, and the dancers moving towards it and away from it (in other words, every movement in a dance is designed to be seen from the theatergoer's angle, so why have camera and dancer do a pas de deux around one another when no member of an audience is able to do so without constantly changing seats?). The result has been a series of TV ballets where the screen gives an extra dimension to the performance rather than detract from it.

Sweden still has a long way to go before she is "self-sustaining" in the dance field. Besides, this objective looks dubious at best: after all, a small country is better served by ready access to a common market of the dance. The higher the rate of interpenetration and international exchange, the more exciting the things that come our way.

For sheer practical reasons, the destiny of Swedish ballet is bound up with a few teachers and choreographers and the institutions they have created. To begin with there is the Royal Opera, which after a Rip-Van-Winkle sleep in the 1950's was aroused by Mary Skeaping and Anthony Tudor. After a few years with the Canadian choreographer, Brian Macdonald, as ballet master, the famous Danish dancer Eric Bruhn is now taking over, which might at last bring the ensemble up to an international standard. The Opera has long vacillated between classical and modern; its versions of the classics and Balanchine ballets have fallen short of the mark for lack of adequate technical polish, and the modern ballets could have been more enjoyable if purposeful training had gone into their production.

The Ballet Academy is the only major school apart from the Opera. It is headed by Lia Schubert, who came from Paris 15 years ago and was quick to appreciate that she had to handpick her teachers in the United States.

The Choreographic Institute started out to train choreographers under the leadership of Bengt Häger, a dance historian, and Birgit Åkesson. However, it has increasingly concentrated on the production of teachers.

Presumably the whole business of training dancers will be cast in a new mold, as the State has already done for the acting profession with its new dramatic schools. The system of recruiting youngsters into a school of ballet at the age of eight and keeping them in harness until they're pensioned off is old-fashioned, to say the least. A new type of training would permit greater competition, a higher degree of interchange between different types of dance, and equal opportunities for those who opt to learn the more modern forms of the art. A big step in the right direction is the new modern-dance ensemble under Birgit Cullberg at the Stockholm City Theater; this is intended to be a permanent company supported by national and local government funds.

During the 'sixties the Swedish art scene has become very much movement-minded. Happenings, puppet shows, pantomime, films, mobile sculpture and musicals all seethe with kinetic energy. But dance somehow keeps playing a lone hand. As always it is either far in advance of the other arts (and then usually without being aware of it) or hopelessly trailing behind them. Up to now, at any rate ...

Bengt Jahnsson

Born in 1928. Author and theater critic. Has made a name for himself as poet and storyteller. Notable work: the Italian-inspired novel, *Gulliver's Sixth Voyage*. As critic is especially receptive towards experimental playwriting.

Theater

At the beginning of the 1960's, "happening" was just another word in the English dictionary, but it soon became known in Sweden as a multi-art form of entertainment. The chief inspiration came from John Cage, Ann Halprin and Kenneth Dewey, who have all been in Stockholm. Dewey, as the first to arrive, also introduced the ideas of the other two in a series of guest stagings during the 1963–64 season. Although short-lived as a fad, the happening has left some significant imprints, especially on the work of three Swedish concretists: Bengt Emil Johnson, Åke Hodell and Torsten Ekbom. Their work with instrumental drama experiments at the Museum of Modern Art in Stockholm was accompanied by considerable literary successes. The resulting increase in prestige encouraged them to continue the experiments. By 1963–64 they and their supporters had succeeded in pushing the theater into the forefront of cultural debate, something quite unusual for Sweden.

The new experimental ferment enjoys a fixed locale in Stockholm's tiny Pistol Theater, launched in the late spring of 1964 by Staffan Olzon and Pi Lind. The Pistol is the only workshop theater in Scandinavia which changes its sets every fortnight and gives its stagers a completely free hand. Teams of authors, musicians and artists with surprising technical gifts have there sought to achieve the ultimate in multi-art with the help of double projections, shadow screens and stereo sound systems. Professional acting is of lesser importance since the "roles" do not lend themselves to character interpretation, and hence they can usually be performed adequately by student amateurs or even by the directors themselves. The established playhouses have caught on.

Later on the avant-gardistes of the Pistol Theater have wedded their experiments with form to an intense interest in international issues. Åke Hodell and Öyvind Fahlström have been thumping the tub for a "politically conscious" theater, intended to put the most socially retarded of our arts into fruitful relationship with the conflicts of our time. The goal is admittedly remote, but the efforts to get there shed a revealing light on the present-day theater situation in Sweden. When Ingmar Bergman assumed the business management of Dramaten in 1963, he may not have been politically motivated, but he certainly wanted to modernize the national theater. Accordingly, he hired the cream of the country's acting talent en masse and proceeded to shoot holes in the conventional repertory. During his two-year reign Dramaten went both musical and Brechtian (until then, believe it or not, Brecht had never been played there), though without turning its back on the classics. Bergman also engaged the services of some of our leading revue writers, despatched Dramaten performances on barnstorming tours throughout the country, and worked hard to build up drama classes in schools. He resigned in 1965 after the authorities refused to increase his budget of around two million dollars. Although his successor, Erland Josephson, is understood to want to pick up where Bergman left off, a more troubling question needs to be answered: Is the art of drama best served by pouring most of the public resources into a single theater? Its very organization becomes unwieldy, say the critics.

To Bergman, the theater has always been uppermost as theater, and not as an instrument for changing society; indeed, his lack of social pathos is striking. This feeling is all the stronger in Alf Sjöberg, who has manifested it in many of Dramaten's finest productions. Gombrowicz's "Yvonne" (1965) and Brecht's "Squire Puntila and His Servant Matti" (1966) were typical specimens of Sjöberg's fantastic inventiveness as director combined with strong social engagement. But in spite of Sjöberg and the winds of change, Dramaten remains a parlor theater, with lots of polish but little inner flame. Since it lacks an experimental stage, Dramaten can seldom present foreign playwrights before their names are in lights on the Continent, by which time they no longer belong to the vanguard. A far more exciting repertory is offered by the Stockholm City Theater, which has put on plays of Dario Fo, Audiberti, René de Obaldia, Kenneth Brown and David Rudkin almost at the same time as they've been discovered in their homelands. In 1964 the young Swedish director, Per Verner-Carlsson, premiered Genet's "The Screens" two years before Paris got around to it, and in a version that was more magnificent and caustic than the French. In the fall of 1964 Michael Meschke gave "King Ubu" at the Marionet Theater, which is coordinated with the City Theater. With Allan Edwall in the leading role surrounded by marionettes and loudspeaker voices, the performance drew such raves as to result in guest tours of Italy, Britain and the United States.

The rural thirst for drama is catered to by two road companies, the National Touring Theater and the Swedish Theater, both fully subsidized, which were merged into one organization in 1966. There are also eight municipal theaters in Sweden (Stockholm's City Theater being one of them) and their standard is uniformly high. One of the best is in Göteborg, with a programming policy that is nothing if not audacious.

A playwright of world stature does live in Sweden: Peter Weiss. All the stages of Europe are open to him, a privilege that is also due to the fact that he writes in German. Swedish-language dramatists are in good enough supply, but they are seldom played abroad, and even less in Sweden—strange as that may sound. None the less, the situation is improving with some determined missionary efforts, chiefly on the part of our Radio Theater, with television, Pistol and the student theaters also in the vanguard. Lars Forssell, Bengt Bratt and Sandro Key-Åberg have been the chief beneficiaries. Key-Åberg's satirical "talkies" have scored meteoric triumphs in the space of only one year, having been translated into some ten languages and already staged in six countries.

Ingemar Wizelius

Born in 1910, Licentiate of Philosophy. Literary critic for Dagens Nyheter since 1944. Also worked as foreign correspondent in Rome and Zürich from 1948 to 1956.

Literature

A Swedish man of letters who wants to make a name for himself abroad has one strike against him before he starts: a language that is spoken by only about 8,000,000 people. He can hardly hope to compete in an international market before his works are translated, which in practice means he can scarcely compete at all.

In this respect, the poet and novelist are decidedly worse off than other word craftsmen, not to mention the practitioners of other arts. Writers of film scenarios have done by far a better job of making a dent on the international scene, and it is no coincidence that a playwright should have achieved Sweden's greatest literary renown: August Strindberg (1849–1912); a dramatic genius, of course, has other than purely linguistic means to get his message across.

Be that as it may, Swedish writers stand a far better chance of attracting international attention today than they have had in a long time. The whole tenor of postwar developments is responsible for this.

During World War II the greater part of Swedish literature functioned as a war commentary, either directly or indirectly. This close identification with the unfolding of events continued for the rest of the 1940's, in response to the hardships which the war had inflicted on such a vast scale and to the oppression of mind and spirit caused by the ensuing cold war. Pathos found great favor, the key word was *angst*, and both poetry and prose contained a strong element of preaching. The formal experiments of that day were similarly motivated: in a tattered world, art also had to have a tattered guise. Realism, which had flourished in the prewar storyteller's art, was mocked in the programmatic essays of Lars Ahlin, who pleaded for a functional fiction that demanded active participation from the reader in order to achieve its fulfillment.

With the onset of the 1950's, the literary atmosphere gradually became more relaxed. A younger generation of writers argued the case for romanticism and graceful melancholy to offset what they regarded as the overly grim-faced visage of their elders. However, some time was to elapse before these "antis" could gain a wider hearing. The 'fifties came to be dominated by a number of already established authors. One of the familiar names to reappear in poetry was that of Gunnar Ekelöf, the classicist of Swedish modernism, who once again set a stylistic pattern with his innovations. In prose, new heights were again reached by such veterans as Pär Lagerkvist with "Barabbas", by Eyvind Johnson with "Days of His Grace" (one of the great novels of Swedish literature), and by Vilhelm Moberg with his cycle of novels about Swedish emigration to the United States in the 19th century: "The Emigrants", "Unto a Good Land", "The Settlers" and "The Last Letter Home". With "Aniara" (1956), Harry Martinson wrote the first major space epic; at one level it deals with a space ship which veers off its course into an eternal interstellar void, but at a more profound level it is a bleak, despairing Utopia filled with cosmically inspired poetry.

Three historical novels and a vision of the future among the dominant works: taken together, they represent the increasing remoteness from the here and now which typified the literary scene of the 1950's, even though "Aniara" indirectly mirrors the nuclear threat and the 1956 uprising in Hungary figures as a leading motif in "Days of His Grace". By long tradition, Swedish literature has otherwise contributed eagerly to the pros and cons of current public debate. By the mid-1950's, however, the material benefits of Sweden's rapidly expanding Welfare State had begun to pale on the writing profession. In consequence, the younger writers have turned in increasing numbers to international affairs, with particular reference to the problems of developing countries. For them, the contrast between the world's haves and have-nots, with all that this entails in the way of racial antagonisms and political oppression, has become a struggle with conscience. Per Wästberg and Sara Lidman have abandoned their native sources of fiction for on-the-spot portrayals of Africa and

Vietnam, which have aroused a good deal of controversy. Sven Lindqvist and Jan Myrdal have also caused an international stir with their eyewitness reports from mainland China. The man who certainly can be said to have shown them the lead is Artur Lundkvist (born in 1906), poet and left-wing polemicist, who is as indefatigable in bringing his country's attention to new foreign literature as he is in his own globe-girdling travels.

But when allowance is made for this hiatus of the previous decade, it should be said that Swedish writers are again concerning themselves with what is happening at home—and with far greater zest in the bargain. They are spearheading what might be called an "agonizing reappraisal" of our basic social values, chiefly in the light of demands for paying greater heed to the wishes of different minorities. Hence a fierce philosophical debate has flared up with Lars Gyllensten as its central figure ("Nihilist Credo", "Cain's Memoirs"). Indeed, writers of fiction play a conspicuous role in today's efforts to summarize and articulate the human condition in a thoroughly secularized society.

This debate has been paralleled by an intellectualization of poetry and a drastic shift towards more radical means of literary expression in general. For the first time every resource of the Swedish vocabulary has been pressed into service and released from the hiding places and poison cupboards of censorship. The flippant witticism is accepted with open arms in circles which were once the headquarters of straitlaced usage. The concretist poets have since gotten in on the act with their irreverent reduction of words to graphic scribbles and of imagery to puzzles whose pieces do not necessarily have to be put together—that task is left to the reader if he feels up to it.

The result is a literary situation which gives writers the maximum freedom of choice. Lines of demarcation between different art forms have become fluid: lyrics are presented as specimens of black-and-white drawing, poems are recited as dramatic monologues, and principles of musical composition are applied to versification. The tendency in prose is to suppress the direct expression of emotion, if not to remove psychological motivation altogether. This approach has been followed with ironclad consistency by Per Olof Sundman ("The Expedition"), whose attitude to reality makes him closely akin in spirit to the new

French novelists. It is also detectable in Sven Fagerberg with his sophisticated analyses of today's consumption-oriented society ("The Fancy Dress Ball"), as well as in many younger writers. On the other hand, the more traditional vein has been successfully exploited by Birgitta Trotzig, whose psychological story-telling technique is informed by her Roman Catholic faith.

In spite of the chains which always fetter a minor language, modern Swedish literature is in livelier touch with foreign currents than ever before. The isolation of a former day has been replaced by a growing international exchange, spurred by the European community of values which has begun to take shape in the wake of relaxed political tensions.

Katja Waldén

Born in 1926, Master of Arts. Journalist specializing in the arts and crafts. Has worked for the Museum of Modern Art in Stockholm.

The Swedish Design for Living

"Swedish Grace", "Swedish Modern" and "Modern Scandinavian" are different slogans applied to Swedish styles of interior design during the past forty years. The first of these was coined with tongue in cheek by a British critic to describe the combination of native craftsmanship and eclectic pastiche which, incidentally, Sweden was not the only country to exhibit at the Paris Exhibition of 1925. "Swedish Modern" referred to the light-colored, comfortable and unpretentious interior settings as typically shown at the New York World's Fair in 1939. And "Modern Scandinavian" (or "Formes Scandinaves") has often served as a common label for Sweden and the other Scandinavian countries in postwar exhibitions of handcrafted and manufactured products.

How would Swedes define a "Swedish style" if asked to do so? Well, we might say that it represents an ideal of great simplicity, verging almost on the homely, yet possessing a quiet distinction. This was certainly the style which prevailed during those periods of our history which we regard as the most originally Swedish: the massive Vasa fortresses; the well-proportioned manors and country estates of the 18th century, with their beautiful, sparsely appointed interiors; Swedish 18th century silver; and the naive, color-sparkling peasant textiles and tapestries of the 19th century. All these artifacts speak a language of simplicity, dignity and moderation—and at times of becoming modesty, too. These very same qualities, moreover, can be found in present-day Swedish design at its best.

However, the descriptions have rendered good service because they are simple and to the point. But in the form of slogans they inevitably leave out essentials and are insufficiently concrete. What is chiefly missing is the social aspect, which has long motivated Swedish design. Besides, the word "style" is somewhat

247

*Horse of earthenware by
Bertil Vallien, also known
as a glass designer.
Photo : Stig T. Karlsson.*

of a misnomer; it would be more accurate to speak of Swedish interior design as a way of experiencing and comprehending the environment: a democratic means of expression, as it were. If one chooses, two apter slogans could be added to the list: "Sweden the Middle Way" and "The People's Home", both in reference to a democratic ideal that is also reflected in the environment.

But let us take a look inside a home in the People's Home. The Swedish counterpart of John Doe, Herr Svenson, is married, has two children, and lives in a city, where he probably rents a high-rise apartment. If he were free to choose, he would much prefer a home of his own. But apartment houses are cheaper, the high rises especially so. And in our day of rapidly increasing urbanization, apartment houses do a better job of accommodating more people on a given land area.

The Svensons presumably had to wait in a housing queue to get their apartment; there are more than 100,000 on the waiting list in Stockholm alone. However, the housing shortage is more apparent than real. Many of the queuers already have leases, but they'd like to trade up to something more commodious. And there is the rub. As recently as 25 years ago, the most common type of dwelling consisted of one room and kitchen; many families

Assembly-line furniture for children in lacquered birch plywood, by Stig Lönngren. Prototypes for industrial manufacture, built by Lars Larsson. Photo: Sune Sundahl.

with children, in other words, were cramped for space. As of 1966 the average family enjoyed more elbow room in a flat of three rooms plus kitchen (totalling about 710 square feet), and four rooms plus kitchen is expected to become standard in the 1970's. So overcrowding is on the way out. In addition, the separate housing needs of the old and young must be catered for.

Attention is also paid to the public environment. Architects are trying, with varying degrees of success, to inject life into the hearts of dormitory towns with local stores, churches, cinemas, libraries and communal facilities of one kind or another. Planners are striving to make our urban culture more child-centered. Countless livability studies have been carried out to determine the housing and environment that will best serve the needs of tomorrow.

Sweating out the queue has its rewards for the Svensons, for the built-in amenities of their dwelling are pretty high by European standards: an electric range, a refrigerator, a sink and

Vases designed by Gunnar Cyrén of Orrefors. Photo: Johan Selbing.

work counter of stainless steel, ample storage space in the kitchen, and a bathroom (still rather Spartanly appointed, we admit). In addition, their house may have a laundry and drying room which serves all the tenants. For these creature comforts the Svensons will have to pay up to one-third of their income after tax.

On the other hand they enjoy one big advantage. When they marry, when they later move to larger quarters to accommodate the growing family, and when they eventually retire and perhaps want to change their design for living once again, they have access to a market which offers a rich selection of furniture and other furnishings, available at moderate prices and of good quality and design.

That may not sound very remarkable, yet it deserves to be considered a minor democratic miracle. A bit of sketched-in background will explain why. When industrialization came to Sweden, it generated a grotesque confusion of styles as the crafted wares of home and artisan's workshop were pushed out by cheap, mass-produced articles. Although all industrial countries have had this experience, they have not always been quick to react. The reaction in Sweden may be said to date from 1845 with the formation of *Svenska Slöjdföreningen* (Swedish Society of Arts and Crafts, now the Society of Industrial Design). Its purpose was to preserve the Scandinavian tradition of sloyd and handcrafts. Other associations dedicated to similar ends were formed towards the end of the 19th century: homecraft societies in the different provinces, Friends of Textile Art, Licium, which specializes in religious art, etc.

Stimulated by the German Werkbund, the Morris movement in England, and the national romanticism of the day, artists, writers and intellectual leaders thumped the tub enthusiastically for improved patterns and textures in furniture and handwork. Although national traditions were upheld, the emergence of Jugendstil or art nouveau was also looked to for inspiration. The arts and crafts exhibitions in Stockholm in 1897 and 1909 gave magnificent play to the new outburst of patriotic styling.

Even then a social and ethical program was clearly expressed alongside the esthetic. The "workers" got in on the act early, though it must be admitted that they were somewhat idealized.

There were special designs called "worker furniture" and "worker porcelain".

Around the turn of the century two distinguished artists, Alf Wallander and Gunnar Wennerberg, joined the country's two largest porcelain factories, Rörstrand and Gustavsberg. They designed Jugendstil-inspired tableware with elaborate flower patterns, as well as objets d'art of glass and ceramics. At the same time two remarkable architects, Ferdinand Boberg and Carl Westman, also drew on Jugend sources in making furniture for the interiors of the buildings they constructed. This combination of industrial design and free expression proved to be a legacy with many heirs.

In textiles such talented women as Märta Måås-Fjetterström, Selma Giöbel and Maja Sjöström achieved a rebirth by the judicious use of traditional patterns. Well-known artists drew originals for tapestries and other weaves.

The next major expo, the Baltic Exhibition in Malmö in 1914, gave evidence of stagnation if not of actual decline in interior design. Slöjdföreningen led the attack under its energetic young secretary, Erik Wettergren, and the social program was reawakened. The clarion call against deteriorating taste and quality was sounded again under the mottoes, "More beautiful things for everyday life" and "Artists in industry". In 1917 a home exhibition was opened at the Liljevalchs Gallery; among other things, it displayed a "worker dwelling" with specially designed furniture: simple, sparsely ornamented, but with noble proportions, well-crafted and of good quality.

Beginning in 1917, Slöjdföreningen acted as an employment service on behalf of artists under the direction of Elsa Gullberg, the textile designer. Among those it placed in industry were Simon Gate and Edward Hald, who joined the Orrefors glassworks; Wilhelm Kåge, engaged by Gustavsberg; and Arthur Percy, who went into Upsala-Ekeby, also a porcelain factory. Their jobs were clearly spelled out: to design attractive utilitarian ware that could be mass-produced at low prices.

In spite of these successful initiatives, the ensuing decade of the 'twenties was not marked by any radical change of attitude or a broadening of the socio-ethical program. Instead, the designers turned to older periods, with a penchant for Sweden's age of stylistic greatness in the 18th century, when native and foreign impulses formed an unusually happy marriage in moderate, beautifully proportioned room settings.

Around 1920 the arts and crafts were given a focal point for their endeavors with the interior decoration of Stockholm's City Hall, designed by Ragnar Östberg and considered one of the finest specimens of modern public architecture. "Swedish Grace" came into being in the shadow of this project. Carl Malmsten, who designed the City Hall furniture, drew on 18th century Sweden and its refined manor-house milieus for his finely handcrafted pieces. The building's textiles were created by Maja Sjöström. These two, together with Märta Måås-Fjetterström in textiles and Simon Gate and Edward Hald in glass, were the principal representatives of "Swedish Grace", in which capacity they scored one triumph after the other at domestic and foreign exhibitions during the 1920's.

Swedish silver had also enjoyed a heyday in the 18th century, and it was revived by Jacob Ängman in his form-expressive flatware, vases and goblets. The same lucidly defined classicism was cultivated by Erik Fleming at Atelier Borgila. Wiven Nilsson at Lund, on the other hand, could be regarded as a harbinger of functionalism with his severely geometric and compact shapes, inspired both by medieval silversmithing and modern cubism.

The death-knell of brittle, decorative "Swedish Grace" was sounded by the Stockholm Exhibition of 1930. Function was now put in the catbird seat. The exhibition's motto was "accept". Accept what? Well, the new functional style that had already swept over Europe. Functionalism lacked roots in Swedish tradition and many people found its unabashed straightness of line hard to swallow. Even so, the exhibition acquired great importance as a catharsis and galvanizer. It encouraged new experiments in ceramics and new approaches to furniture design. Towards the middle of the 1930's G. A. Berg and Bruno Mathsson drew on posture studies for their designs of chairs and sofas, which still remain hard to beat for comfort. These pieces also served to remind us that ours is a country of wood. Furniture makers now began their successful challenge of foreign woods with home-grown birch, elm, ash, pine, oak and beech. Sweden's "blonde" furniture style became an international fact.

However, functionalism did not last long in unadulterated form. A new soft and ornate style took over, as evidenced by Swedish displays at the world fairs in Paris and New York of 1937 and 1939. Flowered patterns enjoyed a field day in the home-furnishing textiles designed by Austrian-born Josef Frank and in the ornamental fabrics of Lisbeth and Gocken Jobs and Stig Lindberg. The firm of Svenskt Tenn, led by Estrid Eriksson with Josef Frank as art director, introduced a comfortable, modern Continental interior style which won wide admiration.

Background to Postwar Developments

The long continuity of Swedish creativeness in the arts and crafts was momentarily halted by World War II, entailing as it did a cutting-off from outside sources of ideas and inspiration. With the arts of interior decoration now entirely in Swedish hands, there was danger that Swedish design might bog down in the overly precious and affected.

Even so, the main trends from 1917 and 1930, with their emphasis on social and functional considerations respectively, were further developed. When Slöjdföreningen (now called the Swedish Society for Industrial Design) celebrated its 100th anniversary in 1945, it pointed up the results of the housing studies which had been made in the 'thirties. The Society's two exhibitions portrayed a future in bright colors, where everyone would live in a commodious dwelling filled with fine furniture.

The winds of international influences and impulses blew fresh again when the borders were reopened in 1945. No time was lost in resuming the familiar activity of taking part in foreign exhibitions. The Scandinavian countries displayed specimens of their arts and crafts at the Triennale in Milan, and two mobile exhibitions, "Design in Scandinavia" and "Formes Scandinaves", were despatched on tours of the United States and Europe.

H55, the name given to the exhibition held at Hälsingborg in 1955, was a recapitulation of the experiences gained during the first ten hectic years of the postwar period. The exhibition was at the same time an exercise in soul-searching. "Man at the Center of Things" became the slogan of the decade. At long last, H55 seemed to say, the hopes of the 1930's have been realized; the "more beautiful things for everyday life" were now within reach of the common man.

Furniture

The ideas behind and impressions from the open-plan, brightly colored interiors shown at the New York World's Fair in 1939–40 persisted into the postwar period. A freer style of furnishing replaced the former obsession of laying out whole living rooms with matched pieces. The home was no longer regarded as static, but as something that could grow and change with its inhabitants. Television did its bit to turn accustomed ideas of interior decoration upside down. Sitting furniture was turned towards the screen and arranged like the rows in a cinema. Sofas and fauteuils were supplemented with stray chairs, footstools, hassocks, pillows on the floor and small tables. A piece of old furniture or an antique will often relieve the modern accent, and indeed enhance its flavor. The surrounding emphasis is on light, undecorated wallpaper and curtains which admit the sunshine that is so precious a commodity in these northern latitudes. It is left to the textiles, paintings and numerous flowers to give color and warmth to the interior.

Consumers are supplied with disinterested facts from various sources: from interior-decoration studies sponsored by Slöjdföreningen, from government-financed research into materials and quality, from informative labelling on merchandise, from regular courses of instruction on interior decoration, and so on. Standards have been drawn up to define the optimum dimensions of chairs, tables, cabinets and other furnishings, and these standards are increasingly used by manufacturers.

It has also dawned on the producers that the very young and the very old have their own furniture needs. The furniture market offers several excellent series, including sturdy chairs of special height, designed to offset the old-age handicaps of aching backs and faltering movements. Children are catered for with playful, curve-edged furniture constructed to scale and capable of taking severe punishment. Not even toys have been immune: boats, trains, swings, tents and games have been revamped by young designers who have evidently tackled their tasks with great relish.

The 800 firms which comprise the Swedish furniture industry are mostly clustered in the southern provinces of Småland and Skåne. They have been exposed to keen competition in recent years and the importation of cheap furniture, especially from eastern countries, has been particularly hard on the small firms. The industry is now trying to consolidate itself by a greater measure of specialization and the implementation of cost-reduction programs. Several firms have formed common marketing organizations for their mutual support, while others present their furniture series in common showrooms.

Another innovation at the selling end is highway retailing. Large sales warehouses have been established on the outskirts of cities. These furniture supermarkets contain just about everything to be had. The overwhelming emphasis is on modern furniture, but space is also given over to newly-made period furniture and to provincial wooden pieces in freshened-up romantic style.

A few of the early pioneers are still active. Carl Malmsten, the grand old man of Swedish furniture design, keeps extending his vistas of the handcrafted art. Of late he has also gone in for semi-industrial production, which bears the same identifying hallmarks of his unique pieces: painstaking attention to detail, grace and restraint. Several of his pupils have carried on in the master's tradition with pleasing and well-proportioned designs. Bruno Mathsson, with his own showroom at Värnamo, has just about exhausted all the ways in which people can sit. Like the Finnish architect, Alvar Aalto, he makes use of molded bent wood, but his forms are softer, thinner and more elegant. His latest creation—in partnership with the Dane, Piet Hein—is the versatile, super-elliptical table, equipped with the revolutionary pre-tensioned leg.

Some of the pace-setting Swedish designers—Carl-Axel Acking, Alf Svensson and K. E. Ekselius—represent a solid, tasteful and handsomely dimensioned style of furniture which one would very much like to call typically Swedish. Other designers, such as John Kandell, Björn Hultén, Börge Lindau and Bo Lindekrantz, specialize in leather pieces mounted on steel or wooden frames which bespeak an orthodox functionalism.

Modular systems have been adopted by Yngve Ekström and Sven Kai-Larsen, among others, for furniture that is meant to serve not only the home, but also schools, hospitals and other public buildings. Their pieces may be combined in any of innumerable variations, are easy to move and stack, and set great store by quality and choice of materials.

Parallel with this quality output, the market has always offered simple and inexpensive pine furniture in forms that have adorned Swedish homes for centuries: open-backed chairs, drop-leaf tables, rustic cabinets and benches. They make very useful fill-ins, not least for the summer houses and bungalows where many Swedes spend their leisure time.

Swedish furniture is not quite as radical as the Finnish, nor does it boast the same fine workmanship and bold originality of the Danish. It is easy to trace influences of the interior-decoration tastes prevalent in Denmark, Italy and the United States. The merits of Swedish furniture derive from other aspects: from consistency, high quality, and the reasonable prices made possible by mass production.

The Artist in Industry

The years which have passed since the end of World War II have witnessed a considerable broadening of the cooperation between artists and industries. In addition to the purely industrial designers, whose output bears no distinctively national character (and accordingly falls outside the scope of this report), artistic advisors and designers are now attached to porcelain factories, glassworks and many textile and furniture factories.

Present-day Swedish design is also enriched by an impressive array of artists who create unique, individual works, though they may at the same time be working under contracts with factories. Craftsmen in the decorative arts are more and more emboldened to push the limits of their domains, and in so doing inevitably poach on the artists' preserves. Most of the raids emanate from *Konstfackskolan*, the Swedish State School of Arts, Crafts and Design in Stockholm. This institution is supposed to train designers for industry, but many of its teachers—among them textile designer Edna Martin, ceramist Stig Lindberg and silversmith Sven-Arne Gillberg—also consider it part of their job to bring out whatever talents their pupils may have for independent creation. As a result, not a few of the graduates dream of their

own studio or weaving loom in preference to the more circum-
scribed work of designing for mass production. This is a trend
for good and ill in a society whose industries will have a tough
row to hoe against foreign competition for some time to come.

In 1964 Slöjdföreningen opened its exhibition, "Form Fantasi",
at the Liljevalchs Gallery in Stockholm. It had three objectives:
first, to define "decorative arts", a term that had been suffering
from inflation; second, to present good prototypes for use by
manufacturers; third, and most important, to enumerate the many
facets of the decorative arts and to underline the esthetic
experiences these arts can give. More than 300 craftsmen from
all over the country responded to Slöjdföreningen's call by sending
in 4,000 objects for display.

Textiles

A new freedom was in the making, and perhaps its most
convincing manifestation was in textiles. Swedish textile art had
long been dominated by the overshadowing figure of Märta
Måås-Fjetterström (1873–1941). Her workshop at Båstad
produces rugs, carpets and hand-woven cloths. Since her death
it has been under the direction of Barbro Nilsson (capably
assisted by Marianne Richter, Barbro Sprinchorn and others, who
each developed their individual styles).

At the same time, local handicraft societies preserved the old
traditions and created new patterns. Local specialities were
cultivated and new initiatives were taken; an example is the
knitwear line of jumpers and sweaters emanating from Bohus
Province.

Ever since the 1920's, moreover, there has existed a tradition of
creating for industry, and many of the country's finest talents
have been engaged in this work. Alice Lund, Sofia Widén, Astrid
Sampe and Edna Martin—to name just a few—have drawn clearly
defined, firmly composed textile patterns in well-matched colors,
and with a firm grasp of structure. In the 1950's a notable
initiative was taken by Göta Trägårdh when she invited a handful
of our best abstract painters to design patterns. A very vital
stimulus has come from the Finnish-born textile designer, Viola
Gråsten, who is particularly noted for her color-riotous pile rugs
and her imaginative curtains and upholsteries.

Sven Kauppi and Kaisa Melanton are two of the artists who have carried textile-making in the direction of even greater freedom and abstractness. A younger generation carries on, with an uninhibited approach which broke out in full bloom at "Form Fantasi", and subsequent exhibitions have confirmed more of the same. Whole fairy tales are narrated in glowing colors of silk, velvet and silver. Free play is given to light between the shifting structures of a fabric; gold, silver and all the colors of the rainbow are employed to create a surface of living beauty. Hieroglyphs wander over a field of dry desert tones, and pieces of cloth are mounted like waving banners. These youngsters seem to recognize no limitations, and perhaps the best way to describe their work is to call it textile painting.

Ceramics

A similar emancipation is on its way in ceramics, an industry which has long been tolerant of innovations. In Sweden, the ceramics industry is largely represented by five medium-sized companies, which compete sufficiently with one another to offer consumers a wide range of everyday articles. All the porcelain factories have studios where artists work not only to production requirements but also enjoy considerable freedom in performing ceramic experiments.

In keeping with the greater emphasis on function, manufacturers are no longer as concerned as in the past to regard tableware as indivisible sets. Instead, they produce tableware pieces as sundries which can be bought individually and combined as the consumer sees fit. Many vessels have assumed different shapes in recognition of new functions, and much of what used to be china's exclusive province has been taken over by plastics. Vessels are often made to serve the twofold purpose of storage and heating, and flameware has come into widespread use.

Stig Lindberg, who succeeded Wilhelm Kåge as art director of the Gustavsberg porcelain factory in 1949, is a man of versatile gifts with a particular penchant for the decorative.

Also employed at Gustavsberg is Karin Björquist, who may be said to represent the other end of the creative spectrum. Originally a pupil of Edgar Böckman, a ceramist of classical austerity and purity, she shows a quiet seriousness and tenderness in her treatment of material, whether it relate to utilitarian ware, unique stoneware or monumental decor in a public setting.

At the Rörstrand factory, where the Danish-influenced Gunnar Nylund (also known as an outstanding animal sculptor) was hired as artistic advisor in 1931, and at the Upsala-Ekeby Group, where Arthur Percy drew for inspiration on the colorful glazed pottery of 18th century Sweden, a long string of good designers stand security for refined, decorative design. Hertha Bengtsson and Marianne Westman have produced excellent sets of tableware, while Carl-Harry Stålhane has analyzed the utensil problems of restaurants and come up with new solutions. Stålhane has also produced abstract art.

Important ceramists also work outside the factories. Ingrid and Erich Triller administer a Chinese legacy with their nobly shaped vases and bowls. Tyra Lundgren, a woman of versatile talents, does masterful representations of animals, especially birds, in her stoneware sculptures.

Many ceramists work in Skåne, a province blessed by nature with fine clays. Signe Persson-Melin turns out household articles, rustic and sophisticated at the same time, and Henning Nilsson has successfully brought off difficult experiments with the oxblood technique. John Andersson has proved that the old potter's art can still pay dividends with his series of tableware known as "Old Höganäs".

Perhaps the most interesting of the ceramic experimenters is Hertha Hillfon, whose work has been described as "a bit of coral, a cathedral in ruins, a Gothic tracery, and a swarm of birds". Anders Liljefors, who used to concern himself exclusively with household ware, has discovered a new method of casting ceramics in a sand mold, and is now working feverishly to extract new and unexpected effects from this material. Many of the very youngest ceramists have been fascinated by the other aspects of the raw material they work with: its ability to be baked, kneaded, shaped, clipped, cut, rolled, and so on. Alternating between surrealistically fluid patterns and glazes on the one hand and gay neo-baroque with swelling forms and the skillful use of glazes on the other, they are creating objects almost completely divested of utilitarian aspects—expressions rather than wares.

Glass

In foreign eyes Swedish glass was long synonymous with the clear and sparkling crystal of Orrefors, especially as wrought by Simon Gate and Edward Hald in their superb pieces. The traditions of this famous glassworks were carried on in the 1930's and 1940's by Sven Palmqvist and Edvin Öhrström in particular, and in recent years Ingeborg Lundin has attracted attention with her clean-lined, abstractly ornamented fancy glass. Young Gunnar Cyrén has launched Orrefors' first "pop" glass in color.

However, the need for a higher artistic standard of production was also recognized long ago by other Swedish glassworks, which like Orrefors are also mostly located in Småland Province and are likewise the bearers of traditions which are just as old, if not actually older. At Kosta, Gunnar Wennerberg was already producing the first modern glassware at the turn of the century. Edvin Ollers, who became Kosta's art director in 1917, specialized in blue and green glass, and during the 1930's the company's reputation was further enhanced by Elis Bergh with his crystal-ground glass. More recently, the facetted color cubes of Mona Morales-Schildt have won great popularity. The virtuosity of Vicke Lindstrand is documented both in household glassware and in imaginative objects d'art.

Perhaps in protest against the excessively virtuosic, ornamental and beautiful in Swedish glassmaking, the new generation of artists has adopted a more irreverent approach, given over to exuberance and free bursts of fantasy, and drawing not a little of its inspiration from rustic folk life. Its leading exponent is Erik Höglund at the Boda glassworks, a man of many gifts who, in addition to glass, has devoted himself to smithwork, furniture design and wooden reliefs. His seals, medallions and glass-tapered candelabra are forcefully done with a somewhat slipshod charm and in a vigorous style that is almost baroque.

The art nouveau style, currently fashionable the world over, has found successful expression in the vases and household glass of Christer Sjögren, which alternate soft, sweeping lines with fluted forms suggestive of cubism, and in the production of the designer couple, Ann and Göran Wärff. That glass readily lends itself to architectural treatment is also shown by Lars Hellsten in his decorative compositions, which are built up with a sure hand.

Silver

During the postwar period Swedish silversmithing has acquired increased breadth, with a handful of smiths showing particularly great force as creators.

Sigurd Persson has brought a strong sense of function to his craft, which represents the mature fruits of his versatile experience of design (embracing objects as diverse as flatware, plastic trays, coffee pots, brushes and furniture). His work is marked by a high degree of purity and a well-disciplined imagination. His jewelry, though amazingly simple in design, is shaped with the wearing woman's personality in mind.

Torun Bülow-Hübe goes many steps farther in liberation and individuality. Her jewelry, watches, bowls and flatware admittedly serve a utilitarian purpose, but it is the esthetic effect as manifested in form and play of lines which interests her most. Her unconventional, at times almost shocking creations, are a kind of freehand sculpture, proving that even a material as heavy-laden with traditions as silver can be revitalized.

In 1965 the National Museum held an exhibition featuring the work of young silversmiths. Of the fifty or so who displayed their wares, only a few revealed the influence of surrealism which now predominates in European jewelry; the majority embraced the simplicity and purity of line traditionally associated with Swedish silver. One of the exhibitors, Theresia Hvorslev, has been influenced by Danish silversmithing with its softer forms and advanced technical skill. Others, such as the "chain masters" in Göteborg, Anders and Sven-Erik Högberg, relate to medieval tradition in their pendants.

In common with the other decorative arts, silversmithing is in the process of shattering its traditional bonds, and further developments promise to be even more exciting.

Anders Rapp

Born in 1927. Docent of physical geography at Uppsala University.
Visiting professor at Pennsylvania State University in the spring of
1965. Has published some 20 scientific works, particularly on problems
of frozen ground in Scandinavia, Spitsbergen and other northern areas.

Lapland–The Northern Wilderness of Sweden

The Kebnekaise mountain range includes the highest peak in Sweden, with an elevation of 6,960 feet. Photo : Gustav Hansson.

Sweden has been called the "land of space". This is particularly true of the northern region, Lapland, with its abundance of mountains, forests, lakes, rivers and mires. Many of the tourists come from the south to see the Midnight Sun and enjoy the bright summer nights of the north. Others are attracted by the wilderness and by the prospect of hiking for days in the mountains or traveling by car in the forest lands without seeing many people.

The wilderness of Lapland is characterized by a very low population density of less than one person per square kilometer in an area more than 600 km (370 miles), long and 250 km (160 miles) wide totalling 118,000 square km (46,000 square miles). This is about one-fourth the area of Sweden and roughly the size of England. Out of a total population of 120,000 in Lapland, about 70,000 people live in the three centers of Kiruna, Gällivare and Lycksele.

For all the vastness of these mountain and forest areas extending to the Norwegian border in the northwest and the Finnish border in the northeast, they have the advantage of being accessible. Even though the northern tip of Sweden reaches north of latitude 69° N, which runs parallel to the middle of Greenland, northern Alaska and northern Siberia, it is much nearer and easier to get to than other subarctic areas, especially for a traveler by train or car from the population centers of central or western Europe. During the peak of the tourist season in July, a hiker on the popular four-day track across the mountains from Abisko to Kebnekaise may fail to satisfy his cravings for solitude if he has to share accommodation with twenty or thirty other hikers in one of the huts along the way. But that is a local and

A panoramic view of Kiruna, Sweden's northernmost city and the world's largest in area. Its origins date back to the turn of the century. Mining, which was opencut right up to the 1960's, now takes place underground. Probably the largest single deposit of iron ore anywhere is concentrated in Kiruna's "iron mountain". Photo: Börje Rönnberg.

temporary exception. If he wants to be by himself he needs merely take off from the main track into a side valley, where he is likely to find a tourist hut with perhaps only thirty names entered in the guest book during the previous year.

The map indicates two entirely different parts of Lapland: the mountain range in the west and the forest lands in the east. These two parts are very different in topography, geology and vegetation, but they are both vast areas of wilderness. The eastern front of the mountain range is very marked and abrupt. After one travels for miles and miles across the eastern high plains or hilly land with forests, swamps and lakes, the mountains are suddenly there, with steep east-facing slopes or cliffs, protruding like bastions between valleys with beautiful lakes. The rapid change

of scenery is about the same for the traveler on a train from Kiruna towards the mountains or in a car on the newly built roads to Stora Sjöfallet, Kvikkjokk or Tärnaby.

Geologically, the mountain range is built of schists, limestones, amphibolites and other sedimentary and metamorphic rocks, which were once deposited as sediments on the sea floor during the Cambro-Silurian periods. The range was folded more than 300 million years ago. Thick sheets of rock were thrust eastwards over the Archean basement of mainly granites and gneisses. This process was part of the worldwide Caledonian folding. It was duplicated in the mountains of Scotland, western Spitsbergen, and parts of the Appalachians in America.

The land was then subjected to the sculpturing process of

nature. Weathering, river erosion and glacial scouring have created the present-day landscape of valleys and mountains in the west, and the vast, forested high plains or hilly land of the Archean gneisses and granites in eastern, pre-montane Lapland.

The latest of the great dramatic events which created the landscape was a series of glaciations during the last million years. Actually, the mountains of Lapland were the core region of Scandinavian glaciations. The first growth of continental glaciers started up here from local glaciers in valleys and cirques, in a situation similar to that of today. Gradually, the expanding ice sheets covered the entire Scandinavian peninsula and reached as far south as northern Germany and Poland. The last glaciation ended not more than 8,000 years ago, when the remnants of the big ice sheet melted in the mountains of Lapland. The glaciation and the melting ice created the topography which is predominant in today's landscape, both in the mountains and forest lands.

One effect of glacial erosion in the main valleys has been the series of beautiful lakes which occupy the valley floors in the eastern part of the mountains and reach out into the forest region: Lake Torneträsk, Stora Lulevatten, Hornavan, Storuman and many others. They are similar to the fjords of Norway's west coast. Like these they were over-deepened by erosion of the main glaciers flowing from the mountains, but here the lakes are less deep than the fjords. Another effect of glaciation was to widen the mountain valleys into broad, flat-bottomed troughs, like the "glens" of Scotland. The troughs break through the mountain range like broad gateways, ideal for the cross-country hiker and for the migrating reindeer herds.

Although the existing glaciers in Lapland are not as large as the biggest plateau glaciers in Norway, the Swedish mountains still have no less than 290 glaciers. Together they cover more than 300 square km (116 square miles), mostly in the highest massifs such as Sarek and Kebnekaise, where several summits are more than 2,000 meters above sea level.

Sarek and Padjelanta are the two largest national parks in Europe. Sarek covers 1,900 square km (734 square miles) of high mountains and was established in 1910. Padjelanta national park dates from 1962 and covers 2,000 square km (772 square miles) of undulating uplands west of Sarek. In recent years there has been much discussion in Sweden about the best way of utilizing the national parks: either build roads through them for a large invasion of tourists, or keep them as remote, untouched wilderness which can be reached only by trained hikers after trips of several days. The solution adopted has been to cater for both schools of thought. Some national parks, like Sarek, are to be kept as inaccessible wilderness areas, where the hikers have to sleep in their own tents in the hunting grounds of bear, wolf, lynx or wolverine. Other national parks in Lapland are meant to be visited by many thousands of tourists every summer; examples are Stora Sjöfallet, which can be reached by boat and car, and Abisko, which is crossed by the railway from Kiruna to Narvik.

In spite of the fact that Lapland is situated as far north as the cold northern tundra lands of Alaska or the ice sheet of Greenland, the climate is relatively mild, due to the modifying influence of westerly winds from the nearby Atlantic Ocean and warm Gulf Stream. The western mountain slopes receive more rain and snow than the forest lands to the east, which lie in a precipitation shadow. The weather station at Riksgränsen, near the international border and on the railway from Kiruna to Narvik, has the highest precipitation record in Sweden, about 1,000 millimeters per year. The country's lowest precipitation, 300 mm, is recorded at Abisko, only about 30 km (18 miles) southeast of Riksgränsen but east of the main mountain ridge. This difference also means that the western mountain areas have a snow cover which is thicker than in eastern Lapland. On an average the snow cover at Riksgränsen stays from early October to early June.

Mean Air Temperatures and Duration of Snow Cover in Three Lapland Weather Stations. Temperatures in Centigrade, 1901 to 1930. Snow Cover, Average Data for 1920 to 1940.

| Station | Mean air temperature | | Snow cover, duration |
	January	July	
Riksgränsen	− 9.7°	+10.6°	October 24–June 5
Kiruna	−11.9°	+12.0°	October 24–May 19
Tärnaby	−10.6°	+12.4°	October 27–June 2

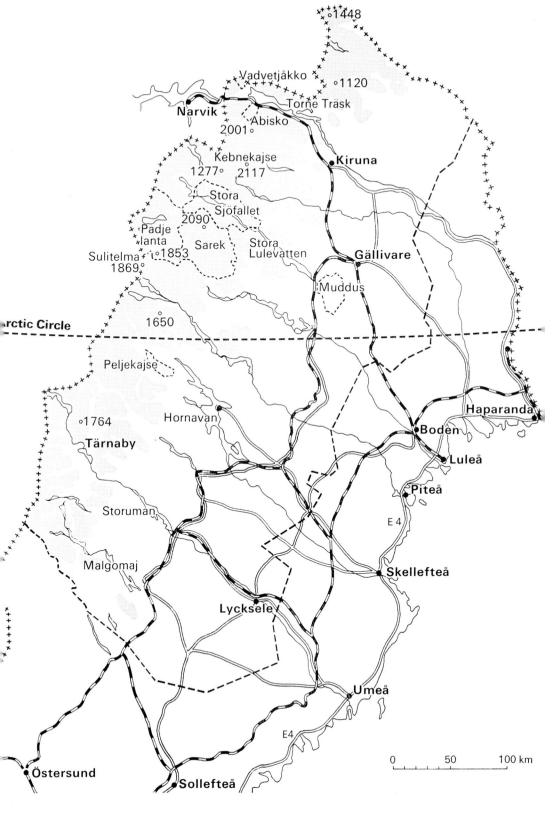

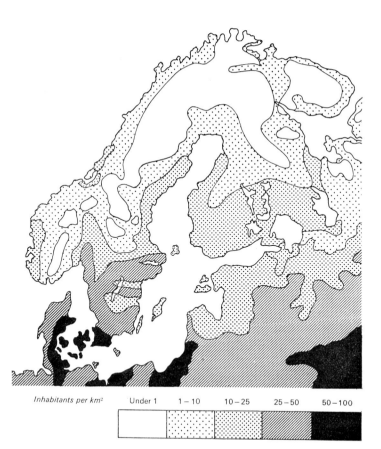

Inhabitants per km² | Under 1 | 1 – 10 | 10 – 25 | 25 – 50 | 50 – 100

Map of population density in northern Europe. Eastern Denmark, like central and southern Europe, has more than 50 inhabitants per square km (125 per square mile). Lapland has less than one inhabitant per square km.

Map of northern Sweden. The light gray marks the mountain range in western Lapland.

In the mountains above timberline, which runs at 500 to 700 meters above sea level, some spells of frost may occur at any time of the summer, but at lower elevations the period from late June to early August is frost-free. Generally the autumn colors begin appearing on the alpine heaths by the end of August and in the upper forests in early September. Many consider September to be the most beautiful time in Lapland, with clear cool air, good visibility and brilliant red and yellow colors in the forests of mountain birch and on the alpine heaths, as well as in the eastern forest-and-mire country.

The winters are colder in the forest lands than in the mountains, and in low sites temperatures of −20 to −30°C are not unusual. Northern Lapland has polar night for four to six weeks during winter, with the sun constantly below the horizon, but by

February there is enough daylight for the tourist hotels to open their skiing season.

The short and intense spring is the most dramatic time of year in these latitudes. In May or early June the snow cover can disappear in a week or two, ice breaks up and flooding occurs on rivers and mountain brooks. The sun shines 24 hours a day and thousands of reindeer migrate from the valleys to upland pastures.

Bird life is particularly rich in delta lands and on the thousands of lakes and swamps in the forest zone. Two famous areas in this respect are Muddus national park and the bird reserve of Sjaunja. Muddus, south of Gällivare, is the only national park in Lapland outside the mountains. It was chosen as a reserve because it has 300 square km (116 square miles) of almost untouched northern coniferous forest. There are also about 200 square km (77 square miles) of mires in Muddus and still more to the northwest in the Sjaunja area, the largest mire complex in Sweden.

In early July these tracts as well as most of Lapland have an abundance not only of birds but also mosquitoes, which were a real plague to earlier visitors. However, there is no longer any reason to fear the attacks of these bloodthirsty insects as modern repellents offer quite effective protection against them.

Lapland is the land of the Lapps. At present about 3,000 Lapps are actively engaged in reindeer breeding in Sweden, while about 10,000 can be classed as Lapps ethnically. Most of them reside in service-center communities and work in subsidiary occupations, such as forestry, road or railway maintenance, and mining. Nor are the reindeer-breeding minority nomadic to the same extent as in the past. Often only a small number of reindeer herders and their dogs follow the herd from winter grounds in the forests to summer pastures in the mountains. But a few Lapp families still move from the winter village to a summer camp in the mountains, usually near one of the large lakes. These lakes teem with fish: trout, char and other species, and fishing is an important source of income in such cases. The fresh fish is flown by hydroplanes several times a week from the scattered summer camps to a freezing plant on the coast or to the cities further south. Today's Lapps are also skillful users of such modern technical tools as aircraft, radio transmitters and snow weasels, which help to make the ancient arts of reindeer breeding and fishing profitable undertakings even in our time.

The natural resources which have opened up Lapland to modern communication by rail, road and air are primarily iron ore, hydroelectric power, and timber. Coniferous forests of pine and spruce occupy enormous areas of eastern Lapland, although lakes and mires can cover up to half the land or even more. Nevertheless, the conditions for forestry are less favorable in the north of Sweden than in the south, due to the long distances and the slow rate of growth in the northern forests. A pine tree requires up to 200 years to reach full growth in the cool, short summers of the north.

The real economic basis of Lapland derives from its huge deposits of iron ore, with iron content as high as 65 percent. Even so, it took the smelting processes of modern times to eliminate the residue of phosphorus and make mining profitable. Knowledge of the ore bodies dates back to the late 17th century, and the first workings were established in the following century. Reindeers and sledges were used in the old days to transport the ore and iron.

The invention of the Thomas process, which also made it possible to produce high-grade iron and steel from phosphoric ores, triggered off an "iron rush" contemporaneously with the famous gold rushes to northern Canada and Alaska. A railway line from the Gällivare mines to the port of Luleå on the Gulf of Bothnia was built and opened in 1888. The continuation of the railway to Kiruna and the Norwegian port of Narvik was opened in 1902. It was a difficult and daring project, as the line had to climb from Narvik along the steep sides of a fjord to the Swedish border, and the work had to continue during the cold and dark northern winters.

Output of iron ore at Kiruna now comes to about 16 million tons per year and at Gällivare-Malmberget to 5 million tons. The Kiruna ore is exported by way of Narvik and the Gällivare ore via Luleå. It is estimated that the ore supplies at Kiruna are large enough for at least 200 years of continuous mining.

The erection of power plants was started before 1914 but has

From Muddus in Lapland. The woods here are characteristic of upper Norrland: somewhat thinned out to suggest parks, and dominated by spruce trees with narrow tops and broad crinoline near the ground. The intervening patches are bogs. Photo: Svante Lundgren.

been intensified during the postwar period. Hydroelectric development has had a considerable impact on nature and patterns of human settlement. The building-up of reservoirs behind dams has submerged many homes and a great deal of arable land. At the same time, of course, new employment opportunities have been created, but the jobs mostly require a specialized technical education. All this has hastened the depopulation of the countryside in the forest areas of southern Lapland.

In the past few years the Lapland wilderness has become attractive not only to tourists but also to the space scientists of

Europe. In 1966 the European Space Research Organization (ESRO) opened a large experimental field for space rockets north of Kiruna.

The increasing pressure of man and his technology on these resources of open space will necessarily call for careful planning. This is also true of the adjacent wilderness areas in northern Norway and Finland. Although the remaining space in north Scandinavia is not unlimited, it is still large enough to serve the rest of Europe as its main northern recreational ground.

Torsten Ehrenmark

Born in 1919. Journalist and correspondent for leading Swedish newspapers in London, New York and Paris. Popular as a writer of light articles for the press and as radio disc jockey.

That's Us Swedes

"The Swedes are the greatest!" We're too modest to say so openly, but that, in so many words, is what we mean. How could it be otherwise when the evidence speaks so plainly: our system of social security, our homes and furniture in Swedish Modern, our free and easy morals, our beautiful girls, our finely engineered products, our matches, our athletes, and our smorgasbord? Until a few years ago, we could just as well have added "our United Nations" to the list. As long as Dag Hammarskjöld was Secretary General, we regarded the UN as being Swedish pure and simple. It came natural to us to guide the world's destinies with becoming modesty. But after Hammarskjöld's death we turned our backs on the UN and no longer take anywhere near as much interest in its affairs.

A goldfish who lives all by himself in an aquarium is easily led to believe that he is the world's biggest, handsomest and smartest goldfish. We Swedes live a bit isolated, with water and mountains on all sides. It wasn't until ten years or so after the end of World War II that we began to explore the world around us on an appreciable scale. We were not impressed. All those years in the aquarium had made us immune. The sole attraction for us was the sunny warmth of the Mediterranean (sun and heat have a rough time of it in our part of the globe, but that's because neither of these elements bear the label, "Made in Sweden"). We are now building Swedish towns and villages in Italy, Spain and on the Canary Islands, replete with Swedish creature comforts, Swedish food, and even facilities for the purchase of the traditional half-liter bottle of aquavit on Saturday nights. We don't mind travelling abroad as long as we can take Sweden

with us. But we smile indulgently when in Sweden the
Americans insist on their ice water and the British on their tea.

With such overwhelming superiority in our favor, we can
generally afford to be tolerant to tourists. The years have taught
us to realize that not everybody can have the good fortune to
be born in Sweden. Being a foreigner, in other words, is no sin,
even though it is a trifle suspect. Above all, we take it as
axiomatic that foreigners should want to see for themselves how
earthly life can be lived at its best.

Nowadays, by far the greater number of Swedes are white-
collar workers. It is part and parcel of the welfare state for
manual labor to disappear or be passed on to immigrants, who
don't know any better. The Swede can be recognized by his
upright walk, briefcase in hand, his short sporty-looking jacket,
tight gray trousers and stylish brown shoes, a little brown hat

on his blonde head, and a brisk, effective gait which dispels all doubts as to his own capabilities. He is rational and he rationalizes everything.

Here's an example: A couple of summers ago the Swedish people suddenly began to complain about the deteriorating quality of fish. When the grumbles got louder, a railway official explained: "We were losing money on these fish hauls by rail, so we switched over to trucks, which are cheaper and more rational."

"Well, why didn't you say so in the first place?" was the general response, whereupon the Swedish people proceeded to eat half-rotten fish to save money for our railways. It was a logically tight argument for an inferior diet.

At the moment we are rationalizing rural Sweden out of existence. Why? Because our briefcase carriers have suddenly discovered that agriculture is a poor-paying proposition. Farmers as a class comprise a ludicrous remnant of our folklore. Why should they be allowed to wallow in muck for sentimental reasons when they could be put to better use in manufacturing industry? Trees should be planted on the fields instead so that we can export more pulp and paper. Before long, no doubt, our taxidermists will get to work, and visitors will be privileged to see the typically Swedish peasant family mounted in a showcase at the Nordic Museum. The briefcase carriers are also bent on eliminating all old buildings, and preferably entire sections of our cities. In their place, slabs of steel, glass and concrete are being erected. At long last, they say, Sweden is going to be a beautiful country. Trees are being felled, lakes drained, and effluents discharged in our waterways—all in the same noble cause. Many of the briefcase carriers themselves come from the outlying towns or countryside, but they arrived in Stockholm a long time ago on a conquering mission. And they have indeed taken over the capital; native Stockholmers are now confined for the most part to ghettoes on the east and south sides of town.

What the Scotchman wears under his kilt is a perennial subject of curiosity, but it would be just as interesting to know what the successful, live-wire Swede carries in his briefcase. The wise money used to bet on sandwiches, but has more recently switched to girlie magazines. Here is a field where the Swede once was a rank amateur, but it hasn't taken him long to attain a professional standard in keeping with his country's pace-setting tradition. With the peculiarly single-minded intensity that characterizes cultural debate in our country (not only is it single-minded, but also in chorus, as if in response to a military command), everything suddenly seemed to be exclusively concerned with pornography. Graying professors would insert four-letter words in their articles just for the fun of it, and our finest writers rushed as one man to their typewriters, like motor racers to their cars, eager to outdo one another in prurient detail. Outside observers shook their heads in bewilderment: what need has a country for pornography when it already enjoys the world's most solid reputation for sin?

It took some time for the bitter truth to dawn on the world: the Swedish male was an erotic illiterate and the Swedish female was more willing than able. Anyway, the pornographic flood has supposedly righted this sorry state of affairs and, if nothing else, the two sexes are now at least highly knowledgeable on the theory of love-making. People in the know say there isn't a single girl in Sweden who hasn't passed her B. E. (Bachelor of Erotics). But then people talk too much as it is. It would probably be closer to the facts to observe that the Swedish woman is as emancipated as the women of other countries would like to be but don't dare become—yet. When that day comes our girls will no longer receive special attention on the pages of "Life" and "Time". The disappointment will surely hurt us just as much as when Ingemar Johansson lost his world heavyweight title. There is nothing in Swedish history to describe the elation that swept over the country when he kayoed Floyd Patterson in Yankee Stadium on that sultry June night in 1959. As a small country, Sweden has an enormous need to assert herself. Before the fight we took the precaution to nominate Floyd as one of the best heavyweights of all time, the better to invest Ingemar with an aura for having vanquished such a formidable opponent. When Floyd later became the first ex-heavyweight champion to regain his title, the quirk of patriotic logic made Ingemar's previous feat look even more remarkable. Floyd was appointed Sweden's first honorary Negro. As for his successors, Sonny Liston and Cassius Clay, we look on them as deplorable examples of how brute strength has also invaded the boxing ring.

Uneasy lies the head that wears a crown. Every top-ranking position comes with its built-in neurosis: "What is to become of me if someone better turns up?" But to go so far as some foreign observers by contending the Swedes are wretched in the midst of all their welfare—well, how bare-faced reactionary can you get? Shame on you for wanting to denigrate the Social Democrats! After all, they've been in power for 35 years, and surely there could be no better proof of our progressive spirit than that. No, we are not unhappy. On the other hand, it would be too much to say that we are happy. Let us just say that we are content with our condition of melancholy.

It angers us to hear Englishmen speak of our Teutonic gloom, thereby suggesting that we are kin with the Germans. Nor are we pleased to hear Frenchmen describe our Nordic stolidity. Still, we don't mind calling attention to these qualities ourselves. If Swedes are a melancholy people, that's because a Swedish summer sunset transcends all other sunsets in the world. And perhaps a lyrical string in our hearts is touched whenever we cite a line of Swedish poetry beginning, "Beauty is most at twilight's close". The only trouble is that most of us usually don't know more than the first line. On all such occasions the foreigner feels himself to be an awkward outsider; he realizes he stands on the threshold of a sacred temple to which he is denied entrance.

Actually, Swedish melancholy is one of our most successful national camouflages. It makes an excellent cover-up for our inability to express ourselves, for our lack of spontaneity, for our coldness of emotion and absence of candor. We smile somewhat sadly when the foreigner asks us for our opinion, because we usually don't hold opinions on a subject that hasn't been discussed by political or cultural writers in our newspapers. It is a smile so forbidding as to make the foreigner feel he has committed a breach of tact. He doesn't know, of course, that the Swede subscribes to a newspaper which feeds him with opinions, and it is only these opinions that he is prepared to discuss. True, he is able to think for himself, but he has rationalized his existence to the point where his opinions are like commodities available in a supermarket. In that way he can completely devote his energies to keeping up with the Joneses which, though admittedly an international occupation, is nowhere pursued with greater eagerness than in Sweden.

It is relevant here to mention that the Swede regards himself as the world's champion sufferer from red tape—a form of tyranny on which, being the good Protestant that he is, he has bestowed the name of St. Bureaucraticus. The chief tasks of Swedish bureaucracy, as he sees it, are to issue arbitrary and contrived thou-shalt-not's, wait for the individual citizen to apply for exemptions, review the reasons therefore and, by means of refusals, to submerge him deeper into the gloom that is his rightful mood.

Melancholy bursts into its fullest flower when the Swede takes a look at the younger generation. In his time, he fought for social equality, the emancipation of women, the removal of ethnic discrimination, and all the other noble causes that his country has embraced. His first reaction, when he sees his children practice by right all the things he had merely hoped for, is one of indignation. But at the same time he is morosely satisfied with himself as belonging to the morally superior generation. Naturally, this doesn't mean that we cannot laugh. Over the years we have grown disaccustomed to bursting out in guffaws at cruel jokes, like slipping on banana peels. We no longer laugh at people because they are Negroes, speak Danish, or go into bankruptcy. Nowadays, we try seriously to organize our laughter —in other words, share the fun with as many sections of the community as possible in order to strengthen our feeling of solidarity. The preferred medium for the concentration of our risibilities is television, which exerts the proper degree of control and makes sure that no abuses occur. Incidentally, there is little risk that Swedish TV will give us a surfeit of humor. We have now learned that joy is easier to bear when it is shared by many, and we never have as much fun as when we are collectively urged by the broadcasting media to go out on the streets and exchange neckties with one another or embark on similar merry pranks. Believe it or not, even the most melancholy Swede badly needs to laugh, and it must be said in all fairness that this canalization of his innermost instinct came in the nick of time. To all intents and purposes, you see, private laughter had fallen under an anathema. How was this possible, especially in Sweden, which unlike the United States or France has no economic pressure groups? We do of course have organized interests, and our country is often jocularly referred to as "Organization Sweden". But these interests tend to be professional, idealistic, religious or oriented to sports and hobbies. It lies in the nature of laughter to single out specific butts, such as a schoolteacher in a joke, a shoemaker in a vaudeville sketch, or a police constable in a film farce. But every time this happens, the spokesman for some organized interest will denounce the portrayal, claiming that to heap ridicule on one member of a trade or profession is to bring the whole lot into disrepute. Gradually, all Swedes were made to appreciate that laughter was a damned serious business which required not only planning and rationalization but, even more important, the purification of that unhealthy miasma known as vernacular humor. It was at this juncture that radio and TV came to the rescue by contriving new forms of mirth, like making us all exchange neckties with one another.

And thus it has come to pass that Sweden has created the world's most enlightened and progressive humor. No one is discriminated against on grounds of his group affiliation, racial origin, or nation of allegiance. The very thought of such discrimination frightens us to death. We dilute our speech with meaningless euphemisms so as not to offend anybody, but the very act of beating around the bush can sound insulting enough. For instance, we can't bring ourselves to say, "The Negro was an unemployed doorkeeper from an underdeveloped country." Instead, we think we phrase the sentence more considerately by saying, "The colored man was a disengaged caretaker from a developing country."

Surely, none of you thinks by now that we are a nation of bores or that life is dull for us? If so, you are completely mistaken. We have a whale of a time in our soberly designed houses, with their tidy attics in this litter-less country of ours. Oh yes, our need for litter is enormous, but we sublimate it in melancholy ("Do you remember Grandmother's rocking chair?"); nothing must blemish the uncluttered surfaces of our live-at-home lives, which we faithfully model after the all-wise counsel of our leading magazines on interior decoration. Swedish design is our heritage, though sometimes we introduce a bold contrast to heighten the formal elegance of our living rooms, such as a pair of porcelain dogs from the Caledonian Market. It also provides us with a splendid opportunity for one-upmanship: "But, my dear, I stopped going to Portobello Road a long time ago. They have much nicer things at the Caledonian." We adore these outlandish names; they make us feel we are throwing our windows open to the world—the wider the throw, the more remote we reach. Even now it is possible to overhear this sort of conversation:

"Well, here I was at the Cloudhoppers Bar in Anchorage, and an Eskimo comes up to me and says ..."

"Eskimo?" comes the response in mildly reproving tone. (That old discrimination bogey again!)

"But it was an Eskimo, I told you."

"So what? It's not his fault. You make it sound like a physical handicap. You ought to say a 'Greenlandish subject.'"

From which it follows that the Swedes do get together socially. Indeed, we go so far as to exchange visits to our beautiful homes, although the obstacles are almost insurmountable—at least in our big cities. Every Stockholmer lives in a suburb, and his best friends live in suburbs at the opposite end of town. Henry Ford's maxim, "Alcohol and gasoline don't mix", is ironclad law in Sweden (and hence out of bounds for ironic comments), which means that Mr. and Mrs. Svenson have to make some hard choices when they visit the Andersons: either they both take the subway or, if they drive, he will do the drinking at the Andersons while his wife stays sober so that she can drive the car home; but this is frowned upon as being sex discrimination. Of course, the Svensons can also go by taxi. But all the Swedish taxis shape up as custom-made models ordered by the Sheikh of Kuwait who later found he couldn't afford to pay for them. They are therefore expensive, and when you arrive home a glance at the taxameter is enough to assure you that you've been taken for a ride. But by standing up to the temptations of the glass, giving in to the wife's nagging, or making the best of chronically taut finances, one can occasionally overcome these obstacles to visiting friends. We never issue formal invitations but rely exclusively on the telephone. The usual gambits are, "Come on over—nothing fancy, you understand," or, "Bring your wife along

and take potluck with us." The potluck turns out to be a four-course dinner with three varieties of wine, served at a table lavishly set with crystal stemware, flat silver, lighted candles and flowers. The host bids his guests welcome with white wine, while the gentleman next to his wife gives the mandatory speech of thanks when the port and dessert are served (long before then, of course, he will have become aware of his seating, with adverse effects both on his appetite and on his speech). The sumptuousness of this "simple meal" is followed by coffee and brandy, whiskey and soda. At one o'clock in the morning comes the "go-to-hell" sandwich—a discreet hint from the hosts that it's soon time to go home. This may take some doing, for after midnight the Swedish guest operates on a supercharger that easily keeps him going until three or four a.m. As the wee hours progress, his stories tend to become more and more discriminating, unless they turn entirely inward on his memories as a soldier and protector of Swedish neutrality during World War II—the unforgettable experience of the middle-aged Swede. By that time the wives, having long since been ignored, are in a corner by themselves discussing the length of skirts in Paris.

The prevailing cuisine at these dinners is French, though modified for Swedish palates. Even so, it is amazing how successfully the Swedes have translated France's culinary refinements, in contrast with many other countries. The only glaring deficiency is the poorer quality of the meat. On the other hand, one consequence of our Gallophilism in this sphere has been to push many excellent items of homely Swedish fare off the dinner table. Here, for instance, is a nearly forgotten recipe: You buy a swede, you peel him, you cut him in pieces, you boil him, you mash him, you eat him together with a lightly salted boiled leg of pork. The Swedish name for it is *rotmos och fläsklägg*, and represents the Swede at his very best.

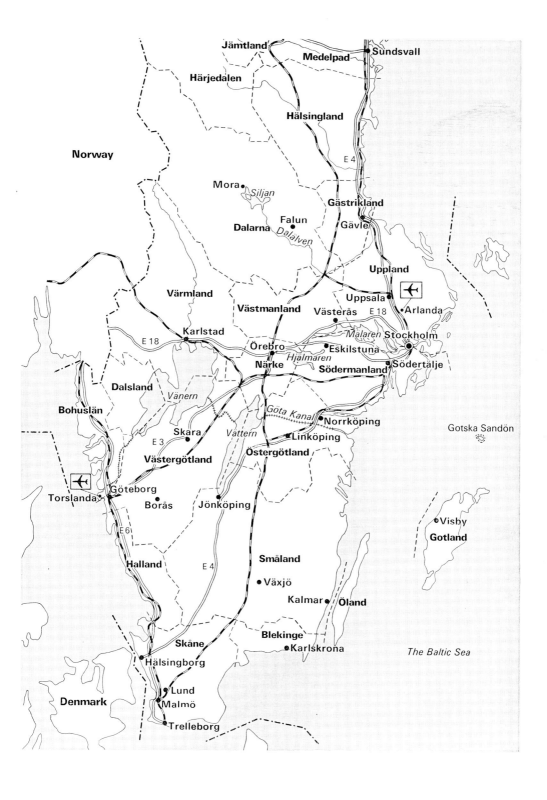

Bibliography

Hans L. Zetterberg
Sweden—A Land of Tomorrow?

Gustafsson, Lars. *The Public Dialogue in Sweden. Current Issues of Social, Esthetic and Moral Debate.* Stockholm: Norstedt/Swedish Institute, 1964. 116 p.

Kälvesten, Anna-Lisa. *The Social Structure of Sweden.* Stockholm: Swedish Institute, 1966. 91 p. Sweden Today E. 97.

Linnér, Birgitta. *Sex and Society in Sweden.* New York: Pantheon Books, 1967. 204 p.

Schmidt, Folke. *The Law of Labour Relations in Sweden.* Stockholm: Almqvist & Wiksell, 1962. 343 p.

Schmidt, Folke. *Organization and Jurisdiction of the Labour Court in Sweden.* Stockholm: Swedish Institute, 1965. 17 p. E. 69. (From: Schmidt, Folke, The Law of Labour Relations in Sweden.)

Schmidt, Folke and Strömholm, Stig. *Legal Values in Modern Sweden.* Stockholm: Svenska Bokförlaget/Swedish Institute, 1965. 86 p.

Per Olof Sundman
A 15-minute Baedeker

Facts about Sweden. Stockholm: Forum/Swedish Institute, 1966. 79 p.

A Geography of Norden, Denmark, Finland, Iceland, Norway, Sweden. Oslo: J. W. Cappelens Forlag. Stockholm: Svenska Bokförlaget, 1963. 363 p.

Maze, Edward. *The Traveler's Guide to Sweden.* Stockholm: Gebers, 1963. 157 p.

Pilkington, Roger. *Small Boat through Sweden.* London: Macmillan, 1961. 227 p.

Travel, Study and Research in Sweden. Compiled by Adèle Heilborn. Stockholm: Sweden-America Foundation, 1965. 277 p.

Zweigbergk, Eva von. *Stockholm to Delight You.* Stockholm: Bonnier, 1961. 96 p.

Kurt Ågren
A History of Sweden

Andersson, Ingvar. *A History of Sweden.* London: Weidenfeld and Nicolson, 1956. 461 p. New edition will appear.

Arbman, Holger. *The Vikings*. London: Thames and Hudson, 1962. 212 p.

Bengtsson, Frans G. *The Life of Charles XII. King of Sweden 1697– 1718*. Stockholm: Norstedt, 1960. 495 p.

Brøndsted, Johannes. *The Vikings*. Hammondsworth, Middlesex: Penguin Books, 1965. 347 p.

Carlsson, Sten. *History of Modern Sweden*. Stockholm: Swedish Institute, 1966. 17 p. E. 74.

Hatton, R. M. *Charles XII of Sweden*. London: Weidenfeld and Nicolson, 1967.

Heckscher, Eli F. *An Economic History of Sweden*. Cambridge, Mass.: Harvard University Press, 1954. 308 p.

Hägglöf, Gunnar. *Britain and Sweden. From the Vikings to the Common Market*. Stockholm: Norstedt, 1966. 44 p.

Oakley, Stewart. *The Story of Sweden*. London: Faber and Faber, 1966. 292 p.

Roberts, Michael. *Essays in Swedish History*. London: Weidenfeld and Nicolson, 1967. 358 p.

Roberts, Michael. *Gustavus Adolphus. A History of Sweden 1611– 1632*. Volume one 1611–1626. Volume two 1626–1632. London: Longmans, Green and Co, 1953, 1958. 585 + 848 p.

Stenberger, Mårten. *Sweden. Ancient Peoples and Places*. London: Thames and Hudson, 1962. 229 p.

Stolpe, Sven. *Christina of Sweden*. London: Burns & Oates, 1966. 360 p.

Pär-Erik Back

How Sweden Is Governed

Andrén, Nils. *Government and Politics in the Nordic Countries*. Stockholm: Almqvist & Wiksell, 1964. 241 p.

Andrén, Nils. *Modern Swedish Government*. Stockholm: Almqvist & Wiksell, 1961. 252 p.

Andrén, Nils. *The Party System in Sweden*. Stockholm: Swedish Institute, 1965. 21 p. E. 4. (From: Andrén, Nils. Modern Swedish Government.)

Calmfors, Hans. *Local Self-Government in Stockholm. A Short Presentation.* Stockholm 1966. 28 p.

The Constitution of Sweden. Documents Published by the Royal Ministry for Foreign Affairs. New Series II: 4. Stockholm 1954. 109 p.

Dahl, Robert A. *Political Oppositions in Western Democracies.* New Haven: Yale University Press, 1966. 458 p.

Håstad, Elis. *The Parliament of Sweden.* London: Hansard Society for Parliamentary Government, 1957. 165 p.

Johnston, T. L. *Collective Bargaining in Sweden. A Study of the Labour Market and Its Institutions.* London: Allen & Unwin, 1962. 358 p.

Langenfelt, Per. *Local Government in Sweden.* Stockholm: Swedish Institute, 1966. 17 p. E. 89.

Langenfelt, Per. *Principles for a New Division of Sweden's Municipalities.* Stockholm: Swedish Institute, 1962. 9 p. E. 39.

Modern Swedish Labour Market Policy. Stockholm: Prisma/National Labour Market Board/Swedish Institute, 1966. 120 p.

Pers, Anders Yngve. *The Swedish Press.* Stockholm: Swedish Institute/ Swedish Newspaper Publishers Association, 1966. 46 p.

Swedish Government Bill. (No. 174) concerning State Support for Political Parties, November, 1965. Mimeogr. Ministry for Foreign Affairs.

Vinde, Pierre. *The Swedish Civil Service.* Stockholm: Ministry of Finance, 1967. 30 p.

Nils Andrén

National Security and International Solidarity

Abrahamsen, Samuel. *Sweden's Foreign Policy.* Washington: Public Affairs Press, 1959. 99 p.

Andrén, Nils, *Power Balance and Non-Alignment. A Perspective on Swedish Foreign Policy.* Stockholm: Almqvist & Wiksell, 1967. 212 p.

Documents on Swedish Foreign Policy. Annual. Documents Published by the Royal Ministry for Foreign Affairs.

Michanek, Ernst. *Sweden's Development Assistance Efforts.* Stockholm: Swedish Institute, 1966. 23 p. E. 104.

Wendt, Frantz. *The Nordic Council and Cooperation in Scandinavia.* Copenhagen: Munksgaard, 1959. 247 p.

Stig Strömholm

The Law and Its Administration

Amilon, Clas. *Survey of the Correctional System in Sweden.* Stockholm: Swedish Institute, 1966. 32 p. Sweden Today E. 23 b.

Amilon, Clas. *Youth Prison: A Swedish Form of Treatment for Young Offenders.* Stockholm: Swedish Institute, 1965. 27 p. E. 22 b.

Bexelius, Alfred. *The Swedish Institution of the Justitieombudsman.* Stockholm: Swedish Institute, 1965. 30 p. E. 95.

Eek, Hilding. *The Swedish Conflict of Laws.* The Hague: Martinius Nijhoff, 1965. 304 p.

Frykholm, Lars. *Swedish Legal Publications in English, French and German 1935–1960.* Stockholm: Almqvist & Wiksell, 1961. (From Scandinavian Studies in Law 1961, pp. 158–217.)

Ginsburg, Ruth Bader & Bruzelius, Anders. *Civil Procedure in Sweden.* The Hague: Martinius Nijhoff, 1965. 491 p.

The Penal Code of Sweden. Effective January 1, 1965. Transl. by Thorsten Sellin. Introd. by Ivar Strahl. Stockholm: Ministry of Justice, 1965. 82 p.

Rowat, Donald C. (ed.). *The Ombudsman. Citizen's Defender.* London: Allen & Unwin. Stockholm: Norstedt, 1965. 348 p.

Scandinavian Studies in Law. Ed. by Folke Schmidt. Annual. Stockholm: Almqvist & Wiksell.

Schmidt, Folke. *The Law of Labour Relations in Sweden.* Stockholm: Almqvist & Wiksell, 1962. 343 p.

Schmidt, Folke. *Organization and Jurisdiction of the Labour Court in Sweden.* Stockholm: Swedish Institute, 1963. 17 p. E. 69. (From: Schmidt, Folke. The Law of Labour Relations in Sweden.)

Schmidt, Folke & Strömholm, Stig. *Legal Values in Modern Sweden.* Stockholm: Svenska Bokförlaget/Swedish Institute, 1964. 86 p.

Bengt Rydén

The Swedish Economy

See Bibliography of the chapter Patterns of Postwar Economic Debate.

Kurt Samuelsson

Patterns of Postwar Economic Debate

Eliasson, Gunnar. *Investment Funds in Operation.* Stockholm: National Institute of Economic Research, 1965. 161 p. Occasional Paper 2.

Gorne, Staffan & Sohlman, Staffan. *Prospects for Swedish Exports 1970.* Stockholm: National Institute of Economic Research 1967. 115 p. Occasional Paper 3.

Johnston, T. L. (ed.). *Economic Expansion and Structural Change.*
A Trade Union Manifest. London: Allen & Unwin, Ltd., 1963. 175 p.

Kragh, Börje, *Financial Long-Term Planning.* Stockholm: National
Institute of Economic Research, 1967. 157 p. Occasional Paper 4.

Labor Peace and Full Employment in Sweden. Stockholm: Ministry of
Health and Social Affairs, 1964. 38 p.

Lundberg, John. *In Our Own Hands.* Stockholm: Kooperativa Förbundet.
(Cooperative Union and Wholesale Society), 1965. 45 p.

Michanek, Ernst. *For and Against the Welfare State, Swedish
Experiences.* Stockholm: Swedish Institute, 1964. 47 p.

Norr, Martin, Sandels, Claes & Hornhammar, Nils S. *The Corporate
Income Tax in Sweden.* Stockholm: Stockholms Enskilda Bank, 1966.
63 p.

Some Data About Sweden. Annual. Stockholm: Stockholms Enskilda
Bank.

The Swedish Budget. A Summary publ. by the Ministry of Finance.
Annual. Stockholm.

The Swedish Economy. (A Quarterly Review.) Stockholm: Economic
Division of the Ministry of Finance and the National Institute of
Economic Research.

The Swedish Economy. Publ. by Skandinaviska Banken. Uddevalla
1967. 63 p.

*The Swedish Economy 1966–1970 and the General Outlook for the
Seventies.* Publ. by the Ministry of Finance. Stockholm 1966. 224 p.

Swedish Export Directory. Publ. by the General Export Association of
Sweden. Annual. Stockholm.

Swedish Economy and Industries. Fact Sheets. Stockholm: Swedish
Institute.

Taxation in Sweden. Publ. by the Law School of Harvard University.
Boston: Little, Brown and Company, 1959. 723 p. (World Tax Series.)

Taxes in Sweden. Publ. by Skattebetalarnas Förening (The Swedish
Taxpayers' Association). Stockholm 1965. 41 p.

Westerlind, Erik & Beckman, Rune. *Sweden's Economy. Structure and
Trends.* Stockholm: Prisma/Swedish Institute, 1965. 98 p.

Åström, Kell. *City Planning in Sweden.* Stockholm: Swedish Institute,
1967. Sweden Books.

Siv Thorsell

Swedish Women Today

Bruun, Ulla-Britta. *Nursery Schools in Sweden.* Stockholm: Swedish Institute, 1965. 14 p. E. 52 b.

The Changing Roles of Men and Women. Ed. by Edmund Dahlström. London: Gerald Duckworth and Co., 1967.

Gendell, Murray. *Swedish Working Wives. A Study of Determinants and Consequences.* Totowa, N. J.: Bedminster Press, 1963. 269 p.

Rössel, James. *Women in Sweden.* Stockholm: Swedish Institute, 1965. 31 p. E. 99.

Britt Marie Svedberg

Welfare from the Cradle to the Grave

Albinsson, Gillis. *Public Health Services in Sweden.* Linköping: Swedish Hospital Association, 1965. 51 p.

The Child Welfare Act of Sweden. Effective January 1, 1961. Transl. by Thorsten Sellin. Introd. by Holger Romander. Stockholm: Ministry of Justice, 1965. 28 p.

Childs, Marquis W. *Sweden, the Middle Way.* New Haven: Yale University Press, 1961. 199 p.

Living and Working in Sweden. Stockholm: National Labour Market Board, 1965. 31 p.

Michanek, Ernst. *For and Against the Welfare State, Swedish Experiences.* Stockholm: Swedish Institute, 1964. 47 p.

National Insurance Act, May 25, 1962. Stockholm: Ministry of Health and Social Affairs, 1963. 57 p.

The Right to Security. Health Insurance—Basic Pensions—Supplementary Pensions. Stockholm: Swedish Institute, 1966. 27 p. Sweden Today E. 96.

Social Benefits in Sweden, 1966. Stockholm: Framtiden, 1966. 64 p.

Swedish Youth. Stockholm: Swedish Institute, 1964. 71 p. E. 87.

Uhr, Carl G. *Sweden's Social Security System.* Washington: Government Printing office, 1966. 159 p.

Gunnar Smedberg

The Religious Organization

The Church of Sweden. Past and Present. A book sponsored by the Swedish Bishops' Conference. Ed. by Robert Murray. Malmö: Allhem, 1960. 286 p.

Murray, Robert. *A Brief History of the Church of Sweden. Origins and Modern Structure.* Stockholm: Diakonistyrelsens Bokförlag, 1961. 116 p.

Scandinavian Churches. A Picture of the Development and Life of the Churches of Denmark, Finland, Iceland, Norway and Sweden. Ed. by Leslie Stannard Hunter. London: Faber and Faber, 1965. 200 p.

Sten Lindroth —
Bo Oscarsson
Science and Technology

Hagberg, Knut. *Carl Linnaeus.* London: Jonathan Cape, 1952. 264 p.

The Intellectual Face of Sweden (Ergo International). Uppsala 1964. 150 p.

Jorpes, J. Erik. *Jac. Berzelius. His Life and Work.* Stockholm: Almqvist & Wiksell, 1966. 156 p.

Scandinavian Research Guide. Directory of Research Institutions within Technology and Science Exclusive of Life Sciences. Vol. 1, 2. Oslo: Scandinavian Council for Applied Research, 1960. 687 p., 486 p.

Swedish Men of Science. 1650–1950. Ed. and with an introd. by Sten Lindroth. Stockholm: Almqvist & Wiksell/Swedish Institute, 1952. 295 p.

Uggla Arvid Hj. *Linnaeus.* Stockholm: Almqvist & Wiksell/Swedish Institute, 1957. 18 + 16 p.

Göte Rudvall —
Ulla Åhgren-Lange
Swedish Education in New Molds

Dahllöf, Urban, Zetterlund, Sven & Öberg, Henning. *Secondary Education in Sweden. A Survey of Reforms.* Ed.: Torbjörn Carle. Stockholm: Board of Education, 1966. 104 p.

Educational Policy and Planning. Sweden. Paris: OECD Directorate for Scientific Affairs, 1967. 448 p.

The Intellectual Face of Sweden (Ergo International). Uppsala 1964. 150 p.

The New School in Sweden. The Comprehensive School, Aims Organization Methods. Stockholm: National Board of Education, 1963. 47 p.

Orring, Jonas. *Comprehensive School and Continuation Schools in Sweden. A Summary of the Principal Recommendations of the 1957 School Commission.* Stockholm: Ministry of Education and Ecclesiastical Affairs, 1962. 154 p.

Stahre, Sven-Arne. *Adult Education in Sweden.* Stockholm: Swedish Institute, 1966. 40 p. Sweden Today E. 98.

State Study Assistance in Sweden. Stockholm: Swedish Institute, 1966. 17 p. Sweden Today E. 155.

Travel, Study and Research in Sweden. Compiled by Adèle Heilborn. Stockholm: Sweden–America Foundation, 1965. 277 p.

Ingrid Arvidsson

Swedish Cultural Policy

Elvander, Nils. *Role of the State in Sweden's Cultural Life.* Stockholm: Swedish Institute, 1965. 11 p. E. 72 b.

Brunius, Niklas, Eriksson, Göran O & Rembe, Rolf. *Swedish Theatre.* Stockholm: Swedish Institute, 1967. Sweden Books.

Carl Henrik Svenstedt

Cinema

Cowie, Peter. *Swedish Cinema.* London: A. Zwemmer Ltd., New York: A. S. Barnes & Co. Inc., 1966. 224 p.

Donner, Jörn. *The Personal Vision of Ingmar Bergman.* Bloomington: Indiana University Press, 1964. 276 p.

Furhammar, Leif & Lauritzen, Bertil. *Film in Sweden.* Stockholm: Swedish Institute, 1966. Sweden Today E. 105.

Ulf Linde

Painting and Sculpture

A Key to the Museums of Sweden. Editor: Gertrud Serner, assisted by Margaretha Cramér. Stockholm: Rabén & Sjögren/Swedish Institute, 1960. 111 p.

Swedish Art since 1945 (Paletten International). Editor: Folke Edwards.

Söderberg, Rolf. *Modern Swedish Art.* Stockholm: Aldus/Bonnier, 1963. 128 p.

Treasures of Swedish Art. Ed. by Pontus Grate. Introd. by Carl Nordenfalk. Malmö: Allhem, 1965. 166 p.

Treasures of Swedish Art from Earliest Times to the Beginning of the Twentieth Century. With an Essay by Gertrud Serner. Stockholm: Forum, 1950. 111 p.

Runar Mangs

Music

Cnattingius, Claes M. *Contemporary Swedish Music.* Stockholm: Swedish Institute, 1966. 40 p. Sweden Today E. 144.

Hilleström, Gustaf. *The Royal Opera, Stockholm.* Stockholm: Royal Opera House/Swedish Institute, 1960. 83 p.

Horton, John. *Scandinavian Music: A Short History.* London: Faber and Faber, 1963. 180 p.

A Short Survey of Music in Sweden. Stockholm: Swedish Institute, 1966. 44 p. Sweden Today E. 49 b.

Swedish Music. Past and Present. Ed. Bengt Pleijel. Stockholm: Musikrevy, 1967. 112 p.

Tracie, Gordon Ekvall. *The Folk Music of Sweden.* Stockholm 1961. 16 p.

Ingemar Wizelius

Literature

Gustafson, Alrik. *A History of Swedish Literature.* Minneapolis: University of Minnesota Press, 1961. 708 p.

A List of Translations of Swedish Literature into English. Stockholm: Swedish Institute, 1964. 38 p. E. 28. (From Alrik Gustafson "A History of Swedish Literature".)

Sweden writes. Contemporary Swedish Poetry and Prose, Views on Art, Literature and Society. Selected and introduced by Lars Bäckström and Göran Palm. Stockholm: Prisma/Swedish Institute, 1965. 225 p.

Katja Waldén

The Swedish Design for Living

Hård af Segerstad, Ulf. *Scandinavian Design.* Stockholm: Nordisk Rotogravyr, 1961. 129 p.

Kontur. Swedish Design Annual. Published by Svenska Slöjdföreningen (The Swedish Society for Industrial Design), Stockholm.

Stavenow, Åke & Huldt, Åke H. *Design in Sweden.* Stockholm: Gothia, 1961. 268 p.

Anders Rapp

Lapland—The Northern Wilderness of Sweden

Lundqvist, Gösta. *Lapland. Reindeer, Lapps and Midnight Sun.* Foreword by Dag Hammarskjöld. Stockholm: Bonnier, 1960. 124 p.

Manker, Ernst. *People of Eight Seasons.* Göteborg: Tre Tryckare, 1963. 214 p.

Ruong, Israel, *The Lapps in Sweden.* Stockholm: Swedish Institute, 1967. 116 p. Sweden Books.

Rönn, Gunnar. *The Land of the Lapps.* Stockholm: Saxon & Lindström, 1961. 111 p.

Torsten Ehrenmark

That's Us Swedes

Austin, Paul Britten. *On Being Swedish—Reflections Toward a Better Understanding of the Swedish Character.* London: Secher & Warburg, 1967.

Connery, Donald. *The Scandinavians.* London: Eyre & Spottiswoode, 1966. 590 p.

Downman, Lorna, Baird, Anthony & Austin, Paul Britten. *The Charm of Sweden. Some Articles on Things Swedish.* Stockholm: Fabel, 1963. 93 p.

Downman, Lorna, Austin, Paul Britten & Baird, Anthony. *Round the Swedish Year. Daily Life and Festivals through Four Seasons.* Stockholm: Fabel, 1964. 111 p.

Fleisher, Frederic. *The New Sweden.* New York: David Mc Kay, 1967.

Lorenzen, Lilly. *Of Swedish Ways.* Minneapolis: Gilbert Publishing Company, 1964. 276 p.

Maze, Edward. *Creative Sweden.* Stockholm: Gebers, 1965. 151 p.

Nott, Kathleen. *A Clean, Well-Lighted Place. A Private View of Sweden.* London: Heinemann, 1961. 207 p.

Scott, George Walton. *The Swedes. A Jigsaw Puzzle.* London: Sidgwick & Jackson, 1967. 163 p.